Remembering
Anna Akhmatova

Paris   1911

Remembering
Anna Akhmatova

Anatoly Nayman

Introduction by
Joseph Brodsky

Translated by
Wendy Rosslyn

A John Macrae Book
Henry Holt and Company   New York

Published in the United States by
Henry Holt and Company, Inc., 115 West 18th Street, New York, New York 10011.
Published in Canada by Fitzhenry & Whiteside Limited,
195 Allstate Parkway, Markham, Ontario L3R 4T8.
Originally published in the USSR under the title
Rasskazy o Anne Akhmatovoy.
Library of Congress Cataloging-in-Publication Data
Naĭman, Anatoliĭ.
[Rasskazy o Anne Akhmatovoĭ.   English]
Remembering Anna Akhmatova / Anatoly Nayman ; introduction by
Joseph Brodsky ; translated by Wendy Rosslyn.
      p.   cm.
Translation of: Rasskazy o Anne Akhmatovoĭ.
1. Akhmatova, Anna Andreevna, 1889–1966—Criticism and
interpretation.   I. Title.
PG3476.A324Z7613   1991
891.71'42—dc20   91-16241
ISBN 0-8050-1408-X   CIP

Henry Holt books are available at special discounts
for bulk purchases for sales promotions, premiums,
fund-raising, or educational use. Special editions
or book excerpts can also be created to specification.

For details contact: Special Sales Director, Henry Holt and Company, Inc.,
115 West 18th Street, New York, New York 10011

First American Edition

Printed in the United States of America
Recognizing the importance of preserving
the written word, Henry Holt and Company, Inc.
by policy, prints all of its first editions
on acid-free paper. ∞
1   3   5   7   9   10   8   6   4   2

Grateful acknowledgment is made to the following for permission to quote from the works listed: Harcourt Brace Jovanovich for excerpt from "East Coker" in *Four Quartets*, copyright 1943 by T.S. Eliot and renewed 1971 by Esme Valerie Eliot; Penguin USA for excerpts from *Personal Impressions*, Isaiah Berlin (New York, 1980); Strathcona Publishing Co. for excerpts from Zhdanov's speech in *Central Committee Resolution and Zhdanov's Speech on the Journals 'Zvezda' and 'Leningrad'* (Royal Oak, 1980); Ardis Publishers Inc. for verse quotations from *Anna Akhmatova: Selected Poems*, Walter Arndt, trans. and ed., Robin Kemball and Carl Proffer, trans. (Ann Arbor, 1979).

Illustrations courtesy of the author unless otherwise indicated.

page ii: 'Anna Akhmatova, Paris, 1911' by Amedeo Modigliani, private collection of the estate of Anna Akhmatova.

Contents

Foreword

Anna Andreevna Akhmatova, a noble and most moving writer, is one of the four great poets whose art dominated and continues to dominate Russian literature during the half century that followed the revolution; her genius and monstrous persecution by the state will be remembered as long as the history and literature of Russia continues to be known. Nayman, who is himself a poet and critic, and during her last years was one of her closest friends, has written a book of unique authority on her poetry, her opinions, personal, literary, metaphysical, and, above all, her personality, which nobody who met her has been able to forget.

His book, together with Lydia Chukovskaya's memoirs of her, is a worthy and, for all interested in Russian literature, most valuable memorial to a divinely gifted poet, and an outstanding figure in the martyrology of her time.

Isaiah Berlin
Oxford, January 1991

Introduction

Lives of poets are interesting in the first place because the ratio between life and poetry is clearly not in the latter's favour. In an ideal library, where each author is allotted a separate shelf, the works of an average novelist, provided he lasted long enough, would occupy far more space than a poet of similar longevity. Think of W. B. Yeats, for example, or of Robert Frost, not to mention T. S. Eliot or Marianne Moore. In each of these cases, a single volume would sit there on that shelf, surrounded by a great deal of emptiness. That would convey to such a library's visitor the ratio between a work of art and a life: the factor of a miracle.

This is not to belittle the significance of prose. Yet poetry, each particular poem, is indeed a miracle: a linguistic one to begin with, and then—if a poet is lucky—a miracle of spiritual intensity and cohesion. To put it differently, as arts go, poetry is not a mimetic but a revelatory one. However, miracles and revelations, as the existence of these very nouns demonstrates, are quite rare in this life, and a poet doesn't write more often than he does. A poem itself, a black square surrounded by empty white space, is emblematic of his predicament.

Hence poets' lives, biographies, memoirs of contemporaries, all sorts of exegesis; hence, too, the publication of their correspondence, diaries, and laundry bills. They all aim at filling in the vastness of margins, at explaining the miracle, at interpreting a revelation. At times they succeed in giving the semblance of the context in which those things occurred. More often, they cut the poet down to the size of his biographer or his public. In Renaissance times, the approach was more direct, and such texts would appear on the same page as the poem itself: it was literally "writing around", pushing the white away. Nowadays this sort of thing takes the form of a book.

Perhaps we've got more paper. Perhaps the demographic reality of our times breeds in us a greater vanity. Perhaps that same reality unwittingly shops for the sternest lessons in humility. Books about poets mushroom like flashing cameras around a foreign dignitary (upon his departure, it must be added, rather than on his arrival). The emptiness darkens with gossip and analysis; the net result, however, is a sharp sense of futility proportionate to the industry of the common in capturing the unique. The dignitary becomes more and more foreign.

A better course of action could be to print more copies of poets' Collected or Selected, and offering them at discount prices in supermarkets, i.e., multiplying, and increasing access to, the miraculous rather than pushing the banal. Yet that's not to be, since miracles seem to be the province of the dead, while their interpretation and its market are the domain of the living. A poet is always outnumbered, especially once he's dead. The number of great poets in a nation is at best something like three or four to a century. That is, of course, if the nation gets lucky, or if it is particularly populous. For instance, this was the ratio in this century in Russia. Which is to say it got lucky in the twentieth century at least in this respect.

Anna Akhmatova was the most senior member of that great quartet which included Marina Tsvetaeva, Osip Mandelstam, and Boris Pasternak, whose centenaries are being celebrated now all over the place. She was born in 1889; they, respectively, in 1890, 1891, and 1892. Two revolutions (1905 and 1917), with the carnage of World War I in between, were the background of their youth. The national upheaval of the civil war, collectivization, and the Great Terror, the climate of their maturity. That climate swallowed Mandelstam. Then followed World War II, shortly after the outbreak of which Tsvetaeva committed suicide. The five-year-long war with its toll of twenty million in casualties, the postwar nadir of Stalin's reign with its punitive crescendos, were what Pasternak and Akhmatova had for their old age. She outlived him by five years and died in 1966. Looking back on her life, she says of her generation in one of her Northern Elegies:

> So that's when we've decided to be born
> In order not to miss a single
> Unprecedented spectacle ...

Indeed, she missed none. The unprecedented spectacles availed her with the benefit of hindsight were many, most of them very bloody. On a personal scale they meant, increasingly, only one thing: forced subtraction of those whom she loved and knew, including, for instance, two of her husbands, poet Nikolay Gumilyov killed in 1921 on Lenin's direct order, and art historian Nikolay Punin, who died in 1953 in prison, and Mandelstam himself. Another subtraction was the eighteen-year-long imprisonment of her only child. The impersonal scale amounted to roughly forty million lives put to an end by the police state of which she was a citizen.

That alone could wrench open the width of the margins surrounding her poems. What marginalized them and their author even further was the banning of her work from publication virtually for decades. Quite apart from what she was writing, the very fact that she kept doing it was in itself a miracle. Thus the emptiness on both sides of her Collected on the shelf in the aforementioned library would also be an echo of the literal one. A poet's life, of course, is rich in this sort of symbolism; in this line of work, being boxed out comes with the territory. Akhmatova's isolation, however, was the isolation of a target.

That's what engenders the current crop of Akhmatoviana (memoiristic, textological, factological, prurient)—the writing around, since it is unlikely we'll ever be treated to her epistolary output or to her diaries. In her time, the smallest scrap of paper had the knack of becoming a piece of evidence. Therefore, she'd put her pen to paper only in the case of linguistic necessity, i.e., because of a poem. Correspondingly, in her speech she was very succinct, aphoristic, free of chatter, witty in a rather drastic way. The best thing therefore we could be treated to would be a collection of her table talk (three volumes of which already exist, compiled by her life-long friend, the writer Lydia Chukovskaya; before long they will see the dark of print in English).

If the book before you should be regarded as next to the best thing, it is only because its author, Anatoly Nayman, knew Akhmatova only during the last five years of her life. Hence its chief virtue, which is the intensity of the author's attention to his subject—intensity proportionate to the limited time fate granted to him. The other virtue is that this book about a poet is written by a poet, i.e., by a person capable of grasping the precedence of poems over biography. For with a life like Akhmatova's, the temptation to put the cart before the horse is very strong indeed. It takes a poet not to succumb to it, and a young poet at that.

Anatoly Nayman

Three times younger than his employer, Anatoly Nayman was precisely that—first and foremost a poet. As a consequence—and presumably in spite of himself, unwittingly—he happened to be a pupil of Akhmatova as much as he was her secretary. A happy contamination as far as this book's reader is concerned, for Anatoly Nayman refuses to distinguish between his subject's line of verse and her casual utterance: to our benefit, he remembers both. This is as much to the credit of his retentive ability as to the quality of Akhmatova's remarks, which are indeed indistinguishable in style and substance from her verses.

Remembering Anna Akhmatova owes its success with the Russian audience to the fact that Akhmatova's own conversation is recorded on practically every other page of the book; and most of this soliloquy is in one way or another about literature. Thus it is a book about literature; depicting not so much the poet herself as her perspective on what she has been at for more than half a century and what it cost her. For this reason, it is a portrait not of history's victim but of its victor: of a triumphant soul and the triumphant word, synonymous in her case and thus offering her readers an existential standard.

The possibility of this equation between soul and word is what lies behind the attraction of poetry, and it is through the prism of what this equation attained that Akhmatova views both literature and reality. "A Russian Sappho" in her early books in the teens of this century, a Cassandra of the twenties and thirties, the Keening Muse for the rest of her life, she went, technically speaking, through all the options available in her time to a poet of her gender and, by the same token, to a human being. Therefore, her direct speech is of great consequence to her public, and not only because it retains the same timbre, grace, and gravity as her poems, but because it is the voice of a spiritual and linguistic norm.

The most attractive aspect of this book is that it is written not in order to understand or interpret Akhmatova but out of love for her, out of love for that norm or—to look at her with the eyes of its author a good quarter of a century ago—for that human maximum. Hence Anatoly Nayman's retentive ability, since love neither forgets nor edits: it keeps its object in the sharp focus of the present tense as long as the one who loves is alive. That's why now, a quarter of a century later, Akhmatova's phrases and the cadences of her voice as recorded here sound at least to this reader as though she spoke yesterday. The other explanation for this effect is presumably that the wisdom of her words and the compassionate warmth of her voice in themselves were guarantors of their longevity, of their ability to reverberate in the hearts and minds of those who knew her, for the time to come. To say the least, a whole generation of Russian poets—a generation to which Anatoly Nayman and the author of this introduction belong—lives within her echo, or, better still, is her echo. This book carries that echo a little further and, as it were, across the water.

The lives of poets are interesting above all because of that they say, not because of what they do. As for doing, for acting in life, a poet's options are as limited as those of any human being, and a political system, illness, or poverty can reduce them even further. Not so with words, which are what a poet's business is and which are not reducible. On the contrary, language has a distinct centrifugal property, and the radius of a word's meaning only widens with its frequent use, because of repetition. As a result, at every given moment a poet depends less on the limitations imposed upon him by his reality or his personal circumstances than on those of the word he is about to put on paper.

Small wonder that often one falls into dependence on one's own utterances, that they start to dictate one's actions and conduct. Words have a habit of setting into motion not only one's thoughts but one's body and inanimate objects as well. Because of this ability of theirs and because of "In the beginning was the Word", a poet stands—in the collective subconscious—for a mini-Creator. That's what lies underneath the popular interest in a poet's biography and that's why it is redundant to search for the clue to a poet's miracles in his personal data.

As with the Almighty Himself (heard through his prophets), a lot more gets revealed through a poet's passing remarks about his *métier*, his craft—about literary matters and tastes, predecessors, contemporaries, likes, dislikes, and sources of inspiration, chief among which is the language itself—than in a chronology of his meagre human efforts. For these are his etymology, genealogy, geology; these are his holy spirits. Had art indeed depended on experience as much as the critical profession wants us to believe, we'd have far more—and far better—art on our hands than we do. A poet is always the product of his—that is, his nation's—language, to which living experiences are what logs are to fire. Of course, when both experience and language are Russian, the fire burns you even in translation.

Joseph Brodsky
New York, January 1991

Translator's Note

Anatoly Nayman's *Remembering Anna Akhmatova* first appeared in the form of extracts and was then published as a book in 1989. It has found a huge audience in the Soviet Union. Some readers were, no doubt, attracted by the disclaimer on the reverse of the title page: "The publishing house by no means invariably shares the assessments and judgements expressed by the authors [*sic*] of this book." Nayman had taken advantage of fast disappearing restraints on publishing to print an appendix of secondary material about Akhmatova including, alongside the hitherto unexceptionable but now embarrassing denunciation of her by Stalin's cultural dictator Zhdanov, contributions by Isaiah Berlin and the *émigré* priest Alexander Schmemann. (Only the Zhdanov speech has been included in the present translation.) There could have been no better recommendation to Soviet readers than the qualms of the publishing house. Nevertheless, the reader presupposed by the book is not the sensation-seeker; it is rather one of those innumerable members of the Soviet intelligentsia who, in Pasternak's phrase, "live by poetry". Through the trauma of Stalinism and the Brezhnev stagnation it was poetry—not, of course, officially approved verse—which gave readers a set of values to oppose to Marxism–Leninism and furnished examples of moral integrity and cant-free language. For these readers poetry was, and remains, a mode of secular spirituality.

The Western reader is fortunate to come to the text with different assumptions, and in translating I have felt the need to amplify some things which the author takes for granted, and to omit detail which the reader might find gratuitous. I have been encouraged to do so by the author himself. Anatoly Nayman is a distinguished translator; he made helpful comments, collaborated on the changes, and I am very grateful for his inventiveness and utterly unproprietorial attitude to the original. Nayman's complex, though elegant, phrasing and his creative use of language are an intrinsic part of the text and I have tried to give a sense of them and not to simplify them out of existence.

Remembering Anna Akhmatova contains many passages from Akhmatova's poems, translations of which I wished to take if possible from one source, so that Akhmatova could be heard as a single voice. I also wanted translations which conveyed some impression of Akhmatova's rhythms. While it is relatively easy to find good translations of individual poems it is much harder to find a satisfactory set of a large number of specified poems. Since Judith Hemschemeyer's complete translation was still in preparation, I turned to Walter Arndt's translations, and when a particular version did not illustrate the point Nayman was making, or Arndt had not translated the poem required, I supplied a version myself.

The text contains many references to places, and where names of streets could be translated into English rather than transliterated, I did so. Names of people are transliterated rather than given their English equivalents, with the exception of Lydia Chukovskaya and Joseph Brodsky.

Finally, I wish to record my gratitude to Elizabeth Robson, who made painstaking comments on an earlier version of the translation and many suggestions for its greater clarity. I am also grateful to the editors of the British and American publishing houses, who dealt resourcefully with a difficult text, and took over the final editing.

Wendy Rosslyn
Marburg, March 1990

Tanquem si homo notus sive conspiciatur oculis, sive cogitetur, et nomen ejus obliti requiramus, quidquid aliud occurrerit non connectitur: quia non cum illo cogitari consuevit, ideoque respuitur donec illud adsit, ubi simul assuefacta notitia non inaequaliter acquiescat.

... if we see or think of a person we know, and, unable to remember his name, we attempt to recall it, then any other name we recall fails to fit, because we are unaccustomed to think of it in connection with this person, and it is rejected until the real name presents itself, on the appearance of which we immediately observe the usual connection of ideas, and are reassured.

St Augustine, *Confessions*, X, 19

One night I had a dream. Suddenly, in an instant, a high white Leningrad ceiling above my head became swollen with blood and then a scarlet river cascaded down on me. A few hours later I met Akhmatova. I could not get rid of the memory of the dream and I told her about it.

"Not bad," she responded. "Generally the most boring thing in the world is other people's dreams and other people's lechery. But you deserve to hear mine. I had my dream on the night of 30 September–1 October.

"There had been a universal catastrophe and I was standing alone, quite alone, on the ground, in the slush, in the mud, I was slipping, I couldn't stay on my feet, the ground was being washed away. And from somewhere above me, spreading out as it approached and becoming more and more menacing, came a torrent in which all the great rivers of the world, the Nile, the Ganges, the Volga, the Mississippi, had come together ... That was all I needed."

❖   ❖   ❖

I first met Akhmatova in the autumn of 1959. I was twenty-three. We had mutual friends; an opportunity presented itself. By that time I had been writing poems for several years. I wanted Akhmatova to hear them, and I wanted her to like them.

At that time she lived in Leningrad in flat 4 at 3 Red Cavalry Street (Horse-Guards' Street before the revolution). This is in the Smolny district of the city, formerly the parish of Christmas. Not far away, in Tauride Street, was Vyacheslav Ivanov's "tower", his sixth-floor flat, where the Symbolists had a salon and where she used to go when she was young. Not far away was the Tauride Garden, where the ghosts of The Year 1913 lurked in blizzard-filled avenues.[1] Not far away either was Tapestry Street, now Voinov Street, with the prison famed for its many famous detainees, which at various times held her first husband, her son, and her last husband ... At any given place in Leningrad something had once happened, someone used to live, someone had met someone. "Do you remember our conversations in February 1914 in Horse-Guards' Street?" wrote Nikolay Vladimirovich Nedobrovo, a man who played a unique role in Akhmatova's poetic and personal fate, in a letter to a mutual friend of Akhmatova and himself. Whenever she and I happened to be travelling in the city and she pointed out some house or other, then another, then a third, she would cut herself short: "Tell me to keep quiet, I'm turning into a professional guide." She had lived a long life, and seen events which had no connection with one another going on in one and the same place, and seen one and the same play being produced in the most various of stage sets. Moreover, she also attracted the most improbable coincidences and the most unexpected doubles.[2] The repetition of an event, its reflection in a new mirror, displayed it in a new way. If a meeting did not take place, a non-meeting did, and for her both were real and magical, substantial and incorporeal. The days of her life, apart from the words, work, and minutes of which they consisted, were also anniversaries and jubilees: tenth anniversaries, silver and golden jubilees. Everything was "as it was then", at some time in the past. The time when I got to know her, and up to the end of her life, was the time of the fiftieth anniversaries: the first published poems, of the publication of Evening, Rosary, and White Flock, joining the Poets' Guild, of her marriage to Gumilyov,[3] and the birth of her son. Space behaved as time did and made a whimsical choice of houses and streets for her. When she was four years old, she lived at Tsarskoe Selo, in Wide Street; her last registered place of residence was Lenin Street in Leningrad, formerly Wide Street. She spent more than thirty years within the walls of the House on the Fontanka, the palace of the Counts Sheremetev; and her body lay in its coffin in the morgue of the Sklifosovsky Institute in Moscow, formerly the Sheremetev almshouse, which bore the same coat of arms and the same motto, *Deus conservat omnia*.

The woman who opened the door to me, and the woman who had been visiting and was just leaving, and the grey-haired smiling gentleman whom I met in the corridor, even the girl who passed quickly at the back of the flat, seemed unusual; their unusual exteriors seemed to carry the stamp and secret of her private life. But she herself was stunningly—I shall use the awkward, but most suitable, word—grand, inaccessible, distant from everything around her, from people and from the world, silent, still. My first impression was that she was taller than me, then it turned out that she was the same height, perhaps marginally shorter. She held herself very erect, as if balancing her head, walked slowly, and even when she moved was like a sculpture, a massive, meticulously modelled—at some moments, it seemed, hewn—classical sculpture: a masterpiece of the art form. And what she had on, something threadbare and long, perhaps a shawl, or an old kimono, was reminiscent of the flimsy wrappings which are thrown over the finished piece in the sculptor's studio. Many years later this impression came distinctly to mind in connection with Akhmatova's writing about Modigliani, who thought that women who were worthwhile subjects for sculpture or painting seemed clumsy in dresses.

She asked whether I wrote poems and suggested that I recite them. One poem contained the line "My short boot [*botinok*] capers like a sleek black fish". When I had finished reciting, she said, "We used to say *botinka*" (that is, the word was feminine, not masculine in gender). A few years later I was reciting my lines about the park at Pavlovsk, "And the leaves whirl round my shoe [*tufel'*] like a wheel". She pronounced, "We would say *tuflia*," again using the feminine. I reminded her of the boot and made some witticism about my miscalculations with footwear, which did not find favour.

The woman who had let me into the flat brought in a saucer on which lay a lonely boiled carrot, which had been peeled perfunctorily and had already dried up somewhat. Perhaps such was her diet, perhaps it was simply Akhmatova's wish, or the result of disregard for housekeeping, but for me at that moment this carrot expressed her infinite indifference—to food and everyday routine, which was almost asceticism, especially viewed alongside her unkemptness and her poverty.

I caught her in her relatively comfortable years. The Literary Fund had allocated her a *dacha* at Komarovo, a little weather-boarded house, which she called, good-naturedly rather than disparagingly, her Cabin, as she did the little hut near Odessa where she had been born. It can be seen even now, one of four on the small promontory between Osipenko Street and Lake Street. She once said that one had to be a rare architect to give such a house only one living-room. Indeed, there was a tiny kitchen, and a room of average proportions if rather dark, and all the rest was corridors, a verandah and a second porch. One corner of the trestle bed on which she slept had lost its leg and bricks had to be put underneath. When she went to Italy in 1964 to receive a literary prize she was obliged to borrow some pieces of clothing; on her return I took a disintegrating woollen scarf to the widow of the rich and famous novelist Aleksey Tolstoy.

Those with whom she shared the flat in Leningrad, Irina Nikolaevna Punina (it was she who opened the door to me), who was the daughter of Akhmatova's last husband, and Anya Kaminskaya, his grand-daughter, could not give her the attention she needed: they had their own families, troubles, and things to do, and selflessness was required in this case. Nina Antonovna Olshevskaya, with whom she most often stayed when in Moscow, Mariya Sergeevna Petrovykh, and Nika Niko-laevna Glen, who gave her shelter at various times, were selfless, genuinely good to her, and attentive. Even so, these were refuges and not her own home. Homelessness, being unsettled, a nomadic way of life. Being prepared for deprivations, disregard of deprivations, memories of them. Poverty, which was taken for granted, which arrested the attention, and was not merely for show. Not cultivated poverty, not tousled hair, not intentionally wearing a dress until it fell into shreds. Not feigned lack of well-being—"This is the third month I've been waiting for them to issue my visa for Paris." Insecurity as a norm of life. And the present stroke of luck in some matter or other only lit up the unhappy overall picture like the flash from a camera. An offer of an "advantageous" poetry translation meant weeks or months of exhausting work and reminded her of her inadequate seventy-rouble pension. The move to Komarovo for the summer began with the search for a distant female relative, a female acquaintance or friend who would look after her and help her. The award of the Italian prize or the Oxford degree emphasised how ill and old she was. In exactly the same way her smiles, laughter, lively monologues and jokes emphasised how sad her face, eyes and mouth were.

In her last years two or three of the people close to her very cautiously and indirectly broached with her the subject of her will. The point was that when her son, Lev Nikolaevich Gumilyov, had been in a labour camp Akhmatova had made a will in favour of Punina, so that after her death, as she expressed it, "the residents' management committee should not come round for the jumble". After her son was released she made a memorandum (in one of her notebooks and on a separate sheet of paper) revoking the previous will, which automatically meant that her son became the sole heir. This memorandum, however, was not witnessed by a notary and she asked me what I thought. I replied that in my view she should not leave a will which excluded her son in any form whatsoever. She immediately exploded, and began to cry out about false friends and being just an old beggar woman. A few days later she started again on the same topic and the scene repeated itself. And a third time. On 29 April 1965, at the end of the day, she suddenly said, "Let's call a taxi and go to the notary's office." She was then living in Lenin Street, and the office was in Moiseenko Street, not far from Red Cavalry Street. It turned out to be three very high flights up a steep staircase. The doctor had forbidden such climbs after her heart attack and I suggested that we return home and ask the notary to visit at a time when no one would be in the flat. She began to climb the stairs slowly. The outer office was empty, there seemed to be one other client. She lowered herself heavily on to a chair. I asked the notary to leave his desk and come out from behind the partition. He had a face and hands scarred from burns and shiny taut skin. Akhmatova said, "I am destroying my previous will." He explained that this must be done in writing. She almost groaned, "I haven't the strength to write much." We agreed that he would dictate, I would write, and she would sign. This we did. On the staircase she or I said something about Dickens. But when we came out into the street she said in anguish, "What inheritance is there to speak of? Tuck Modi's[4] drawing of me under your arm and go." (I should add in passing that after her death people who had no right to Akhmatova's archive but who had it in their possession put up a shameful fight for it, there was a disgraceful legal enquiry and as a result manuscripts found their way to three different institutions; it is, moreover, not clear how many individual pages, and which ones, remained in which hands.)

Poverty is an indispensable part of the poet's fate, at least of the modern poet's fate. Akhmatova thought that it was not fitting for real *artists* and worthy people in general to live in luxury. "Why does he insist on being photographed with such expensive things in the picture?" she remarked, looking at colour photographs of Picasso in a journal. "Like a banker." On her return from England she talked about meeting a person who had occupied a special place in her life. Now, according to her, he lived in a fine castle surrounded by flower-beds, with servants and silver. "I thought, it's not right for a man to climb into a golden cage." When Brodsky[5] was tried and sent into exile in the north she said, "What a biography they're making for our Ginger. As if he'd gone out and hired someone to do it." And to my question about the poetic fate of Mandelstam,[6] whether it was overshadowed by his fate as a citizen, which he had in common with millions of others, she replied, "It's ideal."

People were attracted to her not only on account of her poverty, not only for her intelligence, knowledge and memory, but primarily by the authenticity of her fate. I left school in 1953, three months after Stalin's death and two after the release of the Jewish doctors who had been falsely accused of conspiring to murder government and Party officials. Youth's inevitable dissatisfaction with the older generation, the "fathers" as Turgenev would have said, and its attempts to rebel and get free of their power, were fuelled by the sudden discovery of the fathers' cowardice, blindness, hypocrisy, and impotence, not to mention their degeneracy and servility.[7] Youth, with its all-or-nothing approach, did not want to get involved in understanding the complexity of the reasons; and in its egotism, youth's soul was not prepared to be sympathetic. At the same time youth's inevitable need for authority led to disillusion: on close inspection official authority turned out to be hollow and dissident authority to be on the decline.

Akhmatova's elegy 'Memories have three epochs' was published in the 1956 volume of the Moscow anthology *Day of Poetry*. I could not decide what impressed me most about it: the fact that she was still alive, or its content and beauty. Over the thirty years which have passed since then, this blank verse poem, which I immediately learned by heart, has come to mind many times, with good cause and with none, and has gradually filled with meaning. This was a new Akhmatova, and also a familiar one, glimpsed in her 'Epic Motifs'. The next time I saw 'Memories' was in the 1961 edition of her poetry—nicknamed "the frog edition" because of the green shade of its binding—in a cycle with 'So here is that autumnal landscape' (Akhmatova pronounced the Russian word for "landscape" in the French manner) and the quatrain beginning "No longer will that voice respond". The quatrain was dazzling and for a time it completely eclipsed the elegy. "Rejoicing and grieving". "It is all finished". Nothing was superfluous, the intonation was absolutely right, the power of each word was unquestionable. But the main thing was the sound. I imagined a few of the poets whose poems had appeared side by side with hers in the *Day of Poetry* anthology making an arrangement amongst themselves. One might imagine Pasternak[8] reading his 'A candle burned', then Tsvetaeva[9] her 'Newspaper Readers', Zabolotsky his 'Farewell to Friends' and Akhmatova her 'Memories'. But something in the woman who had had the carrot served up to her went beyond the bounds of this new poem, and all the earlier poems I already knew, and in the words which she spoke from time to time there was a sound which, as I then thought, could not conceivably be captured in poetry. This voice, apparently plucked from the chorus of mourners lamenting someone who had fallen silent, could not sing in any choir of poets. "Where you are no more". At the same time these few parting words did not conceal the artistry with which they were composed: the lines produced "an effect", the line broke off at "And my anthem carries ... "—that is, it is all finished, but the song carries, nevertheless.

My literature teacher at school, none other than the headmaster, a short, physically strong man, with Mongolian eyes and a strong chin, a medal-winner at forty, neither conducted empty conversations about his subject, nor dealt in subtleties. He said of Akhmatova, in connection with the 1946 Resolution of the Central Committee which banned publication of her work, "She's a simple case. She was not beautiful herself, but all her life she loved a very handsome man. He paid her no attention, hence her decadence." His lessons were about planning questions, essays on questions. Any questions. Questions that might come up in the exam—we wrote only a small proportion of those we made plans for. His approach to literature was an honest one. He insisted that we know the set books, and gave us War and Peace to summarise over the summer. I enjoyed doing this, chapter by chapter, and filled up a thick exercise book. He did not insist that we develop a love of literature, which for some reason is considered more of a *sine qua non* than a love of chemistry. He did not insist that we love Gorky's *Mother*[10] and her son Pavel as much as *War and Peace* and Pierre. He dictated essay plans. "The character of Pierre Bezukhov in *War and Peace*". His significance in the novel. Relationships with other characters. Appearance, actions, character traits. "The character of Pavel Vlasov". His significance in the novel. Relationships with other characters. Appearance, actions, character traits. Given his view of literature all books were equal. Strictly speaking, the same held true in physics classes: a falling person had the same acceleration as a falling stone. And in biology: a spider also had a heart, only the blood circulation system was not a closed one. We were not taught the subtleties of *belles lettres*, were not forced to empathise with the positive characters, but on the other hand we were not told, as my children were thirty years later, "Eugene Onegin didn't dress like a Russian." Whether or not you liked Blok's poem *The Twelve*, you had to know that it denounced tsarism and sang of the revolution. You could be enchanted by Akhmatova's 'The Grey-Eyed King' but, woken during the night, report that the poem was decadent and depraved.

Akhmatova said that however many people she met, they could all recall 14 August 1946 as clearly as the day war was declared. This was the day on which the Resolution of the Central Committee censuring the journals *Star* and *Leningrad* for publishing Akhmatova and Zosh-chenko was issued. It was the first year after the war and I had been sent to some relatives in the little Latvian town of Ludza (formerly Liutsin) to be fattened up. My aunt's house stood on the square, and right opposite, on the other side of the pavement, there was a wooden stand, past which processions filed on festival days. I was ten. I was lying on the sun-baked painted boards of the stand, reading something, when my cousin, a citizen of Riga and a sixth-former, appeared with a newspaper in his hand. Making a stern face, he said, "What dreadful things are happening in your Leningrad! You've got out of hand there!" I began reading the newspaper, and even in that highly idiosyncratic rendering of her poems, I caught their charm and, as I would now put it, their dramatic quality, and therefore also their truth. I felt the attractiveness of the figure at whom the stones were being thrown and of course I did not doubt that after the Resolution Akhmatova would vanish for ever.

In short, when I went to Red Cavalry Street I was expecting to meet a great, mysterious, legendary woman who had not surrendered, to meet Dante, poetry, truth and beauty. This meeting "could not happen" and it did happen. I was not disappointed.

Her appearance, words and gestures all expressed the fact that she was doomed, utterly. This came as a surprise but, once recognised, was only to be expected. She had acknowledged her doom, so that it already emanated strength. Like all those whose first visits to her I observed thereafter, I too, in Mariya Sergeevna Petrovykh's subsequent definition, "came out staggering", with only the vaguest grasp of what was what, muttering something and mumbling. I left, stunned by the fact that I had spent an hour in the presence of a person not with whom I had no ideas in common (we had after all been talking about something for that hour), but with whom no one on earth could have anything in common. I caught myself thinking that it no longer mattered to me whether she liked my poems or not—it only mattered that she had simply heard them.

❖   ❖   ❖

"A humble lady, poorly dressed, impressive in her majesty." Standing at the trolley-bus stop after one of my visits to her, I realised that I had been repeating these lines mechanically for some time and immediately grinned at the thought that she was like that "school supervisor" of Pushkin's, as if on purpose. At this point I pulled myself together, feeling that my mockery was one more falsification of "the lucid sense of truthful conversations".

One day she let drop the remark "We do not remember what happened, only what we remembered one day." After her death I began to remember her, and since then I have been remembering my memories. But she left memories of herself which contain secrets. For example, once when she was talking about her non-affair with the poet Aleksandr Blok,[11] she spoke with disgust about the depths and imaginativeness of human banality: someone, on the basis of the lines in her *Poem without a Hero* "And now let's go home quickly down the steps of the Cameron Gallery", had hinted at her possible liaison, if not adultery, with one of the inhabitants of the royal palace. The Gallery forms part of the residence at Tsarskoe Selo.[12] She emphasised how refined the immoral mind can be, and with its particular emphases this observation remained in my memory for many years, together with others in the same vein. But also with various concrete references to Tsarskoe Selo which she made at various times.

On another occasion she recited some humorous Tsarskoe Selo verse, which related to the arrival in Russia of the French diplomat Lubbe, who, not informed of the recent morganatic marriage between Grand Prince Pavel Aleksandrovich and Princess Paley, formerly the wife of Pistohlkors, addressed himself to the Empress thus:

> "*Où est Prince Paul, dites-moi, Madame?*"
> Asked Lubbe, bending low, of course.
> "*Il est parti avec ma femme!*"
> Barked her equerry Pistohlkors.

She described Princess Paley as coming from Tsarskoe Selo, although I do not recall for certain whether she said that she knew her. She said that she had read her memoirs: "Not very interesting—an unobservant, untalented lady." After the revolution her husband was held in the Peter-Paul Fortress. "She used to take a sledge with parcels for him.

Anatoly Nayman

Then one night he was shot in the fortress courtyard. She went to
Sweden; when her daughters set eyes on her they understood everything
and burst into tears. There are two photographs in the book: a young
Petersburg beauty—and a woman in extreme old age, and the difference
is only a few years." Then she briefly recounted the details of the death
of the Princess's twenty-year-old son Vladimir, a poet, who had been
thrown down a mineshaft at Alapaevsk six months after the execution
of her husband.

In her writings connected with *Poem without a Hero* she also speaks
of Tsarskoe Selo, referring to the actress Glebova-Sudeykina, her friend
when she was young: "Olga danced *la danse russe rêvée par Debussy*, as
K.V. said of her in 1913." And also: "*La danse russe* in the palace at
Tsarskoe Selo". The memoirs of another, even older, friend, V. S.
Sreznevskaya, edited, if not partly dictated to her, by Akhmatova,
describe the following episode: "The domain of the past has now
claimed the thickets at Tsarskoe Selo and Pavlovsk, planted in the
manner of Versailles and the English; moonlit nights with a thin little
girl in a little white dress on the roof of the green house on the corner
('How awful! She's walking in her sleep!'); and all the caprices of this
freedom-loving child, bathing her little white (there was nowhere for
them to get suntanned!) shapely feet in the stream near Tyarlevo—and
the affectionate voice of Grand Prince Vladimir Aleksandrovich, out on
his morning walk with his aide-de-camp, 'Will you not catch cold,
young lady?'—and the horrified Madame Vinter, who found out about
our pranks (it was always her) and promised to tell our parents
'everything', and our shyness with the handsome old man who made
this observation to us so nicely." And on the map of Tsarskoe Selo
which Akhmatova drew in her own hand the palace of Grand Prince
Vladimir Aleksandrovich (the father of K.V., Kirill Vladimirovich) is
marked.

Akhmatova made a list of dates and addresses after her note "From 2
to 16—Tsarskoe Selo":

Tsarskoe Selo

The so-called Cold House (1893?), Wide Street, first house after
the station. [...]
Bernaskoni's house, Nameless Lane. (1894)
Evdokiya Ivanovna Shukhardina the merchant's wife's house.

10

[...] To begin with on the ground floor with the Antonovs upstairs. [...]

Then on the first floor, with the Tyulpanovs downstairs. N. S. Gumilyov used to visit the brother, Andrey.

Wide Street, the second house after the station, right-hand side, on the corner of Nameless Lane.

My window looked out on to Nameless Lane. Lived there till May 1905.

Summer 1905. Boulevard Street, Sokolovsky's house. Thence to Eupatoria at the beginning of August (father's retirement and parents' separation).

"Nameless Lane" originally figured in the subtitle of 'Tsarskoe Selo Ode', written at the end of Akhmatova's life. It was followed by two epigraphs, "In the lane there was a wooden fence" from Gumilyov, and Punin's "You are a poet of local (Tsarskoe Selo) significance".

Over the years my consciousness gradually pieced together these memoirs, scraps of information, random observations and jottings until little by little they formed a complete, if fading, picture. And that ancient attack on someone's dirty—and denunciatory—suppositions about the Cameron Gallery began to sound different. Not in the sense, of course, that "something" had indeed happened—no! (I hear the same indignation and disgust in her   about people with degraded, malicious minds, *esprits mal tournés*, who twisted poetry in any way they wanted.) But in the sense that everything is less simple than it at first seems.

And when she wrote in her diary, "'All stone compasses and lyres'—it has always seemed to me that P-n said this about Tsarskoe ...", I think that she *knew* more surely than others that Pushkin said this about Tsarskoe. But she wanted to allude to the "majestic lady"; to Mandelstam's review of *The Muses' Almanach*, where he wrote about "the hieratic dignity, the religious simplicity and solemnity" of her poetry: "after the woman came the turn of the *lady*". You recall: "humble lady, poorly dressed, impressive in her majesty"; finally, about the lyres hung on the branches of someone's garden.

The subtle poison of literary rejoinders incidentally made.

❖   ❖   ❖

There was another reason why young people like me reached out to her. She was the living and, we thought then, the flawless symbol of the connectedness of different periods. A young man is by nature a Futurist: he is dissatisfied with the system as he finds it and in any case wants to overturn and dispense with both the restrictions and the conventions, with which he is uncomfortable, and which get in his way. If his walk of life turns out to be art he also proposes to replace the rules with new ones which he considers to be the sole necessary and right ones. But, having received the approval of like-minded people, the overwhelming majority of whom are his own age, he feels intuitively that his position is insecure, lacking a firm foundation, and he seeks support from "other people", especially his elders. He wants his position to be approved not only by "the present moment" but also by "eternity". This is how the mechanism of tradition works.

Akhmatova met the revolution as a completely formed person with moral foundations and principles which she never had occasion to alter. The sureness of her behaviour explains amongst other things the fact that she and Mandelstam were considered and called old when they were only thirty. She was the product of two hundred years of Petersburg culture, and, more widely, of several centuries of Russian culture. She had assimilated the values of a vast period of history. Her moral assessment of what was happening was that of, let us say, Princess Anna of Kashin, or Princess Anna, wife of Yaroslav the Wise, or Anna the prophetess.[13] She told a story about a friend of hers: several years after the revolution the latter was washing linen in a basin in the communal kitchen of a multi-occupied flat. Her daughter ran in from school and as she passed said lightly, though provocatively, "Mother, there is no God." Her mother, not breaking off from the washing, replied, "Where's He gone then?" Akhmatova was not willing to throw overboard from "the steamship of modernity", to use the Futurists' phrase, the cultural ballast which had now been declared redundant; she would not reject the old, tried and true in favour of the much-advertised new. And so when you called out to her in your seeking and she replied, the sound of her every word awoke an echo which receded goodness knows where into the distance of the centuries, and did not bounce off the nearby wall of modern times.

She had no great respect for the poetry which was read from the stage in the late 1950s and early 1960s. Nor was the quality of the poetry the main reason, as I observed. She could forgive any fallacious discovery if she saw honest searching behind it. What was unacceptable was above all the spiritual qualities of the authors, their moral principles, which reflected only the realities of the here and now, and their debased taste.

A young Moscow poet, an acquaintance of mine, asked me to arrange for him to meet her. I told her about this and recommended him to her, and she asked whether I could remember any of his poetry. I recited two lines from a youthful poem: "Autumn comes to each in different ways—in poems, women, wine." "Too many women," she said. But she agreed to receive him.

Or about a poet who was then fashionable, whom I shall call here Albert Epiphany: "How can a person who performs under a name like that call himself a poet? And not hear that a Russian clerical surname doesn't go with a foreign first name straight out of an operetta?" And when I tried to defend him, saying this was his parents' wish, she responded, "That's what you're a poet for, to think up a decent pseudonym."

Once, the mail was brought to her and she began reading a letter from her sister-in-law Khanna Gorenko, while I began looking through one of the literary monthlies, *New World*. After a little while she looked up and asked what I had found. "Yevtushenko." She asked me to choose a poem and read it out loud. "I criticise him, but I've hardly read him." The poem was about the fact that when memory fails a person, and a second memory (apparently the heart's memory) also fails, then a third still remains: "Let the arms recall such-and-such, let the skin recall, let the feet recall the dust of the roads, let the lips ..." The poem had ten stanzas and I observed that after the third she began to listen distractedly and to glance at the letter, which she had not finished reading. When I got to the end she said, "Khanna's letter enhanced the impression somewhat ... What sensitive feet he has!"

In some other poems which I recited in the train on the way to Komarovo, a Leningrad poet, who was in fashion at that time, was playing forced and not very inventive variations on the theme of the possibility of, as he put it, artificially reconstructing in the next century people who had lived in earlier times. And then the *bad* ones, so to speak, the *reactionaries*, would be reproduced in multiple copies as visual aids for schools, but it would be impossible to sculpt more than one copy of the *good* ones, the *progressive* people. I only recall that there would be almost a dozen and a half Mahomets, but one Mayakovsky.[14]

"Excuse me," said Akhmatova, "that's not only banal, it's also self-serving."

13

Soon after the revolution, and before her very eyes, began a process which called itself with smug profundity "the reorientation of the interests of poetry". However, the superficially convincing formula and the aplomb with which it was uttered were intended principally to deceive readers, and to suggest to them that it was legitimate to betray and reject that which makes verse into poetry. Poets' private opinions, their individual perceptions, in short, their personal attitude towards everything on earth is the sole thing which guarantees the authenticity of their every line. When a poet is universal, like Pushkin, his personal poems acquire the right to represent "everyone", to speak "on every-one's behalf"—more precisely, on behalf of each separate person. That is: I too remember the wonderful moment he speaks of, Leila left me, too, yester night, and in general he said all that "about me". But when a poet is individualistic, even egotistical, like Balmont or Igor Severyanin, he has no option: he speaks only personally and for himself, inviting the reader to admire his exceptional qualities or to ignore them.

The new arrangement—speaking "on behalf of the people", "for everyone"—redirected the poet's view, which now had to look out-wards and not in. Convergence of the two directions was allowed (and encouraged), as long as the new one always predominated. "We" elbowed "I" out of poetry patently and covertly: for example, Yev-tushenko's "I'm different, I'm dead tired and idle" was all right, in spite of the individuality of the event and the experience, because of the implication that this was "like many people", "with other people"; but something like Akhmatova's "We are all revellers here, whores"—was not, for obvious reasons. Many subjects and themes, those described as outdated, or intimate, and which were therefore mocked, became officially taboo, and, what is infinitely more important, taboo of the poet's own volition. It was not a question of the private becoming generalised, in so far as that was feasible; the general had to be adopted as one's own, in accordance with a given scheme. In fact authors went out to meet readers, recruited them efficiently, attracted audiences numbering many thousands, but all the time speculated in poetry like black-marketeers, and gave the readers all that they wanted, and not what they, the authors, had to offer. Akhmatova said of V., whose popularity soared in the 1960s, "I tell you as my considered judgment that not a single word of his poems has passed through his heart."

However, "we" in lyric poetry has quite specific content: I and you, I and he, or she, or a group of friends, more or less close, whom the poet can name. Only thus does the limited "we" become greater and generalised. My friends, how glorious is our unity, we exclaim with Pushkin, we, the students of the Tsarskoe Selo *lycée*, Delvig, etc., and therefore all who are "students", to the extent that they are "students". We live with ceremony and effort, we claim along with Akhmatova, we, the Petersburgers, who recognise each other in the street, and therefore recognise all who are poisoned and captivated by this city, to the extent that they are poisoned and captivated by it. In her wartime poem 'But you, my friends, recruits conscripted at the last' Akhmatova speaks of her duty "to shout out all your names to all the world", and in 'The Victors' she names them: Vankas, Vaskas, Alyoshkas, Grishkas—grandsons, little brothers, sons.

She wrote the poem 'Native Land' in hospital in 1961. It consists to a large degree of cliché formulas, only in reverse: "we do *not* write a sobbing poem to it", "we do *not* cherish it in memory", etc. The poem lacks the sharpness which is typical of her poetry, one seems to have read many of the lines elsewhere, and "we" sounds not at all like Akhmatova—it is vague and has no specific addressee. Except, that is, for two lines, more precisely two words within them, which put everything right. "But we mill and we mash and we crumble, and mix nothing into those ashes." "We mash and we crumble" [*mesim i kroshim*] is a reply from the distance of a quarter of a century to Mandelstam's password "Arabian mash and hash" [*mesivo, kroshevo*] in 'Verses about the Unknown Soldier'. It is, perhaps, the ashes of Gumilyov and Mandelstam, which are intended here, perhaps more widely the ashes of the friends of her youth, "to lament" whom, as she wrote, "her life was spared". The fact that this poem has an addressee is revealed still more clearly by the contrast begging to be made with a poem written less than three years later, 'This land, though not my native land'. It too contains standardised imagery, which is especially concentrated in the last quatrain; however, this derives from Symbolist poetics: "The sunset in the aether's waves is such that I cannot be sure: is day or cosmos at an end, or Mystery in me once more?" Here we have what became a commonplace of Symbolist criticism: "When a Symbolist says 'sunset' he means 'death,'" and Akhmatova's satirical recollection: "If a Symbolist was told, 'This is a weakness in your poem,' he would reply arrogantly, 'But you are pointing to the mystery!'" It is curious that the preceding two lines demonstrate, as it were, the Acmeists tilling the soil which belongs *par excellence* to the Symbolists—sunsets: "The rosy body of the pines is bared when sunset's hour is come."

("We were on the ascent. We were daring, lucky, out on our own," she said. They respected the doyens of Symbolism both at the beginning of their path and in later life, in spite of all their attempts to usurp them, but Symbolism itself was going through a crisis. "We became Acmeists, others Futurists." One day I said in passing that, organisational motives and group principles apart, the poetic platform—and programme—of the Symbolists was in any event grander than that of the Acmeists, who set themselves up largely in opposition to Symbolism. Akhmatova said, more huskily than before and therefore more significantly, "Don't you think I know that Symbolism is possibly the last great movement in poetry?" She may even have said "in art".)

"It should not be forgotten," she emphasises in her *Pages from a Diary*, that Mandelstam said in 1937: "I do not repudiate either the living or the dead." She was breathing the new air, but her lungs were still full of the old, which she had inhaled during her youth. She told me how she happened to be at the station—seeing someone off, apparently Mandelstam—on the very day when the nobility were being deported from Leningrad; they were crowding on the platform and kept greeting her as she passed: "I never thought I knew so many nobles." Through her I got to know a few of her women friends, her "younger contemporaries". I thought then that these sixty- and seventy-year-old women were the natural constant of any society, that elderly ladies and old women of this kind, worn out, but not embittered, wretched with suffering, but not despairing, with bloodless faces and mournful eyes, but selfless, forgiving, and approachable, had always been there and always would be. But it turned out that these were the last specimens of a dying race. Today's seventy-year-olds may have been brought up by them, but they have lived all their lives in a qualitatively different atmosphere and this has inevitably affected not only their psychosomatics, as modern doctors would say, but also the composition of their blood. When Chaplin died Lyubov Davydovna Bolshintsova-Stenich said to me, "I was a private in the army he commanded." What old woman nowadays could say such a thing about any army and herself?

Akhmatova inherited, as she said in her poems, the regal word, Dante's Muse, the swans at Tsarskoe Selo, Dostoevsky's Russia, and her mother's kindness. As she wrote, she "made, perhaps, the best that could be made" out of this, rebuilding the house of poetry in her own way, out of the stone of the house which had come down to her, and leaving it for posterity to inherit. These stones are eternal, and as always, from time immemorial, they are suitable for the next builder to use. They are suitable, but not yet required, not in use: there is a new life-style, new functions for architecture, new materials, and plastic is in vogue—"the deathless veneer", as Akhmatova called it.

❖   ❖   ❖

In December 1962 I read her the long poem which I had just finished. This was in Moscow. It was bitterly cold, but there was no snow. She was staying at the time in the home of Nika Nikolaevna Glen in Garden-Carriage Street and in the warmth and cosiness of this family she looked gentler and more homely. "She's another Matryona," she said of N.N.'s mother, referring to Solzhenitsyn's story 'Matryona's House'. By this time fairly friendly relations had been established between her and me, though as yet without the trust that was to come, without that—"after some hesitation I have decided to write to say that . . ."—warmth, which grew after a few months. She said that she liked the poem, liked "this constant walking on the brink, the more so since it is air, sea, light and earth". She also said, "density of thought", not as a compliment, not in disapproval, but stating a fact, as it were. She said, "It is indubitably a poem, although the metre has not been found", and, "I do not like iambic hexameters combined with pentameters." More than once, both before and after this conversation, she spoke about the role of metre in defining and constructing a long poem, and about the fact that the long poem is more or less the metre; she insisted that the metre (and stanza), say Pushkin's iambs (and his *Eugene Onegin* above all), is not an open door but a barrier, on which many poems have wrecked themselves. Only a new metre could therefore ensure the success of Nekrasov's *Red Nose Frost* and Blok's *The Twelve*. As far as the combination of hexameters with pentameters goes, she was objecting, as I understand it, not to the device as such, which she herself used liberally, but to the arbitrariness of the combination, which was possibly not motivated by my conception of the poem, but was merely the result of a poor ear, or even of no ear at all. One brief chapter she disliked absolutely, and when she talked about this, I became ashamed of having compelled her to listen to these lines which she found so unpleasant. She said, "You will redo this chapter, or cut it," and after a short but sharply defined pause: "Or leave it as it is." A little later she said, "It's a new piece," which I understood not by any means to be a

17

sign of approval, but mainly to mean: not our kind of thing. And finally, as if letting the remark drop in passing, she said ". . . this unified suite", and gave me a sense of the distance between her understanding of what a long poem was and my ideas about the long poem as they then were.

Then, twenty-five years ago, I wanted to hear praise (and therefore did) in her comments on this "youthful" poem. Now I do not flatter myself on this account, and I only note that her critique was business-like, professional, and that it did not contain even a shadow of "old Derzhavin", who, as Pushkin said, gave his blessing to a younger poet as he descended into the grave. But now I also know that this was not one of Akhmatova's customary "gramophone records".

"Gramophone records" was the name she gave to a particular genre of oral narrative, polished by many performances, which had its details, turning points and barbed passages definitively adjusted, but which still disclosed its improvised origin in its intonation and its responsiveness to circumstances of the moment. "Haven't I played you the record about Balmont? . . . about Dostoevsky? . . . about the sparks from the steam engines?" and then would follow a brilliant short *étude*, a lively anecdote in the manner of Pushkin's table talk, with aphorisms applic-able, and subsequently applied, to similar or reverse situations. Once she had written them down—and the majority she did write down—they became more imposing and immutable, but, I think, lost their spontaneity.

So, sometimes—not, by the way, as frequently as may be supposed—people who wrote poetry would come to her to get her opinion. She would ask them to leave some poems, and she would begin to read, and if the poem left her cold—and it was rarely otherwise—she would limit her reading to a few lines, or more rarely to a whole poem. When the authors came for her response she tried not to upset them and said something non-committal which, coming from her lips, could be taken as praise. For this she also had "records", two or three sayings which were used successfully, depending on the circumstances.

If there was a description of a landscape in what she read, Akhmatova would say, "Your poems have a feeling for nature." If she came upon dialogue, "I like it when direct speech is introduced into poetry." If the verse was unrhymed, "It is harder to write blank verse than rhymed." Anyone who after this asked her to look at "a few recent poems" would hear her say, "This is very much you." And finally the universal "In your poems the words stand in their proper places" was always to hand.

Remembering Anna Akhmatova

At the end of the evening when I recited my long poem to her she told me how when her mother, Inna Erazmovna Gorenko, had read some of Akhmatova's poems (or had even heard her recite them?), she abruptly burst into tears, and said, "I don't know, I only see that my little daughter is in a bad way." "Now I too see that you are in a bad way." It was after that day that we began to meet frequently and to talk at length.

In general at that time she did not think much even of the poetry of those young people whose work she had singled out in some way. It was all primitive, at best "graduation from a literacy class", as she once said, putting her seal on the matter. One day we were sitting on the verandah, looking at the pine-trees, the grass and the heather, and she said with a mocking expression on her face, "Kolya was standing tall and straight opposite Gorky, who was also tall, but stooped, and he was instructing him in a mentor's tones: 'You don't know how to write poetry and shouldn't do it. You don't know the fundamentals of versification, you don't hear the metre, you don't feel the rhythm or the line. In a word, this is not your trade.' And he listened meekly. But I watched this scene and felt bored."

Here it is relevant to quote in its entirety a letter she wrote in 1960. She passed it on to me, although it was not written to me, or rather, does not carry my name. It is one of "the letters to X.Y." which Timenchik, one of the most thorough scholars of Akhmatova's poetry, has called epistles "to the bearer". In the last decade of her life she wrote several of them, and several people, of whom I am one, could consider themselves the addressee, pointing to some concrete phrase as proof. The one under discussion lay in an old Italian trunk, a *credenza*, which stood in her room and was full of manuscripts, files, notebooks, old proofs, etc. One winter day in 1964, in the middle of a conversation which touched on the current poetry boom and the new twist in her fate (the publication of *Requiem* in the West, the Italian prize, etc.), she said, "Please open the *credenza* and find me such-and-such a letter in such-and-such a place." I found it, and inside it another sheet of paper, entirely covered with writing. "That is for you." I read both and put the sheets of paper on the table. "That is for you." I thanked her and concealed them in my pocket. She began talking about something else.

In reply to a number of your letters I want to say the following.
I have recently observed that readers are deliberately turning

away from my poetry. What I can publish does not satisfy them. My name will not be amongst those which young people (poetry is always in the charge of young people) will now acclaim.*

Although I have a hundred or so good poems, they will not save anything. They will be forgotten.

All that will remain will be a book of mediocre, monotonous, and, of course, old-fashioned poems. People will be surprised that sometime back in their younger days they had enthused about these poems, and will not notice that they had not enthused about these poems at all, but about the ones which did not get into the book.

This book will be the end of my path. I shall not be part of that upsurge of poetry and interest in it which is coming about so rapidly now, just as Sologub failed to cross the threshold of 1917 and remained forever immured in 1916. I do not know in what year I shall be immured, but that's not very important. I have been on the proscenium too long and it's time for me to go behind the scenes.

Yesterday I read this fateful book myself for the first time. It is good serviceable third-rate stuff. Everything merges together—a lot of gardens and parks. A tiny bit better towards the end, but no one will get to the end. And then how much more agreeable it is to establish for oneself the "total failure" (*chute complète*) of the poet. We know that already from Pushkin, whom everyone shunned (including his friends, cf. Karamz.).[15]

Incidentally (although this is another issue) I am sure that there are no readers of poetry left now. There are copiers, and there are memorisers. People hide scraps of paper with poems on them in their bosoms, and whisper poetry in each other's ears, making each other swear to forget it on the spot and for ever, etc.

The very appearance of printed poems evokes yawns and nausea—people have had a surfeit of bad poems. Poetry has become its own opposite. Instead of "Fire with the Word the people's hearts",[16] rhymed lines fuel boredom.

But in my case things are a little more complicated. Apart from all the difficulties and disasters on the official side (two Central Committee resolutions), I have also lived with constant misfortune on the creative side, and the official misfortune has poss. even partly concealed or taken the edge off the more important thing. I fairly early found myself on the far right (not polit.). Everyone was further to the left, and consequently newer, more fashionable:

20

Mayakovsky, Pasternak, Tsvetaeva. Not to mention Khlebnikov, who is still the innovator *par excellence*. That is why "the young writers" who came after us were always so fiercely and irreconcilably hostile to me, e.g. Zabolotsky and, of course, the others from the Association for Real Art. The Briks' salon fought against me systematically, accusing me, in a manner which stinks of denunciation, of being an internal *émigrée*. Eykhenbaum's book about me is full of fear and alarm, lest he find himself in the lit. cart on my account. A few decades later all this moved abroad. There, for convenience and so as not to tie their hands, they began by announcing that I was a nonentity as a poet (Harkins Encyclopaedia), after which it was very easy to give me short shrift, as e.g. Ripolino does, not without grace, in his anthology. Not aware of what I was writing, not understanding the position in which I found myself, he simply bellows that I have written myself out, that everyone is bored with me, that I realised this myself in 1922 and so on.

This is more or less all that I wanted to tell you on this score. It goes without saying that I could supply a multiplicity of examples which corroborate my train of thought. However, they would hardly be of interest to you.

Leningr./Moscow
22 Jan/29 Feb 1960

* This happened once (and poss. more than once) in the '20s, when my readers from the '10s were still alive. Young people at that time avidly anticipated the appearance of some great new revolutionary poetry and trampled on everything around them in its honour (mem. Gaspra, 1929). Then everyone was expecting wonders of Dzhek Altauzen.[17] [*Akhmatova's own footnote*]

❖　　　❖　　　❖

The majority of Akhmatova's diary entries during her last years are devoted to "the beginning": the Silver Age, the relationships of those years, Acmeism. She was explaining causes, exposing slander and lies, correcting errors and inaccuracies, and, I think, generally making minor corrections to one detail or another of the vanished past—not so as to

21

embellish it, not for the sake of future advantage, but rather *mutatis mutandis*, with an eye to changing circumstances. Too much had begun to sound and look different, and sometimes sounded and looked the exact opposite of what it had originally been. She took note of this and said that the twentieth century had withdrawn certain words, such as "silence", had changed the meaning of others, such as "space" or "infinity", or had altered the implications of others: "When people say the word 'neighbour', no one envisages anything pleasant—everyone thinks of a communal kitchen." One of the most extreme, and most naïve, corrections was made in my copy of *Rosary*: in the line "We are all revellers here, whores" she crossed out "revellers" and "whores" and wrote in "came here from fabled shores"—"We all came here from fabled shores". This would have been laughable, were it not for the newspapers of August 1946, the millions of copies of which carried Zhdanov's description of her as "half nun, half whore", soon to be repeated in thousands of speeches at thousands of meetings.

To what extent did Akhmatova remain "a person of her time", that is, what marked her out from what preceded the 1910s and from what came after? Apart from the socio-political rupture and the shifts which it caused in the most various areas of life, as she watched, time also went through a series of evolutions which were, so to speak, natural, and which changed not the face of the age but the expression on its face. Tastes, aesthetics, and fashions all changed. Firstly, Annensky was the last of the poets whose words were simply defined by their previous usage and not by the biography of the writer; Blok was the last of those who aimed to serve beauty with their poetry, and not culture. Secondly, was the conception of art as craft, as religious rite, as a means of transforming the world, was the essential *sine qua non* of the circle which Akhmatova entered in order to take up her place.

She said that whenever Annensky became enamoured of some lady or other, his wife would sell a birch copse and send him off to Switzerland, from whence he returned "cured". She said, and wrote, that "the blinded children" in his poem 'My Anguish' are those poems of his which were thrown out of the second number of the journal *Apollo*. But these are pieces of information and explanations which may facilitate our understanding of the psychology of his creative work, but they are more imposed upon his poetry than necessary to it. His fate as a civil servant and a schoolmaster adds nothing to his poems. The day she read

Leon Felipe's *Interrogation* she said, "In twentieth-century poetry Spaniards have the reputation of being the gods and Russians the demi-gods—we have too many suicides." (Her immediate reaction was: "*What* an old man!" and "I'm envious that it's not mine" and admiration for Geleskul's skill as a translator.) In that case, is Annensky, whose heart attack she associated with postponement of the publication of his poems from one number of the journal to the next, a "god" or a "demi-god"?

One dazzling Leningrad summer evening in 1963 we suddenly decided to go to Komarovo. Anna Andreevna, Nina Antonovna Olshevskaya, her son Boris and I. It did occur to us while we were running for the brandy, phoning for a taxi, and heading out of town, that it was already after ten, but the sun was high and shone in our eyes all the way. We were elated, the trip was something of an escapade: no preliminaries, none of the usual preparations, we had no idea whether Lev and Sarra Arens, the old couple who were looking after Akhmatova that summer, were at the Cabin or not. Everything was a source of pleasure on the way; the conversation came in bursts with periodic comments and rejoinders spoken fast and playfully, aimed at a receptive and happy audience. Nina Antonovna worked out various combinations of sleeping arrangements. I said, "Let's get there and have a drink and then spread ourselves out." To which A.A. replied, "Are you sure that what you are suggesting is entirely respectable? ... Borya, is that how I brought you and your brother up when you were children?" Boris gave me a sympathetic look. When we arrived it had started to get dark. We lit the candles, it was a warm night, the pine-trees were right outside the open window. I had the strange sensation that we were sitting amongst them and that the light, just as in de la Tour's pictures, was picking out the bookshelf, the table and the icon simultaneously. We had a small brandy, speaking less and less often. I surprised myself by saying, with unexpected emotion, "Somewhere there are poems which are so beautiful that every poem that has ever been written here on earth—forgive me, Anna Andreevna, yours included—is frightfully clumsy, ugly-sounding, tongue-tied. The only earthly word which fits in those poems, although it is the most unlovely, is 'beautiful' ... Perhaps the only verse which can show us what they are like, though the resemblance is not very close, is a few of Blok's lines ..." A few moments of silence followed, which I found quite natural at the time. Then Nina Anto-

23

novna and Boris, seeing that A.A. was silent, began to tease me in the way that we had fallen into in the car. Suddenly Akhmatova said, very seriously, "No, he's right."

On another occasion, when we had got on to the subject of modern French poetry, she said, "I know that Apollinaire is the last of the poets, you don't have to convince me." She may have said "the last of the European poets", but "last of all" is what has remained in my mind. I recall this here because Blok's name came up in that conversation immediately after Apollinaire's and with the same attribute: "last". The idea was that after him—or after them—something new had begun.

The new beginning was poetry which consciously based itself on quotation. Other texts, mostly taken from poetry, documentary texts, and allusions to myths, and also music and painting, began to be introduced into modern poetry on a new basis: for deliberate effect and *de rigueur*. Cultural signs were deployed in the poetry as landmarks, both obvious and concealed, and in the latter case the poet required the reader to find the key to their decipherment.

Our conversations touched more than once on T. S. Eliot: in the 1960s interest in him revived, and he won the Nobel Prize. His time, though short, came, and trained a focused beam of light on his person. His ideas became topical, his articles were reprinted. He was born one year before her and died one year earlier. She spoke about him in some detail, not "apropos of" him but really about him, a few days before he died. (She suddenly spoke about Nehru the day before his death and about Le Corbusier a week before his heart attack, also for no particular reason.) She spoke of him affectionately, as if he were a younger brother who had had to wait a lifetime for success, and had received it at the very end. "Poor thing, he worked in a bank for years, how hard it was for him. But at least in old age he had recognition and fame." Later she showed her guests an acutely moving photograph of him, standing with a slight stoop, behind his wife's armchair; it was in the issue of the journal *Europa Letteraria,* which announced the award of the Etna-Taormina prize to her—her first recognition in half a lifetime, also in old age. At that time I translated a chapter from *The Waste Land*, then a section from the *Four Quartets*. In the *Four Quartets* she marked the lines

> The only wisdom we can hope to acquire
> Is the wisdom of humility: humility is endless.

She often repeated "Humility is endless" in English. And around that same time "In my beginning is my end", also from the *Four Quartets*, appeared as the epigraph to 'Tails', the second part of *Poem without a Hero*.

Eliot introduced quotations into his verse text here, there and everywhere, showing his hand. Akhmatova does not make collages of this kind. She transplanted the quotations, regenerating them so that the foreign tissue was compatible with her own. But both used the same sources: Dante, Shakespeare, Baudelaire, Nerval, Laforgue . . . I think it was the line from Gerard de Nerval's 'El Desdichado', quoted by Eliot, which served one day as the starting point for a conversation about the poem. She recited a few lines from memory, took the slim volume of *Les Chimères* from the shelf or out of the drawer, opened it at 'El Desdichado' and said, mockingly as it were, "Now see what you can do with that." A half line from this sonnet soon became the epigraph of 'Pre-Spring Elegy': *Toi qui m'a consolée,* with a change of grammatical gender to make *toi* masculine.

It should be said straightaway, although it will in any case become clear from what follows, that Akhmatova's allusions to authors, the dialogues she conducted with them through quoting their texts (or quoting her own texts as if they were someone else's) is essentially different from the retelling, even the verbatim retelling, of someone's works or of individual passages from them. I read her one of my contemporaries' poems, 'The Potato Eaters', which poetry buffs liked. It describes Van Gogh's picture from the point of view of the eaters and the idea of the whole piece is summed up in its concluding lines: "Either we consume potatoes In the dark, or he does." She snorted critically "Let him make 'The Potato Eaters' himself, not imitate Van Gogh." One should write, not just describe.

Amongst her early poems she preferred 'You marked with charcoal on my left side', both in itself and especially on account of its last stanza:

> You marked with charcoal on my left side
> The target at which to aim,
> To let the bird, my anguish, fly out
> Into desolate night again.
>
> My dear, you'll aim with no hesitation.
> Not long to suffer now.

25

The bird, my anguish, will then fly out,
Sit and sing from its bough.

So that he who's untroubled inside his four walls
Should open the window and say,
"Familiar voice, but I can't catch the words",
And then cast down his gaze.

She made a comparison between these lines and a seventeenth-century
Korean poem which she subsequently translated:

For when my death is close at hand
My soul will take a cuckoo's shape;
The leafy heart of flowering pears
Will be my midnight hiding place,
And from the darkness I shall sing
So that my lover hears my voice.

She repeated the last two lines and added, "What a blow that Korean
geisha dealt me!" But the piquant contrast and the witticism were beside
the point.

The voice singing words which the listener cannot identify, but
which, however, he clearly recognises—or which he finds familiar—was
Akhmatova's own poetic voice, which she began to train in her very
earliest poems. Nedobrovo wrote to her:

How you sing out in answer to all hearts,
And, opening your lips, you breathe our souls;
In the approach of every human face
You hear the song of reed-pipes in your blood!

playing a variation on one of the main themes of his article "Anna
Akhmatova". It appeared in *Russian Thought* in 1915 and was the first
serious discussion of Akhmatova's poetry and, furthermore, the sole
critique of its kind. This absorbing scholarly analysis is impressive not

only for its acute and thorough observations, its definitive conclusions, and its fresh revelations; it also, as it were, shows the poetess in what other direction she may go, what may prove productive, and which paths promise nothing. Now that we can see Akhmatova's evolution as a whole, we do not perceive the newness of Nedobrovo's ideas as sharply because their source in the poems is so patently clear. But the article was written about the author of the first two books, *Evening* and *Rosary*, and Akhmatova, perhaps accepting Nedobrovo's proposals, subsequently moved in the direction which confirmed his ideas. When I told her my impression of the article which, incidentally, she had herself given me, Akhmatova, who had in previous conversations singled out Nedobrovo from amongst the outstanding people of her time, and recalled the influence he had had on her, said simply, "Perhaps he made Akhmatova."

In her *Pages from a Diary* Akhmatova recalls how, when she read Mandelstam part of the *Divina Commedia*, he wept: "... those words—in your voice." The same can be said about very many passages in her poetry, but if Dante's famous words

> *Tu proverai sì come sa di sale*
> *Lo pane altrui, e com'è duro calle*
> *Lo scendere e'l salir per altrui scale*

(You will discover for yourself how bitter another person's bread is, and how hard it is to go up and down another person's stairs) were spoken in 1922 in her voice in a free paraphrase, as it were:

> Endless compassion for the exile,
> The prisoner, the sick, I feel.
> Dark is the path of homeless migrants,
> Fed with a stranger's bitter bread.

then Dante's exclamation

> *Men che dramma*
> *Di sangue m'è rimaso che non tremi:*
> *Conosco i segni dell'antica fiamma!*

27

(Less than a dram of my blood remains which does not tremble: I recognise the signs of an ancient flame!) forty years later has a resonance that is concealed:

> You ask for my verse with no sham.
> But somehow you'll get by without it,
> Though you'll find in my blood not a gram
> Unsuffused with its bitter contagion.

The presence of the quotation is given away by the rhyme: *dramma/ fiamma* and sham/gram but, having given it away, the rhyme drags us into a dizzy whirl of quotations, for the last line of Dante's tercet addressed to Virgil are the words of Virgil's Dido, faithfully translated by Dante from the *Aeneid*; and the preceding poem in Akhmatova's cycle 'The Wild Rose in Flower' opens with a line from the *Aeneid* and was originally entitled 'Dido Speaks'.

Many works of literary scholarship during the last two decades have been devoted to the "other voices" in Akhmatova's poetry, and it has become a common-place to refer to her use of other texts. The discoveries of such literary scholars as T. V. Tsivyan, R. D. Timenchik and V. N. Toporov, who have managed to look beneath the false bottom of her "fateful casket", to look into one after another of the series of hidden compartments with which her poems challenge the reader, will now always shine through her transparent poetry with their "third, seventh and twenty-ninth" layers, to use her own phrases from *Poem without a Hero*. At one time a veritable hunt for quotations in her poetry began and it seemed a sure winner: something always came to light. It seemed that Akhmatova had read everything, and borrowed from everywhere. The results of the textual comparisons depended principally on the mnemonic abilities of those making the comparisons. Re-reading her poems of 1921–22 I hit upon a Batyushkov vein, for example. It was especially concentrated in the poems written in Bezhetsk during that winter. In particular it turned out that Akhmatova introduced Dante's *pane altrui*, referred to above, into her poetry via Batyushkov's *The Dying Tasso* and not directly from Dante:

> In infancy already exiled,
> Beneath the skies of my sweet Italy I roamed,

Remembering Anna Akhmatova

> And like a poor and homeless vagrant
> All the vicissitudes of fate were mine to know.
> Where was my boat not carried by the waters?
> Where did it rest content? Where was my daily bread
> Not sprinkled with the tears of sorrow?

But what did this and similar finds mean? Did they merely illustrate Akhmatova's aphorism:

> Do not repeat—your soul has wealth untold—
> What others found to say in their creations.
> Or could it be that poetry itself
> Is only one magnificent quotation?

Or did they amount to the tempting hypothesis (there is nothing we like to defend more than a hypothesis which has more proofs than are sufficient, but fewer than are required) that Akhmatova found a volume of Batyushkov in the library of the house at Bezhetsk and read it that winter? In relation to some other poet this might possibly be convincing. But Akhmatova did not write poems in order to illustrate a point; and she found what she was looking for. In other words, "What is she quoting?" is only a first question, unproductive in the absence of a second: "Why is this quoted?" What myth, what plot, what nexus of cultural associations are brought into the poem by the chosen quotation (and conversely: specifically what place in the cultural universe is henceforth, thanks to the quotation included, marked by the new poem)? "So Shakespeare said it all, but I like Horace better," writes Akhmatova. What "all" did Shakespeare say? In what respect does she like Horace better? Why does she recall Shakespeare in connection with such-and-such a theme, and Horace with another? What signal do they both give in Akhmatova's poetry? And what does their unexpected juxtaposition in a single line mean in Akhmatova's code?

❖   ❖   ❖

29

To search for hidden quotations in Akhmatova's spoken speech would be a pointless activity: everyone quotes a multitude of other people, more often unconsciously than consciously. But what a given situation made her call to mind was always unexpected and, as a rule, amusing.

She brought into currency the concept of the "Akhmatovka" for the rush of visitors who called on her. It was at times no easy matter to timetable those who wished to see her: visits ran into each other, arriving and departing visitors bumped into each other in the doorway or in the hall, A must not coincide with B, X was jealous of Y's relationship with Z. In short, it was like a railway junction with a tight schedule and inevitable accidents. This happened less often in Leningrad, more often in Moscow. I once went to see her in the afternoon and she said that she had invited So-and-So to come that evening. "Not So-and-So! Such-and-Such has already been invited—you've got it the wrong way round, upside down." Not in the least concerned, she quoted the last lines of Mandelstam's 'The Decembrist': "All's turned upside down, but it gives pleasure to repeat: Russia, Lethe," and pausing, then syllable by syllable: "Lo-re-lei." My immediate reaction was that this was disrespectful to "classic" poetry, the Decembrists, forced labour, that it seemed a new insult to Mandelstam from one of the young Petersburg women whom he called the "Europeans". But I then saw straightaway that for her this was first and foremost the poetry of her youth—which at one time did not exist, which had come into being during her lifetime, was constantly in the ear and on the tongue, and was probably, like everything else in one's youth, the butt of friendly teasing.

When I was taking my leave she sometimes replaced the usual wishes and pieces of counsel with the final line of a Fet love poem, "Kisses, tears, and dawn—the dawn!" and when I once replied with something like Fet's "I do not know what I shall sing—but song comes to fruition", she said that her favourite Fet poem was 'Alter Ego' and recited:

> As the lily looks into the watery mirror,
> You stood guard and watched over the first of my songs.

She then gave me an offprint of Nedobrovo's article "Struggling against Time (Fet)", which is captivating and full of feeling. Although the aim was to rid Fet of the stigma of the parody on the first line of his famous poem 'Whispers, timid breathing' ("Bispers, whimid treathing"), it succeeds only in drawing attention to it once again. And I thought as I read the article that when A.A. deflated the end of that same poem, she knew, of course, what had also befallen the beginning.

Sometimes when we were about to go for a walk she would say: "Give me my soldier's eight minutes to get ready," and when I stretched out my arm to help her she would lean on it heavily and preface her first step with a line I could not place: "Did Fido take his Fifi by the paw, then?"

In April 1964 we were sitting round the table at the Ardovs' flat in Great Ordynka Street: Akhmatova, Amanda Haight—a young Englishwoman who was then writing a thesis on her poetry—another English girl—a friend of Amanda's—and I. The previous day the girls and I had arranged that they would come round for me and we would go to someone's home, where I would read some of the classics of Russian poetry into a tape-recorder, paying particular attention to pronunciation, after which we would listen to Beatles recordings on the same tape-recorder; the Beatles had recently come into fashion. When the time came to leave and they announced this to Akhmatova, it became clear that she had been counting on spending the whole evening with us. With European courtesy and firmness the girls explained "we cannot not go if people are expecting us". I wavered: I did not want to go back on the arrangement, or miss the planned entertainment. We sat for a little longer, then got up. A.A. looked at us ironically and said plaintively to them, pointing at me: "You're taking him away? More of those enlightened seafareresses!" In *Krechinsky's Wedding* the beaten Rasplyuev laments: "Boxing—that's an English invention ... Isn't it? The English are an educated nation, enlightened seafarers ..."

Her responses were amusing because they were appropriate, and yet more amusing because, given the logic of what was happening, they were not really at all apt. What had Fido to do with anything? She had just been sitting majestic, silent, still, and this very moment was descending the steps, leaning on my arm, as like a statue come to life; she, from whose mournfully closed lips one expected to hear obscure and triumphant words about the rustling of the grasses and the Muses' exclamations—what had Fido to do with it? In that cramped room, where visitors wiping their running noses came in from the cold as did the smell of cooking, and where beneath the trestle-bed lay two cardboard suitcases (manuscripts and clothes), what had the Lorelei to do with anything?

Akhmatova had, as it were, patented a device, almost a rule, of putting her left glove on her right hand—turning situations inside out, deflating high style, exalting lowly things, bringing together phenomena which at first sight could not be compared, putting words at a new angle to each other in poetry. "That was when he arrived at his theory of word-relationships," she writes, speaking of Mandelstam. She held that the poet is always "irrelevant", always "tactlessness personified", and she quoted the example of Pushkin, who printed in the journal *Library for Reading*, alongside a mountain of poems by various poets celebrating the anniversary of the 1812 war and the unveiling of the Alexander column in Palace Square, his 'The merriment of foolish youth is past'—an elegy. "So inappropriate, so tactless".

"A poem should be all inconsequential; society likes order," she wrote.

However, inappropriate recollections and irrelevant comparisons produced an effect of naturalness, almost of reasonableness. The reference to Horace and the allusion to Shakespeare, the yelling in the street and the Muses' exclamations reached her audience, and people were captivated by the intonation, which was highly mundane, ordinary, heard for the hundredth time, and so common that, if one could turn to Zoshchenko's prose to recreate the city speech of the 1920s and 1930s, then Akhmatova would serve to recreate the intonations of Russian speech in the first half of the twentieth century. Akhmatova's intonation had an equally powerful effect on the housewife with no experience of poetry and the structuralist who could analyse texts with exquisite refinement, and this is evident from the fact that they both became attached to Akhmatova's poetry and not, for example, to Vyacheslav Ivanov's or, worse, Voloshin's, although their poetry was no less "cultured" than hers.

Akhmatova was anti-theatrical: she was quite unable to depict people, or to convey their manner of speaking; but her ear was unsurpassed, ideal, as was her memory for the placing of words in rejoinders, phrases and sentences, or, if they were wrongly placed, for how they should have been placed. She said that one could vouch for the complete authenticity of the phrase heard by the young Ivan Sergeevich Turgenev in the lobby of Pletnyov's house. Pushkin, who had put on his greatcoat and hat, turned to the person he had been talking to: "Our ministers are splendid fellows! There's no denying it!" "There's the negro for you!"[18]

Her own speech, however lively in its brilliance, always gave the impression of having been unhurriedly composed of carefully selected words. She could write down an intonation with the accuracy with which musical notation records a melody. The opening phrases of her poems "Ah, it's you again" and "Just think, it's work" are simply accurately pitched musical notes, the sound produced by a keyboard, of a musical instrument tuned to the sounds of "society".

What of mine can I then bequeathe you?
Just my shade? What use is my shade?

When she recorded an intonation she also included expression marks, such as "depressed", "vigorously, but not overly so", "solemnly". And she also provided indications which were virtually stage directions:

(*challengingly:*) I myself am not amongst
Those who fall for others' magic—
I myself . . . (*assertively, but knowingly:*) But not for naught
Do I make my secrets public.

Sometimes the poem conceals the addressee and sounds like a conversation between two people, one of whom is not formally present: the poem is a response to his words which, for the sake of poetic economy, are included in the reply:

Prophetess? Not in the least.
My life is clear as a stream,
But I simply don't want to sing
To the clanking of prison keys.

Similarly, other poems have gestures clearly "written in":

Are we forgotten, forsaken, for ... *(turns round abruptly; in a tired and resigned voice)* Yes?
Who's come to batter the door?
Now I must go to the gateway to meet
Trouble and sorrow once more.

This probably explains the absence of written stage directions in the play *Prologue,* or *Dream within a Dream*, the text of which she was obliged to destroy, and which in her later years she partly reconstructed and partly wrote afresh; however, this omission does not imply that she considered it inappropriate to produce the play on stage—at least she took seriously the telegram she received from a Düsseldorf company requesting permission to produce it. Generally speaking she had a very highly developed sense of the theatricality of life itself. There is a very lively photograph of her and the pianist Genrikh Neygauz sitting on a sofa and talking; it was taken shortly before his death and hers. A.A. made the following comment on the photograph: "It's a scene from a play by some Scandinavian dramatist. She confesses to him, 'Now that so many years have gone by I must tell you that your son—is not yours.' He clutches his hair ... And the son is by now a professor in Stockholm."

She had an extraordinarily expressive face, especially in moments of anger, sorrow, and compassion; she hardly ever resorted to gesticulation. During the winter of 1964 she and I were doing a "co-operative" (as it said in the contract) translation of Leopardi. As spring approached we took up places at the writers' retreat at Komarovo, the House of Creativity, for "the duration", i.e. twelve days; it was explained to us that it was easier to get an extension on the spot than to get a month straight off. She was given a room in the main building, I in one of the outbuildings. When we went out for a walk we took a Finnish sledge with us: at first we walked, then, when she was tired, she would take her seat on the little sledge and I would push it, sending it along the well-trodden paths. On sunny days the snow became softer, but the skiers skied on for all they were worth. The reply to our application for an extension came at the very end: she was permitted to stay for another half-period, I was refused. It was not worth feeling specially bitter about it: one could work in the city just as well. I said something of the sort when I stopped the sledge in an open clearing. She was sitting facing into the sun, outwardly completely calm, even unconcerned. Suddenly she grimaced in unfeigned fury and with an impetuous and somewhat absurd movement of her arm she clenched her hand into a fist, punched the air and shouted "Oh yes! They need places for those women skiers!" It was not clear why it should be the women skiers and not the men, but the episode was horribly convincing.

Perhaps this was a reversion to the uninhibited reactions which she had picked up in her childhood and youth and which were typical of South Russia, especially Odessa, where she then lived. As a seventeen-year-old girl she complains in one of her letters: " ... I am an eternal bird of passage, wandering through alien, coarse and dirty towns ..." Others of her letters from that time provide examples of the conversational style of the period: "Fear not, I shall not snaffle anything, as they say in the south"; "You may imagine that I am stooping to an immoral act"; "in all probability you would say, 'Ugh, what a phiz'". She found much to her taste in the large range of stories and jokes, ancient and modern, in circulation at the home of the writer and humorist Ardov, where she stayed for long periods when she was in Moscow. "In, Mother?!" the host might shout to her as he sat down to play cards, pretending to be her unsophisticated son-in-law. That is, are you in, are you adding your share to the stake? "Yes, I'm in," she would reply indulgently. "Lessons first, dwinks later." She too could pronounce this embellishment in the context of preparing to sit down at table. On the one occasion when, in the course of a scene she was acting with Ranevskaya, a four-letter word had to be uttered, she prefaced it with the warning "For us students of language there are no forbidden words"—but she could call foul gutter language *poésie maternelle*. And the lines

You longed for warmth and comfort.
You know where that is, don't you?

35

smack unambiguously of the intonation of strong language.

❖   ❖   ❖

"Chekhov is counter-indicated for poetry (and, incidentally, poetry for him). I don't believe people who say they love both Chekhov and poetry. Every single one of his pieces is a display from a 'Home and Colonial' shop with a stuffy atmosphere which is incompatible with poetry. His characters are boring, banal, provincial. Even their clothes and the fashions which he chooses for them are extremely unattractive: hideous dresses, hats and cloaks. People will say life was like that, but in Tolstoy for some reason the same kind of life looks different, quite unlike this." Her anti-Chekhovism, which was not so much criticism as an overall position, was something Akhmatova insistently proclaimed; some people were profoundly distressed by it and many were perplexed or found its paradoxicality entertaining. It is difficult to agree with the literary explanations and to make oneself ignore the harmonious rhythm of Chekhov's stories, or the string (in the literal and figurative sense) in *The Cherry Orchard*, and it is difficult to understand why Zoshchenko with his "shop goods" and fashions is not counter-indicated for poetry, whereas Chekhov is. Of the non-literary reasons the psychological one is the most inviting.

The way of life depicted by Chekhov is the real routine in the "alien, coarse and dirty towns" which surrounded and oppressed Anya Gorenko for most of her childhood and youth and which Anna Akhmatova excised not only from her biography but also from her consciousness, replacing them with the wide open spaces of Chersonesus and the Black Sea, and the splendour of Tsarskoe Selo. In her letters of 1906–7, addressed to a close friend, the vein of Chekhov's stylistics is clear to see: "The only good minutes are when everyone goes to have supper at the inn ..."; "This summer Fyodorov again kissed me a lot, swore that he loved me, and smelled of dinner"; "... conversations about politics and fish diets"; "He [Uncle] shouted twice daily: at dinner and after evening tea"; "Of course I can never go to classes again, except for cookery"; "No money. Auntie nags. Cousin Demyanovsky makes a declaration of love every five minutes (do you recognise the Dickensian style?)" One longs to add: the Dickensian style within the Chekhovian. "I suddenly longed to go to Petersburg, where there's life and books";

36

"Where are your sisters? Probably at classes—oh, how I envy them."
"To Moscow, to the university. To finish with everything here and go to
Moscow," echo Chekhov's *Three Sisters*.

These are the letters of one of Chekhov's young women from the
provinces, frustrated with her joyless existence somewhere or other, it
makes no difference where: in Taganrog, where Chekhov lived, or in
Eupatoria. Even the plot line—being in love with an "elegant and so
coldly-indifferent" student from the capital—is typically Chekhovian.
As also is the concrete manifestation of this being in love: "Do you want
to make me happy? If so, send me a picture of him." "It is easy to die." "I
have finished living before I have begun. It is sad, but that is the case." It
was an exceptional situation for Akhmatova to be in (if Akhmatova can
already be seen in the adolescent Gorenko): this is the world, style, and
voice of Chekhov's heroines, introduced into the system of her means of
expression not "by the complexity and riches of the Russian nineteenth-
century novel", not "with a backward look at psychological prose", as
Mandelstam later wrote of her, but by everyday life. This was not
Akhmatova quoting Chekhov but Chekhov quoting some girl called
Gorenko. And in any subsequent assimilation of Chekhov, even the
very slightest, had it come about, there would have been "something
incestuous", as she once remarked apropos of something similar.

But I think the main reason for her dislike of Chekhov was the fact
that their positions in relation to art were diametrically opposed. I
always had the feeling that Akhmatova made the claims she did when
speaking of Chekhov in order to use them as a cover for this unname-
able accusation. Indeed she described Chekhov's plays as the nadir of
theatre. And another time she said that the Moscow Art Theatre owed
its triumph to the fact that, after the failure of *The Seagull* at the
Alexandrina Theatre, Stanislavsky had discovered how Chekhov's
plays should be staged "and they were wildly successful". Lydia
Chukovskaya's notes of her conversations with Akhmatova record an
indignant speech in which she accuses Chekhov of more or less lying:
"Chekhov always, all his life, depicted artists as idlers ... but in fact
being an artist is terribly hard labour, spiritual and physical ... When
the Zamyatins emigrated they left me Boris Grigorev's albums and there
are thousands of sketches in them, just for one portrait. Thousands—
for one ... Chekhov couldn't help going along with the tastes of his
readers, those district nurses and schoolmistresses, and they definitely
wanted to see artists as idlers." She said almost the same thing about the
Soviet satirists Ilf and Petrov: "They slandered writers ... A con man

turns out to be more talented and cleverer than a whole trainful of writers." However, Akhmatova's monologue in defence of artists leads the conversation away from her first and more direct response: Lydia Chukovskaya had made the ironic remark that Chekhov's story 'The Grasshopper' had all that was required by official standards: "a negative heroine and a positive hero ..." "And creative people, artists, are mocked," added Anna Andreevna promptly and angrily. "Quite so, all that is required!" And only a little later did she concentrate her reproaches on the misrepresentation of the hard-working artist.

Why were Chekhov's readers exclusively district nurses and schoolmistresses, and if this is so, why is it still necessary to mock creative people nowadays, when the reading public is radically different? There is no doubt about it: Akhmatova never missed an opportunity to raise the stock of "creative people" in the eyes of society. She neither forgave Voloshin for slapping Gumilyov's face nor Aleksey Tolstoy his gibes at Mandelstam:[19] even if the humiliators belonged to the same fraternity as the humiliated, once they had insulted a poet they became one with the philistines. When *The Literary Gazette* telephoned to explain that they were obliged to hold Akhmatova's poems over to the next issue so as to publish poems by Berggolts, which had turned out to be more topical, she snapped before they had finished: "I do not propose to stand in anyone's way. I know what good literary morals are," and put down the receiver. And so on, and so on. However, for almost fifty years of her life, right up to the very end, creative people were invariably held in high regard and greatly valued—except for those who were officially declared to be outside art, nonentities, parasites, etc., which for the man in the street was no less axiomatic than the "talent and industry" of those recognised by officialdom. And Ryabovsky in 'The Grasshopper' neither undermined contemporary district nurses' and schoolmistresses' faith in the famous Soviet painter Ioganson's "terribly hard labour, spiritual and physical", nor exposed the "idler" Falk, who for the district nurses and schoolmistresses simply did not exist.

"Creative people" are not "mocked" by Chekhov; he states a truth about art which is destructive of art, at least of art in the form given it by the "Silver Age". In 1909 Lev Tolstoy described Andrey Bely and "decadentism" in general as insane delirium: "I cannot communicate with these people. I would like to know what they want to achieve." And: "Anyone can say that 'A Man in Black' is frightening and everyone will understand. But not just anyone can tell how people live and work, and describe their feelings and conflicts." From the point of view of the twentieth century Tolstoy seems old hat, an old man who does not understand the new art. But he was reckoning time differently. Both he and the decadents had forebodings of the shocks which the new age was bringing: revolution, war, depravity, the terror, and, most important, there-is-no-God. Though Tolstoy looked on this courageously, seeking and finding explanations in the eternal character of human nature—like Cervantes, like Shakespeare—the decadents, as if they had taken fright, put this down to the special qualities of the twentieth century and began to create and describe a world parallel to the real one which took in the "Man in Black" and "smelled of sulphur". The concept of the "Silver Age", subsequently invented by its own representatives, latched the new art on to the "Golden Age", both incorrectly and in a purely formal manner: the "Silver Age" seemed not to notice anything that came between Pushkin in the early nineteenth century and Blok at its end. It was only twenty years later that Akhmatova and—less clearly—Mandelstam, as Acmeists, called things by their names, and that was done rather in spite of "the new art", the art "of the twentieth century".

For Akhmatova, and more widely for creative people of the 1890s–1910s, art was service not only in the usual sense of the word but also in the religious sense. In those years so much was said about God in philosophical circles and in theatres, in poems, satirical articles, in restaurants and drawing-rooms, that the very word "God" became like any other, and Akhmatova's close friend Boris Anrep found an epigraph for a poem of his in the spirit of the time:

Let there be light.
God

Theology, which had always been the summit of spiritual achievement and aimed to perceive Truth, was widely replaced by religio-philosophical or ethico-aesthetic speculations, or those based on the feelings of etiolated souls. Gumilyov was able to write: "And in St John's Gospel it says that the Word is God," substituting a profane word in place of Christ, the Word who was with God. Acmeism was also called Adamism, inasmuch as the Acmeists considered themselves followers of their forefather Adam, who, whatever he called each living creature, "that was its name".

Given such a mixture of mysteries and illusions, knowledge and suppositions, truth and opinions, it was now possible to say absolutely anything and justify absolutely anything. Pagan myths satisfied the accepted requirements for credibility just as well—if not better—than the Holy Scriptures. As Blok noted in his diary, "No, it is Christ, even so" about the leader of the Red Guards.[20] Only art undertook to combine these incompatible things, only the magic of art could link idols thrown down hundreds of years ago and icons removed by the disciples of Voltaire or Nietzsche, and put them into the same picture. "As you know, Christianity has not yet been preached in Russia," Akhmatova liked to say humorously.

Art, as she says in one of her poems, "edged into the most secret zones of essence" and certainly did not steer clear of contacts with minor and far from minor demons. Black masses at the home of some or other "creative people" were talked about in lowered voices but not very confidentially: it was almost as if art were laying its hands on the devil, almost as if the devil were laying his hands on art. And the revolution, because it gave material form to the ruins of the spirit, dispelled, as it were, the last doubts about art being the sole source of salvation, and art being the highest value. Art, art alone, justified Akhmatova's lines

> By miraculous icons I swear,
> By the fiery smoke of our nights.

It alone allowed her to call Blok "the Demon himself with Tamara's smile",[21] and not to trouble herself with refuting the fact that

> The Holy Maid watched over
> Her poet absolute.

In 'Thirteen Lines' it threw a delightful veil over dreadful suggestions and the wild violation of that which should be inviolate:

> The world transformed itself for just an instant,
> And wine was strangely altered on the tongue.
> And even I, who was to be the knife

40

By which the godly word would meet its slaughter,
Fell reverently still, lest I make shorter,
When I would yet draw out, its blessed life.

When she summed people up, notwithstanding the fact that in her judgments she was common sense personified, the primary criterion was either their involvement in art or their attitude to it. She ends her hymn to The Poet in *Poem without a Hero* with the words, "He stands accused of nothing, not of this, or of that, or of the other ... In general, sins do not suit poets." She knew that I had no sympathy for this approach, which was especially common amongst younger artists, and which in practice legitimised getting away with things and even encouraged people to gratify their whims. (I tried to persuade Brodsky that a poet should not dare to use his poems to abuse the woman who had left him, since he has been blessed with the capacity to do this in the most effective way possible, and she cannot reply.) Akhmatova avoided the subject when I happened to be present, unless it arose in conversation with a third person, but here are her words as recorded by Lydia Chukovskaya: "... the modernists did great things for Russia ... They left the country in an entirely different state from the one in which they had found it. They taught people to love poetry again ..." Or on Mayakovsky: "He replied, 'What's the point of publishing Khlebnikov now?' That's what he said about his comrade, about his teacher ... So what is the difference between him and the Briks? They don't care about publishing his poems, he doesn't care about Khlebnikov's. There is a difference, a big difference, and it's his enormous talent. He could be just like them, ignorant, and two-faced, and insincere ... But that did not stop him from becoming a major twentieth-century Russian poet." On Stanislavsky: "What I like about him is that he really is possessed by art. Of course he always said to hell with everything else—what mattered was to stage play after play, what mattered was that the theatre should triumph. He simply wasn't bothered about 'life' outside the theatre ..." And similarly on Marshak: "I then understood for the first time where that man's strength came from: he is possessed by art to the point of frenzy." Reading this, I thought for a minute that Akhmatova had used a different word: for a Russian Orthodox, which she was by upbringing, to be possessed is to be possessed by a demon; she says of herself, of the way in which *Poem without a Hero* came to her, that she was "possessed by demonic black thirst": in any event the drift of the

41

emotion is clear. And Annensky, who, as she wrote, "imbibed that poison, drank the stupefaction, and though he waited, did not see his fame ... —and suffocated", fell on the steps of the Tsarskoe Selo railway station when his heart stopped—was murdered, one understands her to say, by the enemies of art, who refused to print his poems on time.

And Chekhov, who only wrote about what he knew for certain, and called dubious what was dubious—"things suggested by intuition", dreams, suppositions—speaks through the mouth of Nina Zarechnaya about "sacred" art thus: "... in our work—it makes no difference whether we are acting on stage or writing—the important thing is not fame, not glory, not what I dreamt of, but the capacity to endure". And before this Trigorin confesses: "One *idée fixe* obsesses me day and night: I must write, I must write, I must ... I write constantly, as if I were carried along by relays of post-horses, and I can't stop myself. I ask you, what have beauty and light to do with it? I see a cloud that looks like a grand piano. I think—I must put that in a story: the cloud floated by, looking like a grand piano ... That's always how it is, always, I can't get away from myself and I feel as if I'm devouring my own life. To make the honey which I give away to someone out there I rob my best flowers of their pollen, I pull the flowers up and trample their roots. Am I not mad? One and the same thing, over and over, and my friends' interest, the praise and admiration—it all seems a trick, I'm being deceived, like a person who has fallen ill, and sometimes I'm afraid that any minute they'll creep up from behind and grab me, and take me away to the mad house ... As soon as it's published I hate it, I see that it's all wrong, a mistake, that I shouldn't have written it at all, and I'm mortified, I feel rotten at heart ..."

Nina Zarechnaya is almost a contemporary of the actress and producer Komissarzhevskaya, the idol of the "Silver Age"; Treplev, the "decadent", of whose work Arkadina says "there are no new forms here, just a bad person", who is laughed at, printed, but not read, is one of the so-called older generation of Symbolists, who were Akhmatova's predecessors, mentors and teachers. And this comes in *The Seagull*, a play in which the interaction between mother and son, playing out the Gertrude-Hamlet episode, always has an eye to Shakespeare, exactly in the manner of Akhmatova. Similarly the allusion to Pushkin's 'The Water Sprite'—"In 'The Water Sprite' the miller says that he is a raven, and in her letters she kept repeating that she was a seagull." Here the piano-shaped cloud begins to look like a parody of Akhmatova's famous poem which begins "High in the sky a little drab grey cloud seemed stretched out like a squirrel pelt".

The new art-cum-religious-rite could "come to terms" with nineteenth-century art-cum-analysis, art-cum-ideas, art-cum-sermon, if only because all of these are "more than mere art". But it was impossible to come to terms with Chekhov, who treated art as nothing more than a craft. The language was the same, the tonality different. Different registers: what Chekhov showed to be amusing, almost vaudeville, Akhmatova began to present with complete seriousness, as drama. The lines of Chekhov's heroines and Akhmatova's early poems are inter-changeable, *passim*, word for word:

> my soul yearned and suffocated, delirious on the verge of
>   death . . .

> you would not have started to torment me—
> there were many torments as it was . . .

> I don't weep and I don't whine—happiness is not for me . . .

> happiness knocks at my window,
> I have only to let it in . . .

> darling, darling, me too! I'll die with you . . .

> let his shade discover how I love him . . .

> oh, how handsome you are, you devil! . . .

> I know how to love and forgive . . .

Whose text a given line belongs in depends on its focus. It is like one of those magic drawings where if you look perpendicularly from above you see the crown of a tree, flowers and birds, but if you look obliquely from one side you see a hunter crouching in the branches. Turn the screw on the viewfinder tight—Anna Akhmatova's cycle 'Disarray'; loosen it—Chekhonte's *The Bear*.[22]

Lidiya Yakovlevna Ginzburg, who visited Akhmatova regularly for

43

many years, said after her death, "Why didn't I ask her the key question, 'How did you start writing *like that*, at the very beginning, that is?'" Perhaps Chekhov offers an answer: in those days young ladies, young women talked *like that*.

In *The Seagull*, Dorn, the wise doctor, who thinks that it is petty to complain about life in old age, who prefers tincture of valerian to all other medicines, and believes in the universal soul only when he gets into a crowd, says of Treplev: "He thinks in images, his stories are colourful and vivid, and I react to them strongly. It is just a pity that he has no definite aims. He makes an impression, but that is all, and impressions alone don't get one very far." Was it this condemnation of the new art; or—inasmuch as art is sacred ("our sacred craft")—was it the [persistent] "profanation of the sacrament" ("Someone's been using sulphur. Is that necessary?"); or was it the purposeful and rigorous deflation of style, calculated, as it turned out, with an eye to the future, particularly to Akhmatova's equally single-minded high style, thereby revealing their common roots; or was it the manservant smelling of roast chicken in every production of *The Cherry Orchard* by the Moscow Art Theatre or any other theatre, which brought back to her the stuffiness and banality of the setting of her adolescence and youth; or was it the sum of all this which caused her to dislike Chekhov? The dislike, hostility even, was permanent. And when I told her that the Leningrad film studios were making a picture based on *Ionych*, Chekhov's story about a doctor, and that Chekhov himself would be one of the characters, she did not miss her opportunity: "Ah! That means there'll be two doctors in it."

❖   ❖   ❖

"May God forgive me! This is terrible," says Anna Sergeevna, the heroine of Chekhov's *The Lady with the Lapdog*, during her first secret assignation with her seducer, and she does not hide her tears. "The peasants say: the devil snared me. I too can now say that of myself: the devil snared me." In a similar situation the heroine of Akhmatova's lyric poems hears in the background the melody of violin music: "Thanks be to heaven—at last you are alone with him." According to Chekhov the young woman's remorse seemed "strange and out of place", but her attitude towards what had occurred is conditioned by the norm of

Christian consciousness. In this sense the attitude of Akhmatova's "happy" heroine constitutes direct and emphatic disdain for the Christian norm, a rejection of it.

Without hesitation or scruple, moreover, the poet introduces this very frank and blatant infringement of Christian law—utterly "strangely" and inappropriately—into the system of co-ordinates of Orthodox life and behaviour, such as prayer in church and at home, confession and communion. She writes in her poems of "A threadbare rug beneath the icon"; "I pray thus at Thy liturgy"; "the priest's dark stole was laid upon my head and shoulders". What is more, the conviction and naturalness with which this alien material is introduced legitimise, as it were, the pleasure of breaking the rules. This pleasure coexists happily with the remorse of acknowledged guilt. In other words, the norm is declared to be none other than this simultaneous infringement and observance of the law. The practice of this combination was already fairly widespread; the philosophy of the period found a basis for it, that is, justified it, and poetry declared it to be Orthodox.

Akhmatova believed in God, and one could not say that she was not a church person. At one time she went to church absolutely regularly:

> My youth was like—Sunday prayer.
> Could I forget it?
>
> Cherubic song
> Trembles by fastened doors;
>
> They got up as if for early mass.

She viewed the Church's ordinances as binding, and after her visit to England in 1965 she told me that she was asked in London whether she wanted to meet the local Orthodox metropolitan. "I declined. Because I could not tell him the whole truth, and one cannot not tell the truth in such cases."

But in her latter years she did not go to church. She might go in, cross herself, and stay to say a prayer; she always had the church calendar in her head and knew it well; and she also knew the services well. On Pardoning Sunday, the Sunday of Shrovetide week, in 1963 she said, "On this day my mother used to go to the kitchen, bow low before the servants and say gravely, 'Forgive me, sinner that I am.' The servants also bowed and replied equally gravely, 'The Lord forgives. You forgive me.' Now I too am asking you, 'Forgive me, sinner that I am.'"

But if we use her own words, she was rather "beyond the church pale", in any event at the end of her life. At times she would say that she could not agree with the general confession, that the introduction of the general confession had driven a wedge between her and the Church; at times she would say, "I want to believe like a simple peasant woman." All the same, these sounded like excuses. But she wrote, "How I envy you in that bewitching countryside of yours outside Moscow, and with what aching regret I remember Kolomenskoe, without which it is hardly possible to live, and the monastery ..."

It is relevant at this point to recall her view that the accessibility of art, in the form of a multiplicity of translations, reproductions and gramophone records, was not progress at all: such ease of access presupposes a casual, easy and superficial knowledge of the manifestations of the profundity of the human spirit, and in this sense facilitates spiritual depravity. "In the past people set off from Moscow on a pilgrimage to Sergiev Posad two days before and stayed the night at Mytishchi. Now the electric train gets to Zagorsk in one and a half hours, but there is too much distraction in a journey like that." On the other hand, when I first came to Moscow from Leningrad to stay for a long time and was beginning to get to know the city, I asked Akhmatova where to start and she answered, "It depends what you're interested in—Kolomenskoe for stones, Ostankino for jumble." And when, on my return from Kolomenskoe, I told her that I had persuaded the caretaker woman to open the disused Church of the Ascension for me, and how unbearably empty and unbearably icy cold it was in there, she asked, "But did you notice how tiny it is inside? What a small court Ivan the Terrible must have had!" Not a word did she say about the Kazan Church, which was one of the few still functioning, as if it simply did not exist.

For Easter 1964 I received a letter from her in which she wrote, "I heard the end of the Russian mass from London on Misha's new radio. A choir of angels. The very first sounds reduced me to tears. That happens to me so rarely."

She also wept another time—when I was telling her about Pasolini's film *Il vangelo secondo Matteo*, which was shown at an Italian film festival. She had only recently come out of hospital after a serious heart attack and still felt weak. I told her that I was sitting in the auditorium behind a young Georgian and when the crucifixion scene began and the first hammer blow and cry of pain were heard from the middle of the crowd, he suddenly put his head in his hands and shook with sobs. Tears filled her eyes and rolled down her cheeks. Then she asked whether the story of the Samaritan woman was in the film: "Though that's in John." This is how the episode is described in St John's Gospel, chapter 4, verses 6–8 and 27:

"Now Jacob's well was there. Jesus therefore, being wearied with his journey, sat thus on the well: and it was about the sixth hour. There cometh a woman of Samaria to draw water: Jesus saith unto her, Give me to drink. (For his disciples were gone away unto the city to buy meat.)"

"... And upon this came his disciples, and marvelled that he talked with the woman; yet no man said, What seekest thou? or, Why talkest thou with her?"

"The remarkable thing," said Akhmatova, "is that the author of the Gospel draws attention to the fact that when he was found alone with the woman no one thought anything of it."

Similar passages from the New and Old Testaments particularly attracted her interest and she read them from the same, or a similar, angle, as best illustrated in her 'Biblical Poems'. She told me with barely concealed triumph that she had caught Dostoevsky out—or the Raw Youth, if Dostoevsky intended the error to appear. The Youth says to Lambert: "If she had married him he would have attacked her the morning after their first night, kicked her and driven her away ... Because that sort of violent primitive love works like a paroxysm ... and as soon as you've achieved satisfaction the scales fall from your eyes and the opposite feeling takes over: revulsion and hate, the urge to crush and destroy. Do you know the story of Abishag?" In fact the story of Abishag from I Kings, chapter 1, verses 1–4 is irrelevant:

Now King David was old and stricken in years; and they covered him with clothes, but he gat no heat. Wherefore his servants said unto him, Let there be sought for my lord the King a young virgin: and let her stand before the King, and let her cherish him, and let her lie in thy bosom, that my lord King may get heat. So they sought for a fair damsel throughout all the coasts of Israel, and found Abishag a Shunammite, and brought her to the King. And the damsel was very fair, and cherished the King, and ministered to him: but the King knew her not."

Akhmatova felt that Dostoevsky must have meant the story told in chapter 13 of II Samuel about the disreputable passion of David's son Amnon for Absalom's sister Tamar, whom he dishonoured and "Then Amnon hated her exceedingly; so that the hatred wherewith he hated her was greater than the love wherewith he had loved her. And Amnon said unto her, Arise, be gone." "[...] he called his servant that ministered unto him, and said, Put now this woman out from me, and bolt the door after her." (Verses 15 and 17).

Akhmatova's choice of plots from the Holy Scriptures (Rachel, Leah and Jacob; Lot's wife; Michal and David; the daughter of Herodias), her treatment of them, and her emphases, reveal a clear tendency: they are all in one way or another devoted to love relationships between men and women—or to be precise, between women and men. The poet does not call upon examples of love in this world in order to cast light upon the prototypes of heavenly love, which we see, according to Christian dogma, "as if through a glass, darkly"; she calls upon them to illuminate the psychological, sensual, "universally understood" aspects of carnal love, albeit of the most exalted kind.

> The Apostles' letters I study there,
> The words of the Psalmodist follow.
> But blue are the stars, the frost all lace,
> New marvels each tryst heaps on,—
> In the Book a red maple leaf marks the place
> Of the High Song of Solomon.

She reads the letters of the Apostles and the Psalms—in general Akhmatova knew the Bible exceedingly well, found her way about it easily, and could find any passage she wanted immediately—but the book falls open at the Song of Songs, a lyrical dramatic poem describing the love of a shepherd girl and a king, in externals no different from a secular poem.

And when Akhmatova speaks to God:

> Thou who sprinkles the dew on the grasses,
> Give me news, bring my soul back to life—
> Not for passion, not for amusement—
> For magnificent earthly love.

the beginning of the quatrain obviously echoes the prayer of John Chrysostom for the eleventh hour of the day: "O Lord, sprinkle in my heart the dew of Thy grace", and the end is in equally obvious contrast to his prayer for the tenth hour of night: "O Lord, fit me to love Thee with all my soul and mind ..." In the context of the poem this "magnificent earthly love" is akin to Karamazov's interpretation of the words in the gospel about the sinner who "had loved much": "... she 'loved much'" (cries Dostoevsky's Fyodor Pavlovich Karamazov), "and Christ forgave her who had loved much ..." "That is not the kind of love for which Christ forgave her ..." (said the meek Father Yosif with involuntary impatience).

Akhmatova's angel's day was 16 February (New Style), and she celebrated her name-day quietly; people would telephone to send their good wishes, and in the evening a few guests would gather round the table. "I am Candlemas Anna," she used to say, and her patron saint was Anna the prophetess, who met the infant Christ in the temple at Jerusalem. Her line "Prophetess? Not in the least" has its origin, of course, in the image of this saint, although it may point to another one: 1909 saw the canonisation of Princess Anna of Kashin who had ended her life in a convent (her husband, Prince Mikhail of Tver, had been killed by the Tatars); icons depict her standing on the bank of a small river; her feast day is 12 June (Old Style), the day after Akhmatova's birthday. As to her birthday—here there was some confusion. To begin with, she wrote in her autobiography, "I was born on 11(23) June," but she celebrated her birthday, as a rule, on the 23rd or the 24th. She sometimes added twelve days to her date of birth to convert it from the Old Style to the New Style on the grounds that this date was in the nineteenth century, but sometimes added thirteen, on the grounds that she was celebrating her birthday on a date in the twentieth. Secondly, she liked to remark in passing that she was born on the festival day of the icon of Our Lady of Vladimir, a festival established in commemoration of the salvation of medieval Rus from her legendary ancestor Akhmat of the Horde, the last to keep Rus under the Tatar yoke. But this day was 23 June according to the Old Style, and 6 July according to the New Style.

Khan Akhmat was, however, more of a decorative ornament, an associate who gave the poet's name and person piquancy and colour which were not superfluous, which meant nothing. There was, though, significance in her assertion, repeated verbally and in writing, that she was born on Midsummer Night, that is, again, on 24 June (Old Style),

7 July (New Style). She gave one to understand, diluting, it is true, the seriousness of her assertions and hints with ironic literariness, that as a result of being born on this day she had assimilated the magic attributed to this night, and its rites—the hunt for the fern with flowers of fire which must be taken on the search for treasure, jumping through bonfires, rolling burning wheels downhill, bathing, etc.; and also the whole set of myths associated with Ivan Kupala, who hides in water, in fire, and in grasses, giving plants the strength of water and the warmth of the sun. The day itself is referred to in her poems not as the festival of the miracle-working icon, or of the martyr Agrippina, or as the eve of the birth of John the Baptist, but as the day of Agrafena-the-Bather, the eve of Kupala's Night. (Moreover, again in combination with a reference to the prophet David who is honoured by the Church.)

This assimilation, as it is now customary to say, of the folk traditions belonging to the cult of Ivan Kupala, and the assimilation of the essentially pagan, i.e. demonic, reality of his cult, was far from innocent. Particularly since it involved an incursion, or intended incursion, into those mysterious forces described mainly in myths deriving from the cults of water or the moon. Akhmatova's line "Thus, stepping like a sleep-walker, I entered upon life" is not a poeticism if we recall Sreznevskaya's recollection of "moonlit nights with a thin little girl in a little white dress on the roof of the green house on the corner ('How awful! She's walking in her sleep!')." Her inner connectedness with the element of water is equally a fact of her biography: she was born near the sea, spent each summer at the sea, and, as she wrote, "made friends with the sea", and "swam like a fish", in the opinion of her sailor brother; the poem 'At the Edge of the Sea' tells too that "The neighbours knew that I could sense water, and if they were sinking a new well, they called me and asked me to find them the place." Hence the mermaid, the princess of the sea, and the woman from Kitezh, the town which disappeared beneath the waters, all to be found in her poems; the sleep-walking gives rise to the somnambulist in *Prologue*, apparently one of Akhmatova's most occult works.

It both was and was not a game. A jest—and the breeding-ground of her poetry. Ancient ruins stylised in the manner of a folk tale—and a nexus of real energy from which her real Muse derived her strength. Her attraction to "the most secret zones of essence", cultivation of the supernormal characteristics of nature, her "sixth sense"—she had prophetic dreams, telepathy, the ability to interpret signs, and "teased out" meetings, news, etc.—were also symptomatic of the fact that she belonged "to her time", to the beginning of the century, with its heightened interest in theosophy, anthroposophy, and occult knowledge. "We know about this," she said one day, putting her thumbs together and spreading her fingers wide: the way people place their hands on the table at a spiritualistic seance. "Until recently you could get five years just for doing that with your hands." This was in Komarovo one winter, when Brodsky, his friend Marina Basmanova and I had been invited to Akhmatova's. We got talking about spiritualism, and I said that two of my friends swore that they had summoned up the spirits of Goethe and the hack poet Lebedev-Kumach, which had appeared simultaneously and got stuck in the doorway. She said that she was opposed to spiritualism and considered it immoral, quoting Modigliani's argument: "Would it be nice for me to discover that someone could summon the shade of my dead mother?" "But anyway," she concluded, "take the S volume of the Brockhaus encyclopaedia and read Vladimir Solovyov's 'Spiritualism' article—it's a very intelligent piece." (Then she gave us a ten-rouble note and sent us to the shop to get some vodka and savouries. It was frosty and the night sky was cloudless and covered in bright stars. Brodsky picked out the constellations, or pretended to, and then asked me, "A.G., why is the Southern Cross not visible in the northern hemisphere? What's the scientific explanation?" I said: "Take the A volume of the Brockhaus encyclopaedia and read the 'Astronomy' article." "And you," he said straight off, pleased with the pun which had come opportunely into his head, "take the A volume of the Brockhaus encyclopaedia and read the 'Atrocious Witticisms' article.")[23]

A world which does not notice the *contradictio in adjecto* in *innocent* happiness coming from *sin*, in *earthly* passion blessed by *heaven*, in the reconciliation of Christ with Belial, is an illusion which poetry alone has the power to create. The creation, the making, of illusion is the meaning of "poetry" in the original Greek.

It has the power to create the illusion, and it must: "the threadbare rug beneath the icon" intensifies one's impressions of the happy sinner and the one will not work without the other: the poetry lies in their necessary conjunction and their simultaneity. Through miserable gratitude for salvation from passion, even if the expression itself is not devoid of blasphemy:

> The King of Heaven healed my soul
> With unlove's icy calm;

through the awareness of temptation, even though in the end she still chooses sin:

> "Those are the devil's pitfalls,
> And his unclean desires."
> "But nothing else could rival
> Her hand, so very white."

the poet becomes master of the illusory space of total permissiveness, in which there are other dimensions and delineations are vague, in which light is like darkness and darkness like light:

> Now I pray to the saints every day
> For our light-hearted friendly attachment.

In 1922 Akhmatova wrote a poem which is exceptional for the frankness with which allusions to *Faust* not only do not veil, but on the contrary reveal, its roots:

> Satan stood by me. I savour acclaim.
> Here are the obvious signs of my prowess.
> Wrench out my heart from my breast with disdain,
> Toss it to ravenous mongrels.
> Fit for no purpose, of no further use,
> I will keep silent, no word will I utter.
> Robbed of the present, I'm proud of the past,
> Though I am stifled by bitter dishonour.

After this admission the next is not unexpected:

> And only once I had the luck to see
> Beside the lake, within the plane tree's shadow,
> Before the sunset, at that ruthless hour,
> The gleaming of the restless unquenched eyes
> Of innocent Tamara's deathless lover.

Shortly before her death we happened to have a conversation about her current situation: about the fame which had recently come to her, and the banality which accompanied this fame; the great authority she exercised, and her powerlessness before newspaper articles, people's memoirs, the Nobel Prize committee, and the Foreign Desk of the Writers' Union; having no home and depending on strangers; old age, illnesses, and dozens of telephone calls and letters. At first she maintained her dignity and repeated: "A poet is someone to whom nothing can be given and from whom nothing can be taken away," but she suddenly crumbled, leaned forward, and said with an expression of pain in her eyes and in a much lower voice, almost a whisper, "Believe me, I would like to go into a convent—it's the only thing I need now. If only it were possible."

❖   ❖   ❖

Nadezhda Yakovlevna Mandelstam reproaches Akhmatova, in the chapter in her memoirs entitled "Opposite Poles", for approving of the image of "the poet on stage". She has the poem 'The Reader' in mind. In fact Osip Mandelstam's opinion that the actor's is a "profession opposed" to the poet's was entirely shared by Akhmatova. The "staginess" of the 1950s and 1960s was almost a dirty word in her usage. But nevertheless 'The Reader', dated 1959, does indeed depict a poet-actor:

> He should not be very unhappy
> And, least of all, secretive. No!
> To be clear to contemporary readers
> The poet is all open wide.
>
> The footlights stick out underneath him,
> All is deathly, and empty, and bright,
> The merciless flame of the limelight
> Has printed a brand on his brow.
>
> But readers are each like a secret,
> A treasure concealed in the earth,
> Not least that last casual peruser
> Who's been silent throughout his whole life.

We find there what nature will bury
Away from our eyes, when inclined.
There someone defenceless is weeping
When time for a meeting is past,

And how much night twilight is found there,
And shadow, and how much brisk chill;
Unrecognised eyes there are ready
To discourse with me before dawn,

For some things they blame or reproach me,
But on one or two things we agree ...
Thus wordless confession flows freely
In dialogue's rapturous warmth.

Our age on the earth is fastflowing,
The circle allotted constrains,
But he is unchanging, eternal—
The poet's unknowable friend.

This image seems to contradict the very foundations of her poetic creed, such as "Without mystery there is no poetry"; "A poet is someone to whom nothing can be given and from whom nothing can be taken away"; and in general to contradict the tragic self-portrait of the poet which arises from her poems. 'The Reader' asserts at the beginning that, in order to be *understood* (liked) by contemporaries—immaterial whether it is by the "philistines" or the "élite"—simply by "contemporaries", the poet *must not* do something.

We talked about the 'Secrets of the Craft' cycle, and about the first six poems; the connections among the remainder had to do with the politics of publication. I said that the poems were descriptive and that mystery was precisely what they lacked, and that I felt that the cycle was second-rate. She replied, "I also dislike them. But I had to write something apart from *Requiem*; and not about launching sputniks, either." I remarked that 'The Poet' and 'The Reader' could be singled out, and that they were not only "made in Akhmatova's studio", but also "by the hand of the master". This was her opinion too, and she answered immediately and with emphasis, "I think that's right."

In August 1959 Akhmatova and Pasternak were guests at the home of

Vyacheslav Vsevolodovich Ivanov. The hosts asked them to recite their poems and Akhmatova recited 'The Summer Garden'. Pasternak was gloomy and aggressive all evening, and delivered some unfriendly comments on the poem. As if paying no attention to this, Akhmatova also recited 'The Reader', prefacing it with a short introduction. (Pasternak seemed to respond approvingly, but morosely, as before. He himself recited little, with an effort, and after several categorical refusals.) Akhmatova gave the impression of *wanting* to recite 'The Reader' to him, come what may.

By that time Pasternak's poem 'Beyond the Turning', which had been circulating in manuscript copies, was already widely known. (When it was printed in 1962 in *Day of Poetry* and I told Akhmatova about the anthology, which she had not yet seen, she said, "It's a remarkable poem.") The topic is the same as in 'The Reader': nature hiding something from outsiders. Like 'The Reader', 'Beyond the Turning' abounds in implications and hints: "hiding *something*", "does not allow *intruders* on the threshold". Akhmatova has "someone defenceless is weeping", Pasternak has "pleas for defence". Finally, Pasternak's "the future" and Akhmatova's "poet" are both "open wide".

No less evident is the echo in Akhmatova's 'The Reader' and 'The Poet' of the "Introduction" and "Theatrical Introduction" to *Faust* in Pasternak's translation, which he recited to Akhmatova section by section as he completed them.

The circle, which was so constricting, fell apart ...	The circle allotted constrains ...
A bit of life, a bit of fiction ... and so on.	A little from devious life And all from the quiet of the night ... ('The Poet');

Akhmatova compiled a list of her public appearances, the last of which date to 1946. Of the thirty-one mentioned in the list at least six fall in this year, and a few of the poetry readings which are enumerated but not dated almost certainly relate to the same time. This accumulation she attributed to the Central Committee Resolution which followed in August. (The last poetry reading in this series, when she appeared together with Zoshchenko before Party and Young Communist League activists, was arranged, she was convinced, for the acquaintance of *persécuteur* with *persécuté*.) Does this not explain, in particular, the tone and lexicon of the first stanza of 'The Reader', which seems to parody the declamatory style and terminology of official documents: resolutions, reports, and leading articles about literature and art?

In April 1946 Akhmatova and Pasternak made one or two appearances together. It is quite probable that on stage Pasternak read his poem 'Hamlet', which, although it had only recently been written, was already very popular. 'The Reader' repeats the situation of 'Hamlet', and also "night twilight" as a concrete description of the situation: "A thousand opera glasses on their axis bring the dark of night to bear upon me."

The contradiction between poet and actor disappears if one concedes that this poet is simultaneously an actor—Shakespeare, or Pasternak–Hamlet, for example. Evidence for this conclusion includes not only Shakespeare's "dual profession", but also the use of the word limelight, which is borrowed from English and which points to the same theatrical epoch. This word is immediately echoed in the next line, where *zakleymilo*, "printed a brand", echoes the phonetics of lime and light. This is a perfectly admissible wordplay given the verbal devices which occur throughout the poem, such as the sound repetitions in other lines as well. Confirmation of the fact that the poem "conceals" Shakespeare lies in the quotation of the statement made by the critic Belinsky about *A Midsummer Night's Dream*, in which he describes the characters as "shades in the transparent darkness of the night".

Midsummer night, Ivan Kupala's night, with its enchanting and eerie magic—such is the landscape, air, and poetic space of 'The Reader', its content. Akhmatova knew her own kind well: these are people who are captivated by the spell of Midsummer night—primarily Shakespeare and Gogol. Belinsky's reference to *A Midsummer Night's Dream* occurs in fact in connection with Gogol's *May Night*. 'The Reader' speaks of the same objects as Gogol's *The Evening before Ivan Kupala's Night* and *May Night*: treasure, which sinks deeper into the ground as one gets closer to it; "everything which was beneath the ground became as visible as if it lay on one's hand"; *weeping* of piteous willows; tears streaming down the face of a young lady who is begging *for help. The reader* is compared to all this formally, as it were: he is a "secret", and this is a mystery.

Lermontov too was essentially one of Akhmatova's *own kind*: he was the bard of the "mermaid" theme, and, moreover, a native of Tsarskoe Selo. But, unexpected as this may seem, the radical Belinsky also figures amongst *her own kind*, on account of his constant penchant in his early writings for ghosts, moonlit scenes, and underwater realms.

In her book *Lermontov's Fate* E. G. Gershteyn, who was Anna Andreevna's friend and whose research over many years was in Akhmatova's sphere of interest, makes a substantial case for identifying the image of the Reader in Lermontov's poem 'The Journalist, the Reader and the Writer' with the poet Vyazemsky. Here too we find Belinsky, in the capacity of an additional variant so to speak. Finally, there is a mention of the comparison between Lermontov's poem and "Belinsky's articles written at the same time, in which he ... speaks of the function of the journal *Notes of the Fatherland* in educating a democratic *reader*".

Akhmatova's poetic thought, entering this world full of mystery, which had beckoned her predecessors and allowed them in, emerged enriched as much with her own experience as with theirs. The poem 'The Reader' is hers, worked outside all previous traditions, a version of the traditional poetic topos "Dialogue between Poet and Non-Poet". The flight of time, its scarcity in the new century, and the quickened tempo of perceiving the world impelled art to economy: "Our age on the earth is fastflowing, the circle allotted constrains." The Poet is doubled and trebled—he is Shakespeare (Pasternak), Gogol, Lermontov; the Reader is doubled and trebled—he is Poets who read (or quote) one another, and Belinsky (now as a common noun) reading the Poets.

These contrasts and comparisons beg to be made not, of course, in order to prove that Akhmatova, when she set about 'The Reader', aimed to "reply" to *everyone*. This is simply what frequently happens in poems which work well: everything and everyone with any relation to the subject turn out to be drawn into them—and this is the evidence that they are good poems.

❖   ❖   ❖

Being with her gave one the distinct sense of being engulfed by three streams of time. The first was the real time—of a day, a year, a state of health, a domestic atmosphere, a political situation, etc. The second, as is often the case with old people, was the time when they grew up and

57

lived, a time in which nothing which was experienced escapes them, a time in which the present visitor or snowfall or change of government takes its place amongst other visitors, snowfalls and changes of government which were once part of real time. Shades, a multitude of shades, would appear, almost materialise out of her memory, interrupt the conversation with their ghostly presence, and correct one's speech and behaviour. "Clothes have changed so much—" she said, "unpredictably and quickly. I can't imagine Kolya wearing a jacket and sweater as you do." And at that moment Kolya, wearing a black frock-coat and white shirt with a stand-up collar, looked me over sceptically. Thirdly, since she conceived of her own life as a constituent part of historical time, even a common-place remark could draw those who happened to be close to her into this river, which has been flowing for thousands of years. When I was a child, I heard an orientalist friend of my parents quote a phrase which in large part determined my subsequent attitude towards history: "In Assyria we impaled people for that." "In Egypt we ...", "in Rome we ...", "we Ghibellines, Elizabethans, we of the Horde"—these were not so much ironic phrases on Akhmatova's lips as immediate experience.

Real time was the arena for real people. Akhmatova's Moscow home was the Ardovs' flat on Ordynka Street, "the legendary Ordynka", as A.A. herself ironically called it, as did, after her, the people who were close to her. The mistress of the house, Nina Antonovna Olshevskaya, put at her guest's disposal a tiny but cosy room which had belonged to her elder son Aleksey Batalov, and she surrounded her with tender and deferential solicitude. Her selflessness, which was full of inward dignity, and her devotion to Akhmatova were repaid by her older friend's confidences and love. Formerly an actress in the Moscow Art Theatre company, then at the Soviet Army Theatre, Olshevskaya, who had had, like the majority of women of her generation and circle, a far from unclouded existence, had a sensitivity sharpened by bitter experience which allowed her to sum up people and poetry equally well. She knew how to do a good deed. Akhmatova used to say: "It is very hard to do good turns; it's easy to do harm, but very hard to do good." I asked Nina Antonovna why she spoilt her granddaughter with such disregard for pedagogy. "When I die, I want her to remember what a kind granny she had." The answer was absolutely serious. Tall, slim, tranquil, a woman of few words, she set the tone of this household, in which her affected mother-in-law and Akhmatova, Pasternak and a vulgar variety artiste, drunken students and the literary scholar Zhirmunsky, who constructed his phrases with academic correctness, might turn up at table simultaneously. Akhmatova intended to write about Olshevskaya's life in a chapter in her book of prose to be called "Victorious after All".

Her husband, Viktor Efimovich Ardov, who knew every joke, anecdote and witticism there ever was, and invented new ones with variable success, earned enough to keep his sizeable family and a never-ending stream of guests and lodgers who came in never-ending succession by selling humoresques, humorous stories and other species of humour to all the papers and journals from *The Herald of the Central Statistical Board* to the more entertaining *The Crocodile*. He knew everyone in Moscow and some compère or satirist up from the provinces was always hovering around him. His expressions were colourful even on occasions when colour was not required, and he had a story to tell, more or less appropriately, at every turn in a conversation. And he prompted his partner in the conversation to tell the same kind of stories. This is a fairly common style of communicating with no aggravation, no inspired moments, nor any disasters: the agents of the conversation are not the people, but the stories they are reminded of, relevantly or perhaps irrelevantly; it is a cross between a debased *Decameron* and a faded *Thousand and One Nights*, something like shuffling cards to while away tedious five- or ten-minute intervals in a game of rummy. And if his partner could not get the mood right and fell into ordinary narration, Ardov would make a show of becoming distracted, drawing on a scrap of paper, brewing the tea, or looking up a phone number in the directory, repeating all the while, quite beside the point, and with a hint of hypocritical sympathy: "Oh dear me. Yes, yes. You know ..." When Akhmatova asked Nina Antonovna what her granddaughter called her stepfather and was told that she called him by his first name, she approved: "That is how it should be. Daddy should be called Daddy, mummy should be called Mummy ..." On his way past, he immediately joined in: "... uncle should be called Uncle, daughter-in-law Daughter-in-law, brother-in-law Brother-in-law. Anna Andreevna, I'll work up a list and give it to you, OK?"

Apart from Batalov, who by that time had a home of his own, they had two other sons, Mikhail and Boris, who were born shortly before the war. Akhmatova saw them grow up, and both were to some extent brought up by her, since she was so often in their home. Mikhail, who had a gift for literature and had picked up his father's liveliness, sarcasm, and wit, she christened with the nickname Shibanov, in honour of the groom whom A. K. Tolstoy praises in his ballad for being faithful to his prince until death. "But the same was his word," he would declaim, helping her into the taxi, and she would continue, straight-faced: "He praises his lord." Boris, an actor with the Contemporary Theatre, was called "the drama artiste", like the character in Zosh-chenko's famous story. He had an unerring nose for hypocrisy and lies and the gift of mimicry which instantly transformed him into a prime minister speaking at the UN, a poetess boasting to Akhmatova about how successful she was, or a police "tail" freezing cold outside on the stairs. The rhyme he brought home

> Foolish, foolish, foolish wench,
> Fool I am, deceived by men.
> For of fools he has a foursome,
> I am just the fifth of them.

she appreciated instantly and it added to her store: "That's me. And my poems." There was another "narrowly parochial" rhyme in domestic circulation which Mikhail had made up when he was a student. This was about academician Vinogradov's visit to Akhmatova, and she gave it her approval:

> Vinogradov came to see me,
> But I shunned that Vinogradov.
> Shout it out with might and main,
> Meshchaninov is my swain![24]

"Misha is unmerciful," she smiled.

Both the Ardov lads had good taste, which expressed itself, it is true, mostly in abhorrence of things which were in bad taste. Much literature and art came to them at first hand: for example, when they were still children they were allowed to remain in the sitting-room when Paster-nak was giving Akhmatova and her hosts a reading of the parts of *Faust* which he had just translated; when he read the scene in the tavern they burst out laughing and were hushed, but Pasternak said that it should indeed be funny. Like the majority of people who have been trained to look upon literature as a living activity and not as books standing on a shelf, they were not in awe of it, did not talk about it in affected voices and were generally layabouts, boozers and adventure fans, rather than bookworms. Especially Boris, who was out at the theatre from the middle of the day until late at night. And so, when he emerged from the bathroom at noon one dazzlingly bright winter day, screwing up his eyes against the light and carrying *The Brothers Karamazov* under his arm, then shut himself up in his room, Akhmatova looked in his direction and whispered to me with mock horror: "Did you see? Dostoevsky!" "So what?" "What do you mean—so what? Mayakovsky never laid hands on a book in his life and then suddenly went and read *Crime and Punishment*. You know what that led to . . ."

They and their friends, who were swashbucklers just like themselves, and had nicknames like Elephant and Lily of the Valley (naturally, Lily of the Valley was even more hefty than Elephant) and so on, learned about life from life and not from literature. Life, in which they were primarily active participants, but of which they were also observers on account of their keen vision, became literature almost without their intervention, most successfully in the genre of the oral narrative. The characters came to them out of brief encounters, one-day friendships, from the company of "girls who were not dear but beloved", as Elephant remarked cheerfully, and from those guests whose regular appearance in their home was due to the host's innate adventurous streak. Vitaly Voytenko was one of the most colourful figures. The criminal law was used in an attempt to restrain his wild and artistic nature, and satirical articles in the press to humiliate him, but without the slightest success. Variety impresario, low-flying fighter pilot, professional accordion player, medical hypnotist (in this last capacity he was exposed by *Pravda* which, however, noted his "irreproachable manners")—these were the main spheres of activity by which, if one went by his own assertions, one might conclude that he had reached the heights. "Don't stuff your faces like that, kids," he bellowed at the young people, who, he thought, reached out too enthusiastically for the meat in aspic after their first glass of vodka. And the same evening, charging out of the host's study and seeing Akhmatova sitting in her usual place in the middle of the sofa beneath the mirror, he fell on his knees, shuffled towards her and cried: "Your dear hand, our little mother, your hand! Allow me to kiss your dear hand!" and, whilst *en route* and kissing her hand, he commented ecstatically to the onlookers, who were shaking with delight, addressing himself to them alone as if she could not hear: "An empress! Exactly like an empress!"

The host's mother was nearing ninety and had moved to Ordynka Street so as not to live on her own—and to let her grandson have her room. "You have observed," said Akhmatova, "that in these circumstances old people become immortal." She not infrequently got things confused, and was capable of putting the telephone on the gas to boil water. A provincial, well-brought-up little old lady, she invited some no less venerable ladies and gentlemen to play cards once a week, and one day when Nina Antonovna took a tray of tea into her room, she found them all stock still and staring fixedly at a single card lying in the middle of the table. She asked what was the matter. "You see, Ninochka," her mother-in-law explained, "someone led with the ace, but we can't remember who." Then again, coming out for breakfast one morning and sitting down opposite Akhmatova, she fixed her gaze on her, looked her up and down at length, and said, interrupting complete silence: "How, even so, Anna Andreevna, how degraded we are all becoming!" Silence reigned again. Seeing from the reactions of those present that she had said the wrong thing, she announced a minute later in a genteel voice, "Yesterday we played preference ..." "You played *préférence*?", Akhmatova had no mercy, "You—are not becoming degraded."

Amongst Akhmatova's close friends with whom she stayed when Ordynka Street was impossible—because the hostess was on tour, or the flat was too full, or for some other reason—were two whom she contrasted: "Have you noticed that Lyubochka is always mentally abroad, while for Marusya there is nothing outside this country?" I had not noticed that Lyubov Davydovna Bolshintsova-Stenich was "abroad", although she was much more interested in international politics than in the juiciest Moscow gossip, for which she also had a taste. She interpreted the events taking place in the world and the way they might affect us, with such common sense and certitude that one would have thought that these foreign governments were composed to a man of her friends from the days of the civil war in the Crimea, or from Petrograd during NEP, and that they were acting on the same level as the residents' management committee. Her husband, Valentin Stenich, who earned Blok's reproof for being a "Russian dandy", was a man of honour, a translator *extraordinaire* who left us model translations of Dos Passos, Joyce, and Brecht, a most intelligent conversationalist, and a brilliant wit who could joke without thought for the consequences in far from amusing situations, and was shot in 1937. People tried to save him, and Zoshchenko and Kataev spoke up on his behalf. His widow, charming, fragile, "porcelain" ("Lyubochka was made of porcelain"—such was Akhmatova's description of her), and spoilt, also turned out to be tough, patient and hard-working, and outlived her husband by forty-five years. Her literary gifts were part of a general giftedness which revealed itself spontaneously in conduct and daily occurrences, but her aesthetic taste, inculcated by her parents, had been refined by her marriage, and her friendships. She spoke several languages and began earning her living by translating American, English and French plays and stories, nor did she disdain literary hack-work; nevertheless her unbusinesslike approach passed into legend. She retired on a negligible pension, but managed to travel by taxi and wore Paris dresses to the end of her days. Fear was her constant companion: fear of searches and arrests—not concrete searches and arrests for something specific, but fated preordained ones; and she fought that fear all her life—with pride, preparedness for the worst, and finally with her carefree disposition. Once in a superficial jokey conversation I asked Akhmatova what had happened to those soft, incapable women who were attractive by virtue of their very helplessness, that is, the weaker sex. "The weak women all died," she said, dropping the light tone immediately. "Only the strong survived."

Mariya Sergeevna Petrovykh rarely went out of the house, brought up her little daughter, smoked, tucked herself into the corner of her couch, translated poetry—from Armenia, Bulgaria, and many other "fraternal and friendly" nations—and from time to time wrote her own poems. A thin woman, with a quiet voice, unhurried speech, a few phrases and then silence, a penetrating glance, she was all attention—and understanding. She did not argue and give way—until things reached a point at which she argued hard and did not give an inch. The poetry translations were done, as usual, from a literal prose translation provided by someone who knew the language. She approached each of these texts with equal conscientiousness and devoted the same effort, unlimited time, and all her skill to each. Nor did she impose her own style or attitudes in the slightest, except perhaps for the time when she was taking pains over a Scandinavian poetess whose erotica she found displeasing: "She was rather disgusting, you know, so I slapped some more filth on." Her translations did not "stink of translation" as my friend put it. In this area she won recognition, fame, and undeclared but utterly undisputed laurels. However, the true scale of her personality is revealed by three things, equally and in combination: her poems, her attitude towards them, and what remained beyond and between the lines of poetry, but was exuded by them. She speaks in her best poems "with ultimate directness" and at the same time with such moderation of emotional expression that they border on a dry statement of fact. She wrote them for herself, and only people who were close to her succeeded in getting her to recite, and that only after ten requests and nine refusals; the reasons had to do with modesty, which feels every poem to be an intimate thing, and the fear that "the darkness which had pervaded the poems might oppress the reader", as she said to me one day. Akhmatova drew the public's attention to her poem 'Say when you'll meet me in this life', which is, I think, overly forced and eloquent. The immensity of that sorrow, anguish, and loss which the human heart cannot contain and which, therefore, poems cannot express but can only point to, is more adequately conveyed by the silence which reigns between one of her poems to the next. The overall impression was one of inner meaningfulness, which was all the more convincing because outwardly it did not manifest anything normally considered "meaningful": solemnity, singularity, or signs of success. Sympathy, tolerance of weakness and pity came through, when only condemnation could be expected. "You, Mariya, are a help to the dying," Mandelstam said to her in his poem, and those words would suddenly come to mind during a conversation with her, evoked only by her fleeting smile and the shy mannerism with which she patted the hair on her temple into place. Hurt by Mandelstam's widow's jealousy and the unproven accusations which she published in editions of many thousand copies in many languages, she did not become indignant, did not write rebuttals, did not avenge herself with counter exposures, but decided never to touch upon the subject again and only observed to me one day in passing: "Of course he was a fantastic poet, and so on, but believe me, Tolya, as far as he is concerned, I . . . "—and then three devastating incontrovertible words, which only a woman who has never loved the man could say about him.

Lyubov Davydovna lived in Korolenko Street in the Sokolniki district, on the fourth floor of a block of flats without a lift: once she had got up there, Akhmatova remained imprisoned in the flat for the duration of her stay. Her room had a wide and tall window, almost the full height of the room, beautiful old furniture, a large oval mirror, and a charming little oil painting: peasants dispersing in the twilight after church with lighted candles and willow branches in their hands. The block was surrounded by roof-high poplars which had luxuriant foliage in spring and summer. The two-storey house where Mariya Sergeevna lived was entirely drowned in greenery: it was one of ten or so absolutely identical cottages built by German prisoners-of-war on the corner of Begovaya Street and the Khoroshevsky Highway—a writers' village, country within the town. Trees, bushes, lawns, summer houses; a wooden staircase to the first floor; one room was very light, the other very dark. In Korolenko Street conversation between hostess and guest had a decided tendency to mention the names of Kennedy, Mendès-France, Sir Isaiah Berlin, Baroness Budberg, Grinberg "the shark of capitalism" . . . In Begovaya Street—the names of the poet and party functionary Surkov, the writer Marshak, the Minister of Culture Furtseva, and the Moscow Gas Murderer Ionisyan . . . Akhmatova was at ease and felt at home in both places. Sitting in a deep armchair, next to an antique mahogony bureau, she looks at the down from the Sokolniki poplars flying by the window and says: "I feel as if I'm very comfortably ill." She sits in front of the mirror, picks up the comb to do her hair, and shouts through the door: "Marusya, he's drawing nigh!" (*He* is the erudite physicist who left his poems for her comments; the hostess is reading them hastily in the next room.) "Tell me quickly: have they got a feeling for nature? Are the words in their proper places?"

This was Moscow. Moscow made out that something was happening in the city every single minute, it stimulated one to take part in what was going on, to be someone, but it reminded one that one was someone *in Moscow*, that one was taking part in *Moscow's* life. Akhmatova called the city "mother Moscow", with a tinge of erstwhile Petersburg arrogance, which, however, did not only not balk at Moscow's current status but added to it by its slightly servile self-reference. Although natives of Leningrad, given the opportunity, underlined their worthiness, aristocratism, and the fact that they lived "with ceremony and effort", they lived quite normally, if more morosely and less actively than in the capital. "What do you expect from this town?", Akhmatova would say when she was angry with Leningrad. "It was finished when it ceased to be the seat of government; now, as everyone knows, it's a major population centre." (This was what Leningrad was called in Informbureau's military summaries.) However, something set the Leningraders in Moscow apart from others, giving them not the idea of belonging to some "Leningrad Society"—that would have been unthinkable—but the feeling that they belonged, as it were, to a recently dissolved quasi-order, quasi-club, the nebulous statutes and hierarchy of which were still being emanated via the climate, buildings and people. The Leningraders who visited Akhmatova in Leningrad thus had an additional reason for visiting her in Moscow—the system of seniority which separated the junior novice from the head of the order was also what linked them together.

In her writings on Pushkin's 'Egyptian Nights' Akhmatova noted: "Little boys, writing poems in everyone's albums, questions about one's latest work—that is what fame amounts to. (That, and no more. Footnote for self.)" Albums had gone out of fashion, questions were now put by newspaper correspondents on anniversaries and not by "the first comer" as they were to Pushkin's Charsky, and but for the "little boys" the note would look like a banal footnote to Pushkin. But it is the "little boys"—not in Pushkin's use of the phrase to mean a child who recites poems, but in Akhmatova's, meaning the young people who are always in charge of poetry—which give it the character of an entry in a diary. "Little boys" was what she would call—in an old lady's indulgently good-humoured tones, and in their absence—a seventeen-year-old student who burst into the hospital to ask her on her sickbed who was the greater poet, Mandelstam or Tsvetaeva; and the twenty-five-year-old "head of the household" who earned enough for bread, vodka and a raincoat with the Chinese "Friendship" label by spending time more or less onerously in a draftsman's office or on a geological expedition. We four, Dmitry Bobyshev, Evgeny Reyn, Joseph Brodsky and myself, belonged to the latter category.

Bobyshev and Reyn, who had not known each other previously, went to the Leningrad Technological Institute and turned up in the same faculty in 1953, that is—a few months after the death of Stalin. Both were serious about their poetry, felt themselves to be poets, were aware of themselves as poets, and looked on each day of their lives as a day in their fate as poets and in the future of Russian poetry—which both depended on them and was shaped by them. I went to the same institute at the same time, but became friends with them only a year later. About three years after that, when we constituted, in the opinion of outsiders and therefore—perforce—in our own too, a literary group, we were joined by Brodsky, who was a little younger. As everyone does when young, we recited poems to each other, and met up during the breaks and when we were cutting lectures. On the sunny spring evening when Bobyshev and I first got talking we walked down Country Street, Vladimir Street and Foundry Street, across the Neva, and down Forest Street to my home not far from Lansky Street, reciting poetry nonstop and stamped up and down outside the gates for another hour, finishing

Bagritsky's 'February' and selections from Tikhonov's *The Horde* and *Mead*. Another time Brodsky, who had been told over the phone by my family that I was queuing for a railway ticket at the booking office, then in the Duma building, came and half-shouted half-sang his newly completed 'Elegy for John Donne': the public went into shock.

Akhmatova also thought of us as a group and said to me: "You four need a poetess. What about Gorbanevskaya?" I thought this most unnecessary; we did not make declarations of our aims, or issue manifestos, did not oppose other groups, and if we set ourselves up against anything, it was against the formlessness of official poetry, or poetry which had ambitions of becoming official. Once Akhmatova called us "Avvakumites" after the priest who refused to recant his beliefs—because of our unwillingness to make any concessions at all for the sake of getting our poetry published and being recognised by the Union of Soviet Writers. We did indeed want to publish, but firstly, not at any cost, and secondly, apart from our almost daily readings to each other, we frequently received invitations to "read a few poems" at someone's home, at so-called Palaces of Culture, at various Litsocs (literary associations), and at poetry evenings. I once performed at the Architects' Union alongside Engibarov the clown and Isaakyan the boa constrictor tamer, who said with an Armenian accent: "The Soviet school of trenning views the animal being trenned as the investigator views the accused, but the Western school of trenning proves to it that man is also an animal, only a stronger one, that is, to put it simply, they beat it." And also: "Pythons are both viviparous and oviposit." In this company I recited a poem about the way in which when sinking into sleep we fall one-third behind the day and time in general, and they applauded, but disconcertedly, as if only the first part of my act had come off and the second—mass hypnosis, let's say—had gone wrong.

We were young, that is, strong, quick, happy with life, and had no doubts either about our talents or about our predestination, and we believed in our stars. We valued the talents of our contemporaries: of Gorbovsky, Eryomin, Uflyand, and of Krasovitsky, Khromov, and Chertkov in Moscow. We respected Slutsky for the seriousness with which he put ownerless words into lines, in the belief that the dry disciplinarian method of putting them together would lead to truth. As for Yevtushenko, his "I am different, I'm dead tired and idle" or "My God, they need a whipping, not a vodka!" was very much for the fans, but there was not a fan to be found who took to "Russia, I have learned from thee sacred faith in youth today". When he and his comrades began writing, or more precisely working, with an eye to success, this became utterly uninteresting, and even the fact that they were our contemporaries became uninteresting.

Neither then nor even now, when our fates have more or less been played out and steps which looked accidental have turned out to lead in a particular direction, links which seemed firm have broken, and those which seemed inconceivable have been made and grown strong, when apparently ridiculous views and reputations have triumphed, I could not and cannot find any system either in relationships between people or in the conflict and development of their ideas. I understand the concepts of "generation", "process", and "place in history" as bits of intellectual-journalistic jargon, obligatory for conducting a certain kind of discussion and writing a certain kind of book but devoid of any real meaning. Olshevskaya talked to Akhmatova, Nadezhda Yakovlevna Mandelstam talked to Akhmatova, Olshevskaya to Mandelstam, and sometimes all three talked together, but each represented no one but herself, and in any case the conversation was the more authentic the less each of them was linked during the conversation to someone not part of it. Every person expresses something which is not individual: his or her family, circle, profession, time—but expresses it, and does not represent it. When "representatives" communicate there is none of that uniqueness and necessariness which attest that the "representatives" are specific people, that is, that they are alive, people, and not, let us say, pages of a text or trees. I was therefore taken aback and dismayed by a furore which I inadvertently provoked. This was at Margarita Aliger's flat, where Akhmatova was staying for a while. I paid her a visit and was invited to dinner by her hostess. We were joined at table by Aliger's two daughters and a Ukrainian poet whose name I do not recall. That day Slutsky had come to the scenario-writing class to tell his audience, myself included, about the social role of contemporary poetry. He emphasised that the demand for books of poetry had grown: editions of 50,000 did not meet the demand, whereas only half a century ago Akhmatova's *Evening* had come out in an edition of 300 copies: "She told me that she had transported them all at one go in a cab." Halfway through a boring and torpid dinner in a big cold room, I had, I thought, repeated what he had said rather appositely. "I?!" exclaimed Akhmatova, "I transported the books? Or does he think I had no men-friends to do that? And he says for all to hear that I said that to him?" "Anna Andreevna," Aliger shouted over this monologue in a high-pitched voice, "he wants to create bad feeling between you and our generation!" "He" was I, but this idea seemed so absurd that I thought there must be some grammatical confusion here. I had no intention of creating bad feeling between Akhmatova and Slutsky, but it had not entered my head to think that Slutsky and Aliger were of the same generation—or of the same anything at all.

At about that time, if not the same day, Akhmatova showed me a new poem in her notebook: "Poetry soaks everything in Moscow, rhyme injects itself in everything ..." It is not directly connected with this episode, and perhaps it does not even take account of it, but the dinner conveyed to perfection the sensation of a thick sticky excess of rhymed lines of poetry, not by any particular poet, but of poetry in general— Moscow poetry, Leningrad poetry, Soviet poetry ... Here we had a hostess who was a poetess, a poet from Kiev, a generation of poets, and 50,000 slim volumes, and this accumulation of roll-calls of names and numbers (socially, but not individually significant) gradually dragged into its joyless orgy both the 300 copies of *Evening* and the name of Akhmatova. "Old Prokop is all right," she said of Prokofev, the president of the Leningrad Union of Writers. "But his poems are a typical *le robinet est ouvert, le robinet est fermé.*" That's from the Goncourt brothers, recalling that when George Sand was an old woman she was astounded by the invention of running water and kept demonstrating it to them: "*Vous voyez*, open the tap and the water flows, close the tap—it's gone."

❖   ❖   ❖

The friend who had taken the cab and transported the parcels of slim volumes with a lyre on the cover turned out to be just as real as those gathered round the table who had been told about him. If not more real: just as three hundred is more real than fifty thousand; just as the Jewish publisher of *Stone* who said to Mandelstam: "Young man, you'll write better and better" is more real than Dymshits who, thirty-five years after the poet's death in a camp in the far east of the Soviet Union, published his poems with the bare phrase: "In 1937 Mandelstam's creative path broke off."

Akhmatova remembered the dead, especially the friends of her youth, in the same tone and with the same liveliness as yesterday's visitor, and often in connection with yesterday's or today's visitor. Although she kept saying: "Now I've turned into Mme Larousse—people ask me about everything", her replies were not encyclopaedic information about the history of literature and art but anecdotes, not critiques but vivid details. She wrote about Acmeism, the conflicts between literary movements, Modigliani, Blok, but when she was speaking, "Kolya", "Osip", Nedobrovo, Anrep, "Olga", Lourié, Lozinsky and Shileyko (who became Akhmatova's husband) appeared; if Modigliani, then as "Modi", not yet famous, her own dear "Modi". She gave the impression that people made her reminisce about Blok, that she was made to speak as "Blok's contemporary", but that he was not one of her own people. Of his wife Lyubov Dmitrievna Mendeleeva she said, "This is what her back was like"—she spread her arms wide to demonstrate. "She was big, heavy, with a vulgar red face"—Douanier Rousseau's Muse materialised. But this did not belittle Blok—on the contrary it increased his stature because the drift of his words about Tolstoy, and about Igor Severyanin and the woman he fired at on Podsolnechnoe Station, published by her in her memoirs, is just the same as the drift of his poetry—but the back and cheeks which he did not see, or which in any event he did not see as a poet, give some idea of the angle at which his poetic gaze was trained on reality. And Acmeism appears in the form of the Poets' Guild, at whose meetings the agendas were sent round by Gumilyov's wife Anna Akhmatova, and where Shileyko joked that she signed them "Anna Gu, Seclitary" because she was illiterate—that is, it appears as the Acmeism of "Kolya", "Osip" and "Mishenka" Zenke-vich, and not as the Acmeism of lit crit. And if so, if Blok is Blok even with a Muse like that, and Acmeism is Acmeism even with frivolity like that, then Pushkin, the central figure of that third "historical time" in which Akhmatova lived, she could describe in a lighthearted moment, and without in the least diminishing his merit, as "a negro throwing himself on Russian women" in Fyodor Sologub's words, and she could say that his Natalya Nikolaevna was a wife of the "blow out the candle" variety—as if speaking of someone she had known while he was still alive, someone really living, and not an arbitrary "if-he-had-been-alive-today" in frock-coat costume.

The present put out fresh shoots of the past at unpredictable moments. Akhmatova talked of the night in 1935 after the arrest of her son and her then husband Punin when she, together with Punin's first wife Anna Evgenevna, née Arens, anticipating an imminent raid, burned in the stove every document which might appear compromising, that is practically all of them, one by one. When towards morning they had finally sat down, covered in soot and worn out, and Akhmatova had lit a cigarette, a photograph glided down to the floor from the uppermost of the devastated shelves: it showed Baron Arens, Anna Evgenevna's father, an admiral of the royal suite, on board a warship, giving a report to the sovereign who had just carried out a visit of inspection—Nicholas II. A.A. began to go through the moves for getting them released, and went to Moscow and saw the writer Seyfullina, who went off to Poskrebyshev, Stalin's secretary, and found out how to hand in a letter so that it would reach Stalin personally. Poskrebyshev said, "Under the Kutafya tower of the Kremlin at about ten, then I'll give it to him." The next day A.A. and Pilnyak drove there by car and Pilnyak handed over the letter. "The wives of the *Streltsy*," she said, referring to the wives of those executed by Peter the Great and providing a commentary on her lines from *Requiem*: "I shall wail like the wives of the *Streltsy* beneath the towers of the Kremlin." That same day Pasternak also wrote a letter to the Kremlin, telling Akhmatova as he did so, "Regardless how much any other person might have begged me to write, I would not have done so, but in your case . . ." Then she wandered through Moscow in a sort of trance and ended up at the Pasternaks'. The host talked all evening about Annensky and what he meant to him, Pasternak, that is. Then they put her to bed. And when she woke up in the morning in a sunny room Zinaida Nikolaevna (P.'s wife) was standing in the doorway and saying: "Have you seen the telegram yet?" The telegram was from the Punins to say that they were both already home. Akhmatova travelled back to Leningrad, to find them very annoyed and angry with each other about something. Recounting his release, Punin said that when they roused him during the night—for the umpteenth time—he thought it was for another interrogation. But when they said that they were letting him go he worked out, although disconcerted by this surprise announcement, that the trams had stopped running, and asked, "Couldn't I stay the night?" The answer was: "This isn't a hotel." "That, Tolya," she said to me, "is the prehistory of my relationship with Stalin. The old cockroach didn't always ask: 'What's the nun doing?'"

The occasions when she talked about Punin were few enough to count. She studiously avoided him to the same extent that she spoke easily of Shileyko, and willingly of Gumilyov. She once said as an afterword to a conversation about divorce ("divorce is the best institution invented by human kind" or "by civilisation") that she "thought she had spent several years more than necessary with Punin". She let me read a copy of the letter he wrote to her in 1942 in which he said that when he was dying in Leningrad during the siege he thought about her a great deal, and this was "completely unselfish, since I did not expect to see you again, of course". "And I thought then that no one else's life could be as whole and therefore as perfect as yours ... I thought then that your life was perfect not because you willed it, but—this I felt was especially precious—because of its organic wholeness, that is, its inevitability, which seems to have nothing at all to do with you ... Much of what I could not forgive in you not only now stands before me forgiven, but even seems the height of nobility ... There is in your being a fortress that seems to have been hewn from stone with a single stroke of a very practised hand." "... But I remained amongst the living and have treasured both that feeling and the memory of it. I am really frightened of losing it now and forgetting it, and am trying to see that this does not happen, so that what has already happened to me in life several times should not happen again: you know that I often wasted the best things fate gave me—thoughtlessly, without even trying, in fact even as if I had been challenging my destiny." He was arrested in 1949 and died in a camp in 1953—Akhmatova showed me a photograph of a flat field studded with geometrically straight rows of little plaques: little plywood boards nailed to pegs, each bearing a number and a few other figures—the figures on the ones in front could be made out. As many plaques as the camera lens could take in: a camp cemetery, and the place in it where Punin's body was thought to be buried.

She spoke of her marriage to Shileyko as a dismal misunderstanding, but she talked about it without a hint of rancour, rather—with cheerfulness and with gratitude to her former husband, in a tone quite unlike the anger and despair of the poems addressed to him: "It was Kolya and Lozinsky. They kept singing a tune for two voices, 'The Egyptian, the Egyptian! ...' So I ... well, I accepted." Vladimir Kazimirovich Shileyko was an outstanding Assyriologist and translator of ancient oriental poetry. He had begun deciphering Egyptian texts as a fourteen-year-old boy. Akhmatova's play *Enuma e lish* which she destroyed (and some impression of which can be gained from the fragments of *Prologue* which she reworked towards the end of her life) takes its name from the first words ("There on high") of the ancient Babylonian poem about the creation of the world, in Shileyko's translation. He was also, I think, the originator of Akhmatova's nickname—Akuma—used by those close to her; though I have since read that Punin named her thus after a Japanese evil spirit. Shileyko was a subtle lyric poet and published poems in *The Hyperborean, Apollo,* and the anthology *Thirteen Poets.* Here is one of his poems, printed in 1919 in *The Siren* in Voronezh:

> In those embittered hardened times
> You were the last exalted sound,
> You were the swan's short farewell song,
> You were the one remaining star.
>
> You were above the poisoned cup,
> In harmony with bitter fate,
> All that was left: my little dove—
> And he, still yearning after you.

Just before the revolution he had been tutor to the children of Count Sheremetev and he told Akhmatova that he had found a document case labelled "Other People's Poems" in the desk drawer of the room allotted to him which was traditionally set aside for the tutor. He remembered that Vyazemsky, the poet and friend of Pushkin, was related to the Sheremetevs and had lived here in his time, and realised that this was his document case, since only a person who writes poems of his own can also have "other people's". Shileyko brought Akhmatova to this room after they had spent the cold, hungry and difficult autumn of 1918 at Third Immaculate Conception Lane. This was Akhmatova's first move to the House on the Fontanka, namely 34 Fontanka: the next came a few years later, when she married Punin who was living there in a side wing, overlooking the fourth courtyard. With Shileyko she also lived in a flat in the servants' quarters of the Marble Palace: "one window facing Suvorov, another the Field of Mars". She recounted the following story about this marriage, with some amusement. At that time it was sufficient for a couple wishing to register their marriage to make a declaration to the house management committee: it was considered valid as soon as the house manager had made the entry in the appropriate book. Shileyko had said that he would attend to this, and soon confirmed that everything was in order and that the entry had been made that day. "But when we were separated and I asked someone to go to the office to inform the house manager of the dissolution of the marriage, they failed to find the entry under that date, which I clearly recalled, or under those to either side, or anywhere at all." She showed me some of Shileyko's letters, written in calligraphic script, in a stylish manner, with the delightful observations of a bookish person, and with passages in various languages. "I have been reading Servius' commentaries on Virgil all day. Wonderful! Here are some *sottises* for you:

> But be polite with haughty boredom.

> Mandelstam

> Nonne fuit satius tristes Amaryllidis iras
> Atque *superba* grati *fastidia.*

> *Ecl.* ii, vv 14–15

And Oska never even tried to see into the Mantuan soul." (The couplet from the *Eclogues* reads: "Did I not have enough of the saddening anger of Amaryllis / And the *proud rejection* of dear Menalcas?") These are the letters of a friend, not a husband, with funny endings such as "Yours, Elephants" and a drawing of an elephant. "That's what he was like," she nodded. "He could look at me after we had had fried egg for breakfast and say, 'Anya, it doesn't become you to eat coloured things.'" I think it was he who told some of their visitors "Anya has a remarkable capacity for combining the unpleasant with the useless." So it was unexpected to discover from her that "the tongue-tied man who celebrated me" was also he.

The early 1960s was the period of Mandelstam's posthumous fame. We read the *Voronezh Notebooks* in about 1955, in a hand-written copy and indeed in a notebook. *Stone*, his early collection of poems, was written out at the front of this notebook, in the same brown ink, already slightly faded, and with the same pen, which produced thick lines when pressed upon, and the first impression given by Mandelstam's first poems, that is the first impression of the poetry of Mandelstam as such, was incomparably more acute than the impression given by, let us say, his 'Verses about the Unknown Soldier', which, though they struck a tragic note, did so against the background of the amazing, amazingly fresh sound of those first poems. A typescript of *Fourth Prose* soon began to circulate, and to stun us with its combination of ego-centrically aggressive refinement and bad language, which was derived from persecution and therefore devoid of individuality. For a young man this added up to a manner which was supremely attractive, and which answered his own literary pretensions in the best possible way. In particular my first experiments with prose also took their direction from it: it was tempting to see universality in it, and, therefore, some very promising perspectives. "That is for you, for your vengeful prose"— Akhmatova concluded her or my description of an event or person whose appearance was in direct contrast to their essence. It was then that she wrote a passage which she intended to insert into her *Pages from a Diary* (and on which she even noted "Insert into text, p. ", though she did not designate the specific place): "And the children turned out not to have been part of a promised sale to the pock-marked devil like their fathers were. It turns out that promises of sale cannot be made three generations in advance. And now the time has come when these children have come, found Osip Mandelstam's poems, and said,

'This is our poet.'"

In the winter of 1962 I interested Brodsky in taking a trip to Pskov. On the eve of our departure Akhmatova suggested that we should visit Nadezhda Yakovlevna Mandelstam, who was teaching in the Peda-gogical Institute there, and give her her good wishes, but she did not know her address, and could only tell us who would help us to locate her. We spent three days in Pskov, scrutinised the town, walked across the river Velikaya on the ice, travelled about the area, and spent a day wandering round Izborsk. On one of our evenings there we set off to see Nadezhda Yakovlevna. She was renting a little room in a communal flat from a landlady whose surname was Netsvetaeva (literally: "Not Tsvetaeva"), which under the circumstances sounded less amusing than ominous. She was tired, a semi-invalid, and lay on the bed on top of the blanket, smoking. There were more pauses than words and one had the distinct feeling that tiredness, ill health, lying on a made bed, and a lightbulb with no lampshade were not the trappings of the moment, but were her whole life, decade after decade, with no way out, in corners of flats which were not her own, in towns which were not her own either.

When she finally moved to Moscow several years later she became a different person: she bustled about and was always making arguments for something which was beside the point, or communicating some apocryphal fact, completely unlike that woman who had been exiled officially or covertly to the end of her days, who had nothing to lose, and for whom it was unthinkable and humiliating to be seduced by the trivia in the carefree lives of those women who were at liberty. And her husband, who arranged this fate for her and countersigned it with the phrase "Who told you that you should be happy?", began to be transformed from the poet-genius Mandelstam who perished in the icy wastes into the famous Muscovite holy fool "Oska" and the outstanding figure of Petersburg's intellectual and aesthetic circles, "Osip Emilevich". During the next "tightening of the screws", either when Khrushchev went off the deep end about literature and art, which were up to the devil knows what, but were not depicting the Russian forests, which were particularly beautiful in wintertime, or when the Sinyavsky and Daniel case[25] was getting going, a frightened Nadezhda Yakovlevna came to see Akhmatova to consult her about how to react. She had by then finished the first volume of her memoirs and large numbers of people had read it in manuscript. She was still living with friends, but attempts to get a flat for her were gathering momentum and Akhmatova had also joined in, sending a letter to Surkov, who was on the board of the Union of Soviet Writers ("For a quarter of a century the widow of a poet who fell victim to the arbitrary rule of despotism has been wandering the country with no home of her own. However, this nomadic life is now beyond her: she is an old woman in need of medical attention"). Nadezhda Yakovlevna was in terror lest the powers-that-be in the literary world should hear rumours of the existence of her memoirs, or get hold of a copy of the manuscript, which was being duplicated and was, therefore, beyond her control. Akhmatova reassured her as well as she could, but after she had gone she said, "What does Nadya think—that she can write books like that and in return they'll give her flats?" I asked how accusatory the book was, and whether it was indeed such a danger to its author as N.Ya. thought. She glanced at me with a look which said that she found this a strange question and whispered, "I haven't read it." Pleased with my amazement, she added, "Fortunately she didn't offer—and I didn't ask." After Akhmatova's death Nadezhda Yakovlevna also wrote and published *Hope Abandoned*. Its main device is a subtle well-measured dose of untruths dissolved in truth and there is no means of removing the malignant matter without damage to the tissues. She says, in passing and as if in fun, "that fool Bulgakov"; and follows up with conclusions which are neither uncontentious nor susceptible to logical refutation, but which lose all meaning if Bulgakov is not a fool. Akhmatova is presented as a capricious old woman who has lost her sense of reality. The only element of truth here is that she was an old woman; the rest becomes plausible as the result of phrases such as "in reply to Akhmatova's words I only burst out laughing"—something which is improbable, given the hierarchy of relationships which prevailed. I think that Nadezhda Yakovlevna began by deflating the images of Mandelstam and Akhmatova by dint of showing their "everyday routine" and then in her last years came to believe sincerely that she surpassed both in intelligence and was not far behind, if at all, in talent. Perhaps she needed compensation of this kind for the pain, horror, and humiliations earlier in her life. After she had closed the door behind Nadezhda Yakovlevna, who had been delivering rapid monologues for a quarter of an hour to an expressively silent Akhmatova on the topic of the place in pre-revolutionary Petersburg culture in which she insisted on setting Mandelstam, Akhmatova related the following episode, apropos of that same question: "In the mid-1910s a society of poets called Fiza was formed with the particular aim of demolishing the Guild. Osip, Kolya and I were on the ascent, but as for the Guild, it was bound to come to a natural end. 'Fiza' was the title of a narrative poem by Anrep which was read at the first meeting of the society in the author's absence: he was in Paris at the time. One day they invited Mandelstam to give a paper. After the paper I went to the station by cab with Nikolay Vladimirovich Nedobrovo, who had moved to Tsarskoe by that time to live closer to me. On the way Nedobrovo said, 'God knows what sort of a paper that was! Firstly he confuses participles with gerunds. And secondly he said "All twelve Muses", but actually there are nine.' Mandelstam had no need whatsoever to know more than he already knew. He said that he was three when he heard the word 'progress' for the first time, and he guffawed uproariously. He imparted life to everything he touched, everything his glance lighted upon. Of course he corrected 'Phaedra the poisoner' when Gumilyov and Lozinsky asked him 'But who did she poison?' But there is no need to present him as a university graduate when at best he went to eight lectures. There is no need to link him with Solovyov's philosophy and turn him and Blok into twins, like Tweedledum and Tweedledee." On another occasion something made her recall, "Mandelstam said, 'I'm a sense man, and that is why I dislike trans-sense language.'[26] And also, 'I am someone who anticipates, and that is why internal exile seems all the more terrible.' "

By the time she told me about Fiza I had heard a great deal about Nedobrovo from her, had read his article about her and the poems he addressed to her, and had heard her say, "Perhaps he made Akhmatova," but when she mentioned his name this time she found it necessary to say emphatically, "He was Acmeism's first adversary, a follower of Vyacheslav Ivanov, someone from his Tower." There was a picture in her photograph album of Nedobrovo, taken in a studio in Petersburg at the beginning of the century. Hair carefully combed—not, apparently, especially for the photograph, but habitually so; head raised high; a very slightly arrogant look in his almond-shaped eyes, which in combination with the long high eyebrows and thin aquiline nose make this thin face with its heavy outline look like a portrait; ascetic dress—in short, an exterior which hides the essence within and does not express it, like a "lifelike" image on the lid of a sarcophagus. He looks like a strong, though also elegant, person, but his chest seemed to me to be overly constricted by his frock-coat; perhaps he was simply narrow in the chest, or perhaps I noticed this because I knew that in 1919, a few years after the photograph was taken he died of tuberculosis in the Crimea at the age of thirty-five. Akhmatova saw him for the last time in the autumn of 1916 in Bakhchisaray, where the stone mile posts which had run towards them so many times on the road from Petersburg to Tsarskoe Selo came to an end, and were now sadly recognised by them both:

> Where I said farewell, and whence
> To the realm of shades you went,
> You who were my joy and solace.

Akhmatova said that Nedobrovo considered himself one of the central figures of what was subsequently called "the Silver Age", never had any doubts about whether he had grounds for so thinking, and behaved accordingly. He was convinced that his correspondence would be published in separate volumes, and apparently kept the drafts of his letters. Akhmatova dedicated or addressed to him a small number of remarkable poems and the lyric digression in Poem without a Hero which ends:

Remembering Anna Akhmatova

Will you not tell me again
The death-
               conquering
                             word
And solve the riddle of my life?

with the later omitted stanza:

He who stood over my turbulent youth,
Gentle friend I shall never forget,
Dream which came that one night only,
He whose strength at one time shone,
He whose grave is quite forgot,
Just as if he had never existed.

"N.V. Nedobrovo—idyll at Tsarskoe Selo", reads the opening of one of her prose pieces from her last years.

In 1914 Nedobrovo introduced Akhmatova to his old and closest friend Boris Anrep. They soon started an affair and by the spring of the following year Anrep had pushed Nedobrovo out of her affections and her poetry. The latter took the double betrayal very hard and made a permanent break with the friend he had until then loved and greatly valued. Anrep took advantage of every mission or period of furlough in order to leave the front and see Akhmatova in Petrograd. One day during the February revolution he took off his officer's shoulder-straps and, risking his life, walked across the frozen river Neva to see her. He told her that he was leaving for England, and that it was "the calm English civilisation of reason, and not religious and political ravings" that he held dear. They said goodbye and he left for London. In 1923 she wrote,

And seven years have passed. October's tragic storm
Has scattered people's lives like yellow leaves in autumn;
The hindmost urgent vessel bore my love away
From these stark shores as flames devoured his mother country.

For Akhmatova he became something like an *amor de lonh*, the distant love of the troubadour, always desired and never attained. More of her

79

poems both before and after their parting are addressed to him than to anyone else. Abroad he became known as a mosaicist, and A.A. showed me a photograph—black and white—of his mosaic on the floor of the vestibule of the National Gallery in London: amongst the many figures it contains is "Compassion", which Anrep modelled on Akhmatova's portrait. In 1965 they met in Paris after the Oxford honorary degree ceremony. On her return Akhmatova said that all through the encounter Anrep was "wooden, and had apparently suffered a stroke not so long ago": "We could not look up at each other—we both felt like murderers."

Reminiscences about the composer Arthur Lourié usually came to Akhmatova by association with someone else: with Mandelstam, with Olga Sudeykina (the "heroine" of *Poem without a Hero*) or the Stray Dog cabaret. She became intimate with Lourié at the very beginning of the 1920s, the time at which he emigrated to Paris with Olga; many years later he wrote, "We lived together on the Fontanka, *à trois* ... Anya is now seventy-three. I remember her at twenty-three." She described with amusement how "Arthur had sent a request from America": could she make use of her connections to get his ballet *The Negro of Peter the Great* produced in the Soviet Union? "Over there he couldn't think of anything more intelligent than a ballet about a negro amongst whites"—this was the time of the race riots. In another conversation the name "Arthur" dredged up from her memory "the old servant woman in Olga's house". In her view the mistress and her lady friend were not doing well: " ... At first Anna Andreevna did at least hum to herself, but now she's stopped. She'll let her hair down and roam like a deer. Top scholars come with a smile on their faces and leave looking grim."

As she lived each new day, opened a book, or went out into the street, she could not help finding herself unexpectedly back in the past, just as when she was caught by an air-raid siren in August 1941, she went down into the nearest shelter, and found herself in the cellar which had once housed the Stray Dog. Nevertheless she did not retreat into the past, but, inasmuch as that which had only recently been the future was now transforming itself into the past, she sent it on a counter-current into the distant future. Not by means of memoirs, which are intended to tie the past down once and for all, but by means of an all-embracing awareness of the fact that the future with its myriad possibilities becomes the one single past precisely so that it should abide forever. Nor is there any place here for variants: what ought to be a fact must be a fact, and what ought to become a legend must become a legend. When Morozova's memoirs appeared in *New World*, Akhmatova suspected that they were inspired by the "legendary" Pallada (as Kuzmin's hymn to the Stray Dog had it: "Love alone is all her pleasure, both where right and not where right; she will never, never, never, never answer 'Not tonight' "), Pallada Olimpievna Gross, and she was furious when she read that the memoirist saw her at the Comedians' Halt cabaret: "I never once crossed the threshold of the Halt! I only went to the Dog!" I thought then, what's the difference? These were artistic cabarets from almost the same period; many of the people who went to the Stray Dog also turned up at the Comedians' Halt later on ... But if for some reason you have *not* gone somewhere—perhaps you promised someone not to go, or thought it quite impossible, and you refused invitations to go, and let everyone see that you never went, as in the case of Blok and the Stray Dog—and then you read that you *did* go, then all the is's and isn'ts in your life change places, your whole life in other words.

The people who said, or now say, that she "corrected her biography" in her last years do so out of the conviction that a document—and they call any note a document—is more trustworthy than a later correction. And that by drawing on documents they can recreate the *true* status quo. And that subsequent interference with the document, which somehow or other distorts the picture they have built up, is an infringement of the truth and can be explained by the desire to improve the part played in the past by oneself or those one holds dear, and to blacken one's opponents. But Akhmatova had worked for several decades with archival documents and knew the dangers of coming to false conclusions, involuntary or premeditated, on the basis of them. She did not believe that an Akhmatova specialist was cleverer than Akhmatova, and she showed herself, through her reminscences and the corrections made in her last years, to be the first Akhmatova specialist, with whose *objective* opinion all later specialists would have to give particular weight.

She had a special way of adjusting opinions held about her in the desired direction. One day she gave me a manuscript to read, an article with the banal title "A Coal Burning with Fire" (culled from Pushkin's famous poem), written by a certain Leningrad critic. The article was well-disposed, but although it touched on Akhmatova's latest poems, it added nothing to what was already known about her. She said, "Never mind, I'll invite him round and float some ideas. I have a way of unobstrusively floating my own thoughts to people. And in a little while they sincerely believe that the ideas are their own." She probably "floated ideas to" Nikita Struve in precisely this manner when she was talking to him in London, though, to extend the metaphor, he "did not take other people's things": "Is it true," she asked him, "that you wrote to someone in Russia about my memoirs and said, '*Je possède les feuillets du journal de Sappho*'?" "I never wrote such a thing in my life." "Oh well, so much for believing people." I think she was using the same method when she declared, "It is said that in twentieth-century poetry Spaniards have the reputation of being the gods and Russians the demi-gods." Who said that, and whom was she quoting, if not herself? Or when a large group of poets went to Italy at the invitation of their Writers' Union and she was not allowed to go, she said, smiling artfully, "The Italian newspapers are saying that they would rather see Alighieri's sister than his namesake." And to make this seem more plausible she repeated in Italian "*La suora di colui*" ("His sister"). By "namesake" she meant Margarita Aliger, who had gone to Rome, but there was no point in enquiring which Italian newspapers had said this. *La suora di colui* is the Moon in canto XXIII of *Il Purgatorio*, his sister—the Sun's. And I interpreted what she said in the same way when, returning from doing an errand for her on my bicycle at Komarovo, I heard, "Not for nothing do some people call you Hermes." There were no other "people", apart from herself, to be seen.

In editing her friend V.S. Sreznevskaya's memoirs she wrote: "... an obstinate mouth with a strongly defined upper lip—thin and supple as a withy—with very white skin—she was an excellent swimmer and diver (especially in the waters of the Tsarskoe Selo bathing pool), having learned at the Black Sea where they spent several summers. She seemed to be a mermaid who had accidentally swum into the dark still waters of the Tsarskoe Selo ponds [Akhmatova adds: *and to this day she calls herself the last inhabitant of Chersonesus*]. It is no wonder that Nik. Step. Gumilyov fell in love straightaway with this fateful woman of his Muse. Her image burdens upon the poet's heart, sometimes a cruel, cold, and distant queen before whom he casts the 'rubies of divinity' [Akhmatova corrects: *of magic*]—sometimes a green seductive and strangely familiar sorceress and witch—in *Pearls* and in *The Quiver* [Akhmatova deletes *The Quiver*] and much later the recognised and irrevocably lost ghost of the beloved who will never return. In order to demonstrate that these are not 'hypotheses and suppositions' (as happens not infrequently in the biographies of major poets) but the real living truth, I quote not only my many years of happy friendship with both, but also the more convincing and unquestionable traces of this love in the poetry of N. S. Gumilyov [here Akhmatova inserts the titles of the poems addressed to her, beginning with *The Path of the Conquistadors*]."

Valeriya Sergeevna Sreznevskaya, née Tyulpanova, was her oldest friend; as far back as Tsarskoe, when the Gorenkos moved from the ground floor to the first floor of Shukhardina's house and the Tyulpanovs moved into the ground floor flat, and Gumilyov, who was at school with "Valya's" brother Andrey, used to come to see him. Akhmatova stayed with her in Petrograd at 9 Botkin Street (a house belonging to the clinic where Dr Sreznevsky worked as a physician) from January 1917 to autumn 1918, that is, through both revolutions, her parting from Anrep, and her marriage to Shileyko. She later stayed in Sreznevskaya's flat several more times and dedicated one of her best poems, 'Instead of wisdom—experience', to her. She recalled that once they were both in a cab, one complaining to the other about something, when the cabman, who was "so old that he could have had Lermontov for a passenger, suddenly said: 'Your grievance is very raw, young ladies'—it wasn't clear whose." When Sreznevskaya died in 1964 A.A. said: "Valya was the last person with whom I used the familiar form of address. Now there is no one left." She was the last remaining witness of those earliest years in which the chief knots in Akhmatova's fate were tied, and she had begun to write her memoirs—under some pressure from Akhmatova. In the extract just quoted Akhmatova leaves "burdens upon" as it is (instead of "weighs upon", an error upon which she pounced in other cases) and "woman of his Muse". By inserting the "inhabitant of Chersonesus" and the titles of Gumilyov's poems she does not change the status of the memoirs as the writer's own self-expression or as a document, but merely makes a loan from the memory that was common to both women—not just from her own—to those who do not have that memory; she fixes the torn-off corner back on to the certificate.

Her memory, which was "predatory" and "golden", to use the words she used to praise other people's memories, was apparently organised in a very special way: it retained what had happened in *specific* situations, and simultaneously what ought to happen in situations *of that kind*. This was, moreover, not an understanding arrived at by analogy with what had happened to her on one or more occasions, that is—it was not the result of experience, although it did also rest on the whole of her enormous experience; it was, as it were, inherited at birth from some unknown person and lay in the very depths of her being. To be precise, Akhmatova did not *know* certain things which she had not herself witnessed; she *remembered* them. The mechanism of recollection which she describes in connection with Blok, "Blok's notebook gives me little presents by extracting half-forgotten events from the abyss of oblivion and returning their dates to them," extended in her case to events which were registered in her Ur-memory. "I was once in Slepnyovo in winter. It was magnificent. Everything seemed to have receded into the nineteenth century, almost into Pushkin's time. Sledges, felt boots, bear-fur travelling rugs, vast sheepskin coats, resonant silence, snowdrifts, diamonds." This was not a conception of Pushkin's times fed by knowledge; it was recognition. The same thing used to happen when she read books: in pages describing things which she could neither confirm nor refute from her own experience she would come upon a line about something she "remembered", the authenticity or fraudulence of which she "recognised" from her "memories", be it Hemingway, or Avvakum, or Shakespeare, or Plutarch. "Of course!" she exlaimed, pointing her finger at a preparatory prose translation of a papyrus, which she was looking over, amongst others, before agreeing to translate some Egyptian lyrics, *Pyramid altius.* "For Horace pyramids were an abstraction, but this man looked out of the window and saw nothing else." "This man" was the scribe who celebrated the scribes of distant antiquity: "They did not build themselves pyramids of copper or gravestones of bronze." She said with the same assurance that her grandfather on her mother's side, Erazm Ivanovich Stogov, "a colonel of gendarmes", had walked past Pushkin in the suites of rooms belonging to the Third Section, the secret police (although she could only know that he served as a gendarme officer of field rank in Simbirsk from 1834).

The method which led her to certain discoveries in Pushkin studies, particularly later on, was akin to this "recollection": first she "recognised" that this, and not that, was the case, and indeed the necessary evidence soon began to gravitate towards it as if magnetised, a process diametrically opposed to fitting the facts to the hypothesis.

Having at her disposal "someone's" memory "gratuitously given" to her, Akhmatova was generous in using it, together with her own, for those in need. It is true that people sometimes said behind her back that she did not do this disinterestedly, that she was not dispassionate, that she interpreted facts in her own way, and imposed "subjective" opinions. I did not observe her trying to prove her own case; on the contrary, her references to people and things were—at least on the surface—light-hearted, humorous and casual throughout: believe me if you like, not if you don't—with which words, incidentally, she often finished what she had to say. She did not "pull the blanket over to her side", did not retouch the history of literature, and she was quite content with its summary account of her fate, her poetry and her place in Russian and world culture, as also with its account of the fates and creative work of her contemporaries. If she went on the attack or defended herself, this was principally for the sake of justice. When we were young, Brodsky enjoyed the instinctive good will of the very same people who were instinctively hostile towards me. If he promised to go to the station to meet someone from another town and forgot, they blamed the latter: why did he have to come anyway? If I was taken into hospital with a heart attack, they said, now he's done it. "It depends on what is preordained for whom," Akhmatova explained. "However vilely Kuzmin behaved—and he treated people dreadfully badly—everyone adored him. And however nobly Kolya behaved, everything went wrong for him. There's nothing that can be done about it." But she could lash out wildly in her irritation: "Perhaps pederasts respect Kuzmin ..." (in connection with her question "Who respects Vyacheslav Ivanov nowadays?").

She said, "Bunin made up an epigram about me:

An assignation with Akhmatova
One cannot but bemoan:
However much one puts one's arm around her
A stone remains a stone.

What do you think? I think it's good."

And with the same enjoyment: "I was born to unmask Vyacheslav Ivanov. He was a great hoaxer, a Count Saint-Germain. His wife, Zinoveva-Annibal, is dying of scarlet fever: they're out in the country and she dies in a few days, simply suffocates. He starts living with her daughter by her first husband, aged fifteen. She has a child by him and some cleric in Italy marries them illegally. And then Sir B. and Sir B. solemnly explain that this was his wife's dying wish ... The Europeans think that Blok was a person who 'visited Vyacheslav Ivanov's famous Tower'. 'Vyacheslav Ivanov taught Akhmatova to write poetry.' He left little old men lamenting him in Baku, in Italy, everywhere." With a little note of vengefulness: "But not in Russia. He latched on to people and then wouldn't let them go—'a fisher of men'. In the Oxford edition of his *Evening Light* there is a portrait of him at eighty-two, an old man with an ecclesiastical exterior but neither intelligence, nor peace, nor wisdom—just their likenesses."

"Haven't I played you my gramophone record about Balmont yet?

"Balmont came back from abroad and one of his admirers arranged a soirée in his honour. He invited the young people too: me, Gumilyov, and someone else. The admirer was a general in the communications corps: a luxurious Petersburg flat, luxurious refreshments, and everything just so. The host sat at the grand piano and sang 'In my garden roses glimmer, white as snow and r-r-red'. Balmont was the reigning monarch. To us all this was completely unnecessary.

"After midnight they decided that those who had a long way to travel, like us for example, who had to get to Tsarskoe Selo, would do better to stay until morning. We went into the next room, someone sat down at the piano, and a couple started dancing. Then little ginger Balmont suddenly appeared in the doorway, leant his head against the jamb, put his feet in this position [at this point she folded her hands crosswise] and said: 'Why am I, such a sensitive person, obliged to see all this?' "

She used this remark with ironic sadness either when she saw something which she found sympathetic but which general opinion considered unworthy "of Akhmatova" (for example, when she came out on to the verandah of the little house at Komarovo and found the young people she had invited getting on bicycles two at a time to go swimming in the river Sestra) or when she saw something which she did not find sympathetic, but which did not warrant a more serious reaction (for example, when her eye alighted on a magazine containing photographs of Elizabeth Taylor playing Cleopatra).

Somehow her accounts of people from "before 1913", that is, the older ones, including those whom she knew well, carried them back into the nineteenth century, via Tolstoy to Turgenev, Fet and Nekrasov. They functioned as a link between her past and the past of history. In just the same way people who had not been part of "1913", as she described it in *Poem without a Hero*, were carried into the present, even those of her own age who were already dead by the time she spoke about them—Pasternak, Pilnyak, Bulgakov. They turned out to be completely incorporated into the Soviet period, were as understandable to us as our then still-living mothers and fathers, and fulfilled the function of signs of Akhmatova's twenties, thirties and forties in her biography ... I was going to a party at the home of my friends from Georgia. She remarked in passing that some people, like Pasternak, "are devoted to Georgia" (one of her customary turns of phrase—of the Leningrad crime-writer German, for example: "By that time German was already devoted to the police ... "), but she herself "was always a friend of Armenia". I replied that there were as many Moscow Georgians in this circle as there were Tbilisi Georgians, and that a Tbilisi Georgian in Moscow was about the same thing as a Leningrader in Moscow. She said that she knew some of the Moscow Georgians. I mentioned the name of Boris Andronikashvili. "How odd ... He must be your age. When Pilnyak was in America he bought a car and shipped it to Leningrad by sea. Pilnyak came to Leningrad to drive it on to Moscow and invited me to accompany him, and I agreed. We set off during one of the White Nights. When we got there he found out that his wife had had a son. That was your Boris Borisych ... Pilnyak was unlucky with his wives: one of them, not Boris's mother, seems to have had something to do with his arrest. But it was his closeness to the NKVD which was his undoing, and Babel's. They both felt the attraction of associating and boozing with high-ranking NKVD officers: 'real power', titillation, and anyway it was the fashion. They were bound to be sucked down the funnel." She was silent for a moment and then said, "For seven years Pilnyak asked me to marry him, but I was rather against it."

And a few days later: "I was coming home with Pasternak from a Georgian feast just before dawn—this was soon after the war. We were going the same way, to the Zamoskvoreche area, and he took me by the arm and talked all the way about Spassky, the poet from Leningrad, and what a remarkable poet he was; we crossed the bridge and just here, in Ordynka Street—she nodded in the direction of the river (she and I were standing at the gates of the block where the Ardovs lived)—he was getting quite choked: 'Spassky! Spassky! Anna Andreevna, you can't imagine such poems, what rapture ...' And at this point he took to embracing me in an excess of emotion. I said, 'But Boris Leonidovich, I'm not Spassky, you know.' That was typical. Dear Boris."

One sunny winter day I popped round to Ordynka Street and found Anna Andreevna at the sitting-room table which was covered with a dazzling white cloth, together with Nina Antonovna and two other elderly people, a stately elegant man and a charming fragile lady, whom I took to be husband and wife. Akhmatova introduced me, and added with a smile, "Anatoly Genrikhovich is a great admirer of *Theatrical*

Novel." *Black Snow: A Theatrical Novel* had just come out in *New World* and everyone was talking about it. The lady looked at me, and also smiled. They all smiled from the very outset, except for the man. I took Akhmatova's remark as an invitation to pursue the subject and said how much I liked the novel and why. Everyone's smiles, which were cordial but merrier, I felt, than my words warranted, together with the sarcastic smile of the man, spurred me on to less sincere and therefore more impassioned praise. The woman's risibility and the man's hostility, which had already manifested itself in hems and the remark "Really!", increased still further. I began to feel uncomfortable, but did not want to surrender, and so quoted some of the best examples of Bulgakov's style. Akhmatova interrupted me, "Let me introduce Elena Sergeevna Bulgakova." Discomfiture on my part, general delight, disbelief on the part of the man: "He knew of course; and if he didn't, he could have guessed." This was Mikhail Davydovich Volpin, a play-wright and a man with a sharp, rather peevish mind and a biting tongue, who had hissed Akhmatova off the stage at poetry readings in the 1920s out of loyalty to Mayakovsky, and who was one of the penny numbers of people who had heard her read *Requiem* in the late 1930s. During the war he and his best friend, the playwright Erdman, both found them-selves in Tashkent and visited Akhmatova, both in military uniform. They knew the whereabouts of the house only vaguely and, according to her, everyone of whom they asked its whereabouts was convinced that "they had come for her" and hastened to make some denunciation. So that when they emerged from the house holding her respectfully by the arm, and returned five minutes later with large bottles of wine, those who had gathered by the verandah were embarrassed and profoundly disillusioned ...

As she was leaving that winter day Elena Sergeevna turned to me and said, "If you like, I can give you another of my husband's novels to read, at my house of course." In her flat, with its shining, apparently wax-polished, floors and its late eighteenth-century furniture, in a block near the Nikita Gates, I read the two files containing *The Master and Margarita* in three days. I admitted to Akhmatova that these sweet hours of reading, the more captivating because the reading was done in this extraordinary setting so uniquely suited to it, had finally settled within me as a wearisome disenchantment. According to the writer, the captivating, vital, "Bulgakov" layer of Soviet Moscow should have been enveloped by a timeless layer, but as it turned out the former brought the latter down to its own level and, taking the form of stylised historical fiction written, moreover, without ulterior motives, it enveloped it itself. She replied unwillingly, "That is more and more terrible," but not in those exact words, perhaps, and then she asked tauntingly, "OK, you didn't guess she was his widow, but do you at least realise that she's Margarita?"

She called Bulgakova "a model widow", that is one who had done everything in her power to save and affirm the memory of her husband. She spoke of the devotion of this young, beautiful, spoilt woman to her semi-disgraced and then terminally ill husband. One day the conversation turned to the "Decembrists' wives of the twentieth century"— Nadezhda Yakovlevna Mandelstam's term, I think; then to the wives who had shared their husbands' fates during their lives and after their deaths, about Bulgakova and Bolshintsova-Stenich; then to the wives who denied and betrayed their husbands. The name of X's wife came up; nature had intended her for the wife of a holder of the title "Honoured Artist" and for the three years that X was Honoured, she was happy. Then they gave him a "People's Artist" and she dissolved into non-existence. Her place was taken by another, who was well suited to being the wife of a People's Artist. Then X was slandered, arrested, and stripped of his title, and he found himself alone. "There was no lady made just for that role," said Akhmatova grimly.

Pilnyak was born in the same year as Mayakovsky, and Bulgakov three years earlier, but in her conception Mayakovsky was an epoch older than them. She put great store by his poetry of the 1910s: "A young man of genius, who wrote *A Cloud in Trousers* and *The Backbone-Flute*." She remembered the young Mayakovsky with kindliness, almost with tenderness. She said that she was once walking down Nevsky Prospect with Punin and when they turned the corner into Sea Street they bumped into Mayakovsky, who was coming out into Nevsky. Mayakovsky was not surprised and said straightaway, "I was walking along and thinking I'd meet Akhmatova at any moment"—and that was as late as the 1920s. She said often that if it had happened that his poetry had been cut short before the revolution he would have been like no one else in all Russia, a vivid, tragic poet of genius. "But writing 'My militia cares for me' is just beyond all bounds. Can you imagine Tyutchev, for example, writing 'My police force cares for me'?" "However, I can explain something to you. He understood everything before anyone else. In any case, before all of us. That is why he wrote, 'The shops display provisions, wines and fruit', that is why he ended as he did."[27]

With her unexpected juxtaposition of Mayakovsky and Tyutchev she was pursuing several goals: she was measuring each figure's stature by making a comparison or, more usually, a contrast; she was seeking each figure's place in a historical perspective by transferring it into a different time context; she was conceiving of time as a unity, not as layers, or as separate epochs. She resorted to this same device when the conversation touched on Marshak, a then famous writer, two or three weeks after his death: "When an old writer dies there should be a collapse, a spiritual revolution, like the demise of Tolstoy—but what do we see in this case?" She said of Fyodor Sologub, one of the few older writers whom she respected, and with whom she maintained friendly relations until his last years, "Sologub never envied anyone, and generally speaking never demeaned himself by comparisons with anyone at all—except Pushkin. He said that Pushkin was overshadowing him, getting in his way." She described having dinners at the Sologubs' in a big, cold, gloomy dining-room with dusty laurel wreaths on the walls; these had been bestowed upon him at various times at poetry tournaments and benefit performances. Occasionally a lonely leaf would detach itself and glide slowly down to the floor. She was also friendly with Anastasiya Nikolaevna Chebotarevskaya, his wife and assistant, whom he loved dearly and who did away with herself in a fit of insanity: she disappeared in the autumn of 1921 and her body was found the next spring when the ice melted, in the river Neva under the windows of their flat.

In general conversations about nearly all the "older" people began: "We didn't like him, but ..." On 11 October 1964 she gave me a photograph of herself, by saying, "We didn't like Zinaida Gippius' poems, except for one splendid quatrain—I've written it out for you." On the back she had written:

> Do not part as long as you live,
> Not for the cause, nor either in play.
> Love will not suffer without revenge,
> Love will take her gifts away.

Then in brackets "Z. Gippius", then the date, then, by way of a signature, a lower-case letter *a* as large as a capital letter with a horizontal stroke through the middle.

❖   ❖   ❖

"We spend our years as a tale that is told. The days of our years are threescore years and ten; and if by reason of strength they be fourscore years ..." the Psalter attests unequivocally. Then the children remember the deceased for twenty or thirty years more until they die themselves, and that is the human span, a hundred years. After that it is "Remember, O Lord, all those who have no one to pray for them."

Being remembered "from generation to generation" is achieved by people who live holy lives and those whose memory is long-lived, but their deeds evoke great resistance on the part of Providence. The position in which poets are placed is rather special; as Pushkin writes:

> No—death is not my master. In this lyre my spirit
> Will long outlive my ashes and escape decay,
> And I shall be renowned,

on one indispensable condition:

> as long as just one poet
> Lives on beneath the moon's bright rays.

Poets are placed in a special position, not because they leave books behind them, things which remain in use thenceforth; and not because a poet from a later generation may stumble on such a book, or seek it out, and value it as he should; or even because he may use these poems by one of his forefathers. The poet does not entirely die, as Pushkin says, not only on account of some fragment of a random anonymous line which time has arbitrarily preserved, but also on account of poems which are now lost forever, but which were assimilated by some poet at some time in the past, and which by means of further acts of assimilation have been handed on at third, tenth, or hundredth hand to one of his descendants. In principle the poet remains "renowned" ("And I shall be renowned"), that is he has a reputation and is remembered, whenever any poet reads any poetry, poetry in general; and he is remembered inasmuch as he is contained in it, he composes it. In other words poetry is also a memory of the poet, but in order to become such it must necessarily be assimilated by one other poet, though it is a matter of indifference whether this occurs "in his own generation" or "in posterity". And it is assimilated "on the level" of reading and "in the process" of reading.

When a poet is read by someone who is not a poet, the poet remains "renowned", but this is renown of an entirely different kind: non-poets are merely receivers, consumers of poetic energy; the motive force of the poet's creativity extends to, and ends with them. In her notes in the margins of Pushkin's poems Akhmatova writes of "the remains of French rhyme": Pushkin turns the common rhyme *rivage* (bank)/ *sauvage* (wild) into the recurring image "the wild shore". And the difference between these two kinds of renown (in the eyes of the reader who is not a poet, as well as the reader who is) is like the difference between the French assonance, sweet to the ear as it is, and the independent image. Non-poets are grateful to the authors they read, they find them moving, they feel they possess them; but poets put them to work. It is work they need them for, not ornamentation: one of the columns can be taken as it is from a pile brought from the excavations, from those lying about in the ruins, or from those that a neighbour has to spare—this has always been done and is still done in the course of constructing a building; but the column must be load-bearing and not merely decorative. Non-poet readers embellish their speech with poetic mouldings: "Some are no more, and others are far off, as Saadi once remarked"—Pushkin provides an example of this kind of assimilation by appropriation. But "the wild shore" is a building block which is pure Pushkin, even though elements of other people's architecture have gone into it. The poet-reader does not assimilate in the conventional sense of the word. That is to say the assimilated poetry is doubly renewed: via poems which did not exist hitherto, and through the enrichment of the poems they reflect. One can compare poetry to building, but only for the purpose of illustration: the poetic "column", unlike the architectural one, is erected in the new building while still standing in the old. The creative assimilation of poetry, by virtue of the fact that it is at once preservation and transformation, is reminiscent of metamorphoses in ancient cultures—with the proviso that Philomela transformed into a nightingale continues to be Philomela. It follows that, if the one poet does not die so long as the other lives, both are alive in poetry at all times. This life is not eternal: dependent on human memory, it exists only "as long as". But memory is a likeness of immortality, an attempt to attain immortality "by one's own efforts", and since there is no better likeness in this world, it proposes that we consider it real immortality and hushes up the fact that it is, even so, only an imitation.

> The gods, I know, made people into objects
> But left their consciousness alert for ever.
> To give our wondrous sorrows life eternal
> You were made into something I remember.

Thus spoke the young Akhmatova. At some point, if not at the very outset, all her creative work became subject to one desire—the desire to turn the dead into the living. In her poetry the magic summoned up by poetry borders on necromancy: she wanted to speak with the living voice of the dead. Her efforts reached their greatest intensity in *Poem without a Hero*. "It is their voices I hear . . .", she writes of her friends who died in the siege of Leningrad, "when I read the poem aloud . . ." and one has the impression that she heard these voices not only in her memory but also in reality.

"Quoting" her poet-predecessors in her poems, Akhmatova consciously takes on the function of the future poet whom they foresaw—and who lives in order to keep them alive. Amongst the few books in her library, those she always kept to hand were the Bible, Dante (in an Italian anthology published at the beginning of the century which concluded with poems by the compiler: "That's why he compiled the anthology," she commented), a complete Shakespeare in one volume, and the collected Pushkin. Quotations from them, more or less coded, are so frequent and, thanks to their delicate transplantation into the tissue of Akhmatova's poetry, often so difficult to catch, that one should speak of a pervasive biblical, or Dantesque, or Shakespearean layer in her poetry. Nevertheless, I do not think we should take 'The Muse' for a mere stylisation after the classics:

> And now she comes. And throwing back her veil
> She fixes an attentive look on me.
> I asked if it was she who then dictated
> *Inferno*'s lines to Dante. "Yes," said she.

This attentive gaze of the Muse is just as concrete as all the "glances" and "looks" in her poems, such as that of Blok, for example:

> Clear the gaze my silent host
> Lucidly directs at me!

She liked to repeat what people who passed Dante in the street whispered to each other when they saw him: "That's the man who's been *there*." The words "She fixes an attentive look on me" take the description of the Muse's arrival out of the sphere of the imagination, just as Dante's contemporaries did not *imagine* that he had been *there*, but were sure that he *had* been.

In the year which saw her return from evacuation to a maimed Leningrad, the year she celebrated her fifty-fifth birthday, Akhmatova wrote a poem which should be classed as one of her "final" ones, i.e. one of those which could claim to be the crown of a poet's work—not a poem like Pushkin's 'I remember a wonderful moment', but like his 'If I walk through noisy streets'—what is known as poetry "about the last things".

> This sacred craft of ours
> Has existed for thousands of years ...
> It could brighten a world deprived of light.
> But not one poet has ever said
> That there is no wisdom, no old age,
> And possibly no death.

The last lines presuppose at least two different readings. "Not one poet has ever said" this, because wisdom exists, old age exists, and death exists, and denial of them, or, more precisely, victory over them, is the business not of poetry but of faith. However, one or two devices—the contrast between "wisdom" and "old age", the calculated unexpectedness of which, not to say its discourtesy, is intended to nonplus the reader; and the use of the hesitant affirmation "and possibly"—bring another sense to the fore: "not one poet has ever said" this, but a poet could have done so. Could at least have risked doing so. The last line is syntactically separate and is an artful question: if poetry does indeed

94

shine in the darkness, then perhaps there is no death either? It is possible to arrive at this only by calling the poet's craft sacred and the sacred a craft. "Sacred craft" does not distinguish between words inspired by God and those inspired by Apollo. In that case the hexastich may have Ecclesiastes in mind, and be an oblique polemic with his "... wisdom excelleth folly, as far as light excelleth darkness ... And how dieth the wise man? as the fool ... Remember now thy Creator in the days of thy youth, while the evil days come not nor the years draw nigh, when thou shalt say, 'I have no pleasure in them;'" (chapter 2, verses 13, 16; chapter 12, verse 1). But if Ecclesiastes concludes by saying "For God shall bring every work into judgment, with every secret thing, whether it be good, or whether it be evil", then why has "not one poet ever said", ever dared say, these words of hope before the day of judgment? This, it seems, is what the poem hints at. Akhmatova's favourite line in *Antony and Cleopatra* was "I'll give thee leave to play till doomsday," the queen's last words to her devoted maidservant.

She began reading Shakespeare (in the sense that a poet does so; literary scholars would say that she began *working* on Shakespeare) in her youth, and she read him to the end of her days, reading various things at various times, or paying attention at various times to different passages in one and the same play. *Macbeth* was one of the works she studied exhaustively and used repeatedly, and motifs from *Macbeth* find their way into her poems both directly, from the tragic circumstances of real life in Stalin's Russia which reproduced the bloodthirsty situations in the play, and via Pushkin, whose borrowings from Shakespeare she discovered as early as the 1920s. *Requiem* and, more generally, the requiem-like poems from the period of terror which engulfed very nearly forty years of her life, are pervaded by the words and spirit of *Macbeth*. The tragic October which scatters people's lives like yellow leaves in the quatrain addressed to Anrep, and the trees voting in the garden in the epigraph to the poem 'And now, in spite of that ...' echo the motion of Birnam wood, the "moving grove" which brings destruction to the murderer-king.

She said that some young Englishman had been complaining of the difficulty of reading Shakespeare, the archaic language and so on. "But when I started reading English I began with Shakespeare—that was my first English language." She remembered putting a dot in the dictionary next to any word she had to look up, and another when she had to do so again, etc. "Seven dots meant I had to learn the word." "I read the majority of English and American literature when I had insomnia in the

1930s," she mentioned one day. Two of the writers concerned were Joyce and Faulkner. She read English almost entirely without a dictionary, but spoke it with great difficulty, haltingly, and with faulty grammar and pronunciation. Sir Isaiah Berlin writes that when he heard her recite Byron he managed to catch only one or two words, and he draws a comparison between this and the contemporary reading of Greek and Roman classics, which similarly would be all but incomprehensible to those early scholars. Once, when she wanted to tell me something not destined for other ears, she suddenly broke into English, supposing that the person who might overhear us outside the door could speak French, and I made some kind of reply. Her next few phrases were also spoken with a struggle, although more fluently, and there the episode ended, with the conversation passing on to another topic. A little while later she said, "You and I were talking like two old negroes."

She found Pasternak's translations of Shakespeare better suited to the theatre, but preferred Lozinsky's, which conveyed "the text" more faithfully. She said of *Hamlet* that the ghost of his father should appear on stage only fleetingly, making the audience think they had imagined it. In this connection she observed that "In general everything on stage should be in a constant process of flux." A note in her diary reads "Found quotation in *Hamlet* (Frère Berthold)" means, if I am not mistaken, that Claudius' words:

> ... so, haply, slander,
> Whose whisper o'er the world's diameter,
> As level as the cannon to his blank
> Transports his poison'd shot, may miss our name,
> And hit the woundless air.
>
> (Act IV, scene 1)

are echoed in Pushkin's *Scenes from the Age of Chivalry* in the phrase "*La pièce finit par des réflexions—et par l'arrivée de Faust sur la queue du diable (découverte de l'imprimerie, autre artillerie).*" (The play concludes with discussion—and with the arrival of Faust on the devil's tail [the invention of printing, a kind of artillery].) Thus Faust's invention of printing is here equated with Brother Berthold Schwarz's invention of gunpowder, and is compared—via metaphor—to slander.

One of the lines from Shakespeare which she knew by heart and could quote when appropriate was the line from *Romeo and Juliet* spoken by Romeo: "For nothing can be ill, if she be well." Her response to this line, "There was no Romeo; there was, of course, Aeneas," is not a fragment of an unknown or unfinished poem but an aphorism, complete in itself, which can be universally applied to the whole area of love relationships, as she insisted with a barely discernible note of playfulness: there are no men as devoted to their beloveds as Romeo; there are innumerable men who desert them "for business reasons" like Aeneas. She used this aphorism in conversation and correspondence more than once, and tried to use it to preface her sonnet 'Fear not—I can still more truly', but it did not take as an epigraph.

She liked to quote two other passages from *Antony and Cleopatra*: Cleopatra's words about herself, "I am fire, and air; my other elements I give to baser life"; and about Antony: "... his delights were dolphin-like, they show'd back above the element they liv'd in". She extended this simultaneous attachment to two elements to herself as well: she recalled the phrase her sailor brother Viktor used to evaluate her prowess at swimming: "Anya swims like a bird"; and another time she said: "I swam like a pike." And one calm, warm, overcast day when we were sitting on the bench outside the house she said, "When I was young I liked architecture and poetry, but now I like music and earth."

Generally speaking, every trace of Shakespeare in her poetry is like a knot tied in a handkerchief to jog the memory, and signals the presence of "the theme of England". From 1945 onwards her "distant love" for the lover who had sailed away to London (Anrep) was connected, intertwined with, and, on the literary plane, enriched by, her feelings for another Russian who had also emigrated from Petersburg—but as a boy with his family, first to Latvia and then to England. In the autumn of that year the literary scholar and philosopher Isaiah Berlin came to Moscow for a few months as an adviser at the British Embassy. The two countries had been allies in the recently ended war, and his arrival coincided with the crest of a wave of mutual sympathy. His meeting with Akhmatova in the House on the Fontanka was, she was convinced, the cause of all the disasters which soon came down upon her head (including the deadly thunder and the long echo of the 1946 anathema, and even—in conjunction with Churchill's Fulton speech—the Cold War which broke out that same year), but it reconstructed and amplified her poetic universe and brought new creative powers into play. Her cycles 'Cinque' and 'The Wild Rose in Flower', the third dedication of

Poem without a Hero and the appearance in it of the Guest from the Future are directly connected—as are, less obviously, the turning-points of certain other poems in addition to individual lines—with these meetings, one of which lasted a whole autumn night and the other of which was a short farewell just before Christmas, and also with his departure, which "repeated" the departure of Anrep and the events which followed.

Akhmatova always spoke of him happily and respectfully (apart from the time when she uttered the phrase about "the man in the golden cage"); she thought that he was a very influential figure in the West, and argued, albeit with a chuckle, that "Taormina and the gown", i.e. the Italian literary prize and the honorary Oxford degree were "the work of his hands" and that it was he who was "now lobbying for a Nobel" for her, although he categorically denied this when he met her again in 1965 and in subsequent writings. She gave me his little book *The Hedgehog and the Fox* on Tolstoy as a historian; it begins with a line from the Greek poet Archilochus, "The fox knows many things—the hedgehog one big one," and puts various writers in these categories: Dante, Plato, Pascal, Dostoevsky and Proust are hedgehogs, and Shakespeare, Aristotle, Goethe, Pushkin and Joyce are foxes. She had underlined the following in her own hand: "Tolstoy was by nature a fox, but believed in being a hedgehog" and "the conflict between what he was and what he believed". It is not impossible that she heard in these words an echo of some of her own, which she never tired of repeating, and which censured Tolstoy for having double standards: his personal morality, and that which reflected the opinions of his circle, family and society. She had specifically spoken of this to Berlin during their many hours of conversation and he later quoted them: ". . . he knew the truth, yet he forced himself, shamefully, to conform to philistine convention."

In conversation she often called him "the lord" with ironic respect, less often "Sir": the queen had given him this title for his services to Britain. "Sir Isaiah is the best *causeur* in Europe," she once said. "Churchill likes to invite him to dinner." On another occasion, when I had been playing football with friends who were visiting Komarovo, and had forgotten the time, I rushed in all hot and bothered, and she muttered crossly, "You seem to be a sportsman by profession," saying "sportsman" in English, and a lightning association of ideas made me ask what Isaiah Berlin looked like. "He has a paralysed hand," she replied angrily, "and while his contemporaries were playing football," ("football" now with a French accent) "he was reading

98

books, which is how he came to be what he is." She made me a present of the flask he had given her as a farewell gift—a British Army brandy flask.

In Akhmatova's poetry the theme of England, or as they say in lit. crit. the English myth, is not solely encompassed by the traces of Shakespeare in her poems. Byron, Shelley, Keats (directly and via Pushkin), Joyce and Eliot are connected with the cycles 'Cinque' and 'The Wild Rose in Flower' and with *Poem without a Hero*, no less than Virgil and Horace, Dante, Baudelaire and Nerval. But the appearance of Isaiah Berlin on her doorstep, her conversation with him that night in her room and her continuing conversation with him "through the aether", as she wrote in 'Cinque', were not only meetings with a concrete person, but a real escape, a flight from the closed routes by which she commuted between Moscow and Leningrad out into the open sparkling intellectual space of Europe and the world, into the future, from which he had come as a guest. Similarly, the Shakespearean current which runs through her poetry did not link it specifically with Romanticism, or Individualism, or Modernism, but with "England" in general, and this current sucked her poetry into poetry in general, culture in general, into "it all"—if we bear in mind her line "So Shakespeare said it all ... "

She made use of her Shakespearean material to shift her personal situation so as to re-focus the reader's view and show her multi-dimensionality. In her daily life these shifts bore witness to her philosophy or her fundamental stance (which in her case were one and the same especially in her later years); and in her poetry they became one of her major and recurrent devices. The most frequent shift was achieved by putting sexes and ages together the wrong way round. In one letter she sent me when I was still a young man she wrote, "... we shall simply live like Lear and Cordelia in a cage ..." There is an inverted mirror image here: she is Lear in age and Cordelia in sex, and the addressee vice versa. Her observation that "we were talking like two old negroes" exemplifies the same arrangement of the constituents of "we". The observation probably draws on Pushkin's note in *Habent sua fata libelli* (an entry in Akhmatova's diary bears the same title): "... Othello, an old negro, who captivates Desdemona with tales of his travels and battles".

The shift in grammatical gender in her teasing reproach to the English girls—"More enlightened seafareresses!" suggests, if we recall the "red-haired beauties" in one of her early poems and "the red-haired arrogance of Englishwomen" in Mandelstam, a comparison with a similar shift in the lines of a poem she wrote in 1961 about a ghost: "A red-head, young and lithe was he—he was a woman." On the same principle she amended the phrase "an inhumanly beautiful secretary", a tired cliché of those times, and introduced "an inhumanly handsome secretary" into her tragedy *Enuma e lish*. This was also the mechanism behind some of her jokes: "Did Fido take his Fifi by the paw then?" when she leaned on my arm as she left the house. Or "Incidentally, Columbine is seventy-five," as she observed when she read a madrigal presented to her by a young poet.

The shifts in function have a more complex structure. The key to their decipherment may be found in the comparatively simple example of a piece of dialogue from Joyce's *Ulysses*, "You cannot leave your mother an orphan", which Akhmatova used as an epigraph to preface several of her pieces, including *Requiem* and, ultimately, the cycle 'Fragments of Pottery'. The result of this shift is that Akhmatova's lyric heroine performs a multiplicity of functions and roles simultaneously, a device which is particularly evident in the cycle 'Midnight Verses', perhaps to the maximum extent possible.

The appearance of Ophelia in 'Pre-Spring Elegy' ("Ophelia seemed to be singing"—when Akhmatova read the line aloud she pronounced the name as in English) is directly connected with the quatrain which opens the entire 'Midnight Verses' cycle. The first two lines of this quatrain:

> I roam through the waves and I hide in the wood,
> I glimmer on virgin enamel ...

can be related both descriptively and textually to the "blue enamel" scene in Annensky's *Thamyra Citharoedus*:

> Without a place to lay my head, I hastened
> Along the cliff slopes, through unpeopled woods,
> Through banks of sand and out into the waters.

The heroine of Annensky's lines is the nymph, who is both the mother and the beloved. The "beloved" Ophelia is also a nymph: "The fair

100

Ophelia! Nymph ..." says Hamlet, and the winter landscape which she inhabits in Akhmatova ("The snowstorm was stilled 'midst the pine trees") obviously refers the reader to "... be thou as chaste as ice, as pure as snow ..."

This device is refined still further in the poem 'Behind the Looking Glass'. The orientation of the 'Midnight Verses' cycle towards English sources is both insistent and ostentatious:

—the first poem refers to Ophelia;

—the third refers to what is behind the looking glass (Lewis Carroll's *Through the Looking-Glass*);

—the fourth mentions "the birches' sacred canopy" (in Akhmatova's notebooks there is an episode called 'The Birches': "... huge, mighty and ancient as druids ...");

—and finally the seventh "and last" poem begins:

> It was above us like a star at sea,
> Whose ray seeks out the ninth and fatal wave ...

and echoes the lines

> The Neva's bank was black as pitch without its lights ...
> And then you came to me, as though led by a star ...

from the cycle 'The Wild Rose in Flower' addressed to Isaiah Berlin.

Some explanation of the enigmatic poem 'Behind the Looking Glass' can be offered if it is read in this same "English" context.

> O quae beatam, Diva,
> tenes Cyprum et Memphin ...
> *Horace*

> The pretty thing is very young,
> But not of our late age engendered,
> We can't stay two—that third which entered
> Forever made between: among.

101

You draw her chairs across the floor,
I share my flowers with her unstinting ...
Unsure of what our acts are hinting,
We find each step alarms us more.
Like men released from prison cells,
We know some horror of each other,
We're in a ring of Hell's, or rather,
This may not even be ourselves.

The line from Horace taken as the epigraph, while retaining the sense of an address to Venus, also describes Britannia as "the ruler of the waves" (in 1878 after the partitioning of Turkey, Britain assumed power over Cyprus and Egypt), and it specifically calls to mind the greeting in *Othello*: "Ye men of Cyprus, let her have your knees.—Hail to thee, lady!" (Act II, scene 1.) In Akhmatova's poetry "armchairs"—the chairs mentioned in the poem being armchairs—always imply a traveller's resting place. ("Not in an armchair like a stately traveller" in the poem 'Just as she is'; and more clearly still the "fine ceremonial armchairs" in *Poem without a Hero*.) Thus the line "You draw her chairs across the floor" not only does not contradict the image of the "ruler of the waves", but in fact intensifies it. And the lines "The pretty thing is very young, But not of our late age engendered" are echoed by the "century-old enchantress" from part 2 of *Poem without a Hero*, which serves as the epigraph to 'Midnight Verses'. The enchantress is "the narrative poem of the nineteenth-century Romantics" (essentially Byron's and Shelley's), as Akhmatova herself said, revealing the secret identity of this "English lady", as the poem calls her.

Parallels thus run throughout the cycle: between the nymph from *Thamyra* and Ophelia (and also their creators, Sophocles and Shakespeare, who may be glimpsed behind them); Venus and Britannia, linked in the epigraph (Horace and Shakespeare—again); and birches "as the altar of Pergamon" (in the study mentioned above) and "as druids". Perhaps these parallels can be compared to the children's guessing game: "if there's a time, it's antiquity; if there's a place, it's England." I think Akhmatova was asserting precisely this, although in different words, when she said after her visit to Italy, "Florence is the same as the 1910s were here," that is, the attributes of a place's culture are equivalent to the attributes of a period's culture.

The same parallel between antiquity and England resurfaces in the poem 'No doubt you're someone's spouse ...', which appeared at the same time as 'Midnight Verses':

Rosa moretur

Horace I, last ode

No doubt you're someone's spouse and also someone's lover.
My casket's themes suffice without including you,
All day I've been entreated by the flute celestial
To make a gift of words as partners for her sounds.
And you were not the object which seduced my gaze.
So many avenues the night extends before me,
So many sad chrysanthemums September gives.
. . . .
So Shakespeare said it all, but I like Horace better:
He grasped life's sweetness in his own mysterious way ...
But when by chance you caught that rarest intonation
Everything that should not happen came to be.

(At this point it is relevant to mention something about the circumstances in which the poem was composed. Akhmatova originally intended to incorporate it with 'The Last Rose' and 'The Fifth Rose' into a cycle called 'Three Roses'. For each of the poems she chose an epigraph from poems dedicated to her: Brodsky's "You will write your sloping lines about us" for 'Last Rose', and my "Your words are bitter and divine" for 'No doubt you're someone's spouse ...' 'Fifth Rose' was written about a bouquet of roses given her by Bobyshev: four of them dropped straightaway, but the fifth, she said, "glowed and perfumed the air, and all but flew". Shortly before, Bobyshev had dedicated his poem 'The Magnificent Seven' to Akhmatova. It contained such lines as "O to hijack in your honour an electric train full of dictionary silver" but he thought it was insufficiently "elevated" and offered her as the epigraph a quatrain about a rose which he had initially addressed to someone else. A.A. allowed him to write the quatrain down in her notebook, but deviousness immediately won through—'Fifth Rose' remained devoid of an epigraph. "My" rose soon acquired the name *Rosa moretur*, 'The Dallying Rose', taken from Horace, and this phrase

103

was both the title and the epigraph. But the poem would not bear two epigraphs (nor would the sonnet in 'The Wild Rose in Flower') and mine migrated to the still unpublished 'Forbidden Rose', which contains the lines "The union they call parting And one of the rarefied torments", which are obviously connected with "that rarest intonation" in *Rosa moretur*. In preparing Akhmatova's posthumous volume, the editor printed the line from Horace as the epigraph, but not also as the title.)

The line "So Shakespeare said it all, but I like Horace better" from this poem does not merely serve to define "place and time" in 'Midnight Verses', nor does it constitute a formulation of the author's designs. It is an indication as well of Akhmatova's special method of incorporating into her poems texts by other authors inside other texts, also borrowed. Her poem 'Cleopatra' is written on the theme of Shakespeare's *Antony and Cleopatra* and wears its debt to the plot of this play on its sleeve, thereby obscuring another Cleopatra—from the thirty-seventh ode in Horace's Book I:

> ausa et iacentem visere regiam
> voltu sereno, fortis et asperas
> tractare serpentes, ut atrum
> corpore conbiberet venenum.

(She who dared to look upon the fallen kingdom with a serene expression and to press the cruel snakes to herself, so that she should drink their black poison into her body.) Specifically, that is in connection with the rose, Akhmatova's line may have in mind Hamlet's words about Gertrude, whose betrayal

> ... takes off the rose
> From the fair forehead of innocent love
> And sets a blister there, makes marriage vows
> As false as dicer's oaths ...

But even if Shakespeare said "it all" about this, as also about all other affairs of the heart, Akhmatova still likes Horace better, since "he grasped life's sweetness in his own mysterious way":

Remembering Anna Akhmatova

mitte sectari, rosa quo locorum
sera moretur.

(cease searching for the place where the late rose dallies).

Simplici myrto nihil adlabores
sedulus curo: neque te ministrum
dedecet myrtus neque me sub arta
vite bibentem.

(Do not toil to add anything to the simple myrtle, I beg you sincerely: the myrtle does not disgrace you, the servant, nor me, who drinks beneath the thick vines.) Myrtle—Aphrodite's plant and the symbol of married love—and myrtle—the adornment of the dead—blossoms and withers in Akhmatova's poem in the form of chrysanthemums: "So many sad chrysanthemums September gives." "Flowers everywhere—just like a funeral," she said on her birthday, when gifts of bouquets and baskets overflowed the room.

Her poems run between the mysterious Horatian charm of the fleeting moment and the irrevocable verdict with which Shakespeare forever chained this moment to words, veering first towards the one bank and then towards the other. Most often towards that which is most lasting and least prone to destruction, towards that which is best preserved and most like a memorial. One July day in 1963 she took a little bottle of perfumed oil from Bulgaria labelled "The Valley of a Thousand Roses" and poured out a few drops for a young woman, capturing this gesture with the line "I share my flowers with her unstinting." She loved flowers, roses most of all. When a bush suddenly bloomed tempestuously under her window as autumn came, she said affectionately and gratefully, "The rose has gone mad." So that "this is all confided to the roses' very depths"—the depths of live roses. But she would observe at the same time: "Flowers fare badly in Russian: 'bouquet', 'bud', 'flowerbed', 'petals'—almost entirely unusable. Try and write a poem after that!" The following emerged from her meeting with Isaiah Berlin in 1945:

The wild rose smelled so very sweet,
It even turned into a word,

105

And I was quite prepared to meet
The emissary of snow-white cliffs.

The fragility of these words evidently inspired apprehension: the fateful
minute threatened to become a fleeting one; and in order to say "it all"
in this connection, she underpinned the foundations the more firmly—
albeit at the cost of "life's sweetness":

And I was quite prepared to meet
The ninth and last wave of my fate.

❖   ❖   ❖

Akhmatova's "abroad" was of two kinds: the Europe of her youth, and
the place of residence of the Russian *émigrés*. The "abroad" of big
names, new movements and trends, well-being and good living was
alien to her and in general bored her. Politics, which always interested
her, she explained in terms of specific people and their relationships,
habits and styles, and this was incomparably more compelling than the
struggle for freedom or raw materials.

    She went abroad for the first time at the age of twenty-one. Her
impressions were collected half a century later in her essay 'Amedeo
Modigliani' and the writings associated with it, which (together with
Pages from a Diary) are the nucleus of Akhmatova's prose. Her memoirs
about Modigliani were completed and arranged as I watched—I was
then helping her since she had no secretary—and the passages which
were cut, though they seemed less substantial than those which were
included, were particularly intriguing, because one wanted to establish
why they had been omitted. Incidentally, one thing she inserted into the
text was that Modigliani "was interested in aviators . . . but when he met
one he was disillusioned: they turned out to be mere sportsmen (what
did he expect?)". Apropos of this she told me the following story. "The
six of us Russians went off to Montmartre to some house. It was not an
entirely respectable place, rather dark: people kept going outside to
look at something, others came in. I sat down straightaway at a table
with a long cloth, right down to the floor, and took off my shoes—they
were hurting my feet like mad—and looked round at everyone imperi-

106

ously. On my left sat Blériot, the aviator, who was then a real celebrity, and his mechanic. When we got up to go I found Blériot's visiting card in my shoe." There was a similar story about a colonel in the French GHQ who took her to Luna Park and showed her all the attractions. As they came to each he infallibly asked the attendant, "*Est-ce que ces attractions sont vraiment amusantes?*"

The following fragment was left out of her memoir of Modigliani: "He wrote very good long letters: *Je tiens votre tête entre mes mains et je vous couvre d'amour*. Of course, he had to draw the address on the envelope with great care because he did not know the Russian alphabet." I once told her about a famous actor who was asked to play Tristan by some Italian film people. I observed that his head was rather like Modigliani's. "But how tall was he?" "Average height." "But Modigliani was not very tall." (Or even—"rather short.") I said, "They couldn't find a Tristan in Italy." "They've all got too much nose."

This period was mentioned one day after a visit from Simon Markish, with whom she was on good terms, and whom she consulted from time to time as a classicist. In her youth she had known his father, the famous Jewish poet Perets Markish, who was shot in 1952, and she said that "he was fantastically handsome", so that when he found himself utterly penniless in Paris in 1913 he entered a beauty competition he had seen advertised and won first prize.

Emigrés, as she once proclaimed, consisted of those "who left their country for enemies to tear apart" and "deportees", but these were not two separate categories, for "those who left their country" overlapped with the "deportees". Over the years her feelings shifted towards compassion for the "deportees", who had been overtaken by the fate of Ovid and Dante and amongst whom she numbered herself during her evacuation from Leningrad: "But the happy word 'home' no one knows anymore, all look out of a stranger's window, some in Tashkent, some in New York . . ." she wrote in *Poem without a Hero*. At the same time emigration was a source of constant irritation and alarm. *Emigrés* took away with them "their last day" in Russia, and published information based on it which she had no chance of refuting. These publications shaped the opinions of both ordinary readers and literary scholars, and were referred to in theses and books. She said of one book—Robert Payne's, I think—"It says that I was in Paris in '37. However crazy that may seem to us, knowing what was being perpetrated then, there is an explanation for this nonsense. Someone told him about Tsvetaeva, who really was in Paris then. And that an American should suppose that there could be two Russian women on the face of the earth writing poetry at the same time, is too much to ask." She therefore took advantage of any foreigner she met to put one or two things right, or to clarify a point, and to restore the truth. That is why she worked for such a long time with Amanda Haight, who was writing a thesis about her work, and why she gave her the materials she needed, supplied her with dates, and put her on to sources. Haight's profound and vivid book *Anna Akhmatova A Poetic Pilgrimage*, published in Oxford in 1976, and her two-volume thesis are unique not only because even now, twenty and more years after Akhmatova's death, they are the only complete biography of her, but also because they convey the direction of her thinking and her "last will" and because phrases here and there convey her voice.

There was not a trace of Russian xenophobia in her, or even suspicion of foreigners. She was repelled by the spy mania which had invaded the hearts and minds of the public by the end of her life. (On the other hand she was not immune to the poison of tail-o-mania: perhaps she did not think straight enough but she convinced herself and those close to her that such-and-such a woman "had been attached to her", that So-and-So was "clearly an informer", that someone was cutting open the spines of her files, that someone had disturbed the hairs she had deliberately put into a manuscript to see if they would be moved and that there were microphones in the ceiling, etc. Perhaps she did not think straight enough—but she did not in any event think about it with any great ease: firstly, there was indeed a glut of all this spying, and secondly, such suppositions were torment for her. As for global "international espionage", one of her favourite arguments against its existence was Somerset Maugham's spying mission to Russia in 1919: "As you see, it's exceptionally difficult to find the right person: they found no one who could spy in a devastated country, more or less safely and without reprisals, no one, except a famous writer." And similarly on Rubens: "I translated his letters—it turns out that he was a double, if not a triple, agent. That's the sort of people spies are, not shopkeeper tourists clicking their cameras.")

She herself was sometimes taken for a foreigner ("a mamselle has come to stay at the big house in Slepnyovo" in 1911) and foreigners constantly figured in her circle during her youth in Petersburg, and even during her childhood in the Crimea. She said that when she was an adolescent she swam so well that she used to swim for long periods far from the beach "and I swam so well that my brother, who trained for naval college and could swim in full kit in icy water, said, 'I swim almost as well as Anya.'" A French wine-grower who had set up a cognac distillery in the Crimea watched her one day and complimented her on her prowess when she came out of the water. Then he introduced himself and said, "*Je suis de Cognac, c'est connu, n'est-ce pas?*" "And at that time it was a matter of complete indifference to me ..."

"The Italians think their language is difficult—not at all, they only say that to feel important"—only a person who had not only read the *Divina Commedia* but had also strolled through the streets of Florence, Venice and Genoa could have said this. It was an observation in the same category as "Italians have too much nose". Her trips in 1964 and 1965 were the direct opposite of the travels of her youth: then she went where she pleased, now she was taken; then she gazed on the world, now they gaped at her. They fêted her, and she thus proved that her chosen path had been the right one, she was victorious; but the palazzo Ursino was slightly reminiscent of a burial vault, the Oxford gown of a shroud, the ceremonial solemnity of a funeral. It was not a matter of old age and debility, which only put the finishing touches to the picture; the point was that everything which had once been full of life had now turned to stone and lost its soul. Punina, who accompanied her on her first trip, took her to a shop to buy a suitcase to bring back presents for people at home. The shop assistant set about throwing the best-quality items from the shelves down on to the counter. Punina pointed to one of the suitcases and asked if it was a strong one. Instead of answering, he threw it on to the floor, took a short run, and jumped on it with both feet ...—the suitcase caved in. He seized another, but they stopped him, bought the first one that came to hand, and hurried to get themselves out of the shop. Akhmatova told this amusing story, but without amusement in her voice: this was one of her few vivid impressions of Rome, but it was not like one of those "dreams which you remember all your life", as she wrote of her impressions of Italy in 1912.

It took several months to process her documents before each of her trips, and the ticket for the train to London was issued on the day she was to leave. She said, "What do they think—that I won't come back? That I stayed here when everyone was leaving, that I've lived my whole life in this country—and what a life!—in order to change everything now!" She growled, "Before, one had only to call the yardman, give him a few roubles, and he'd bring a foreign-travel passport from the police station at the end of the day."

It was a bit like "the visit of an elderly *grande dame*": on her travels she was not Anna Andreevna but, more formally, Anna Akhmatova.

She had to behave like "Akhmatova", and did so. On her return she showed us some photographs: the ceremony in Sicily, a palace, a large table, a lot of people; in the background there was a classical bust with a fairly animated—and ironic—expression on its face. She commented: "You see, he's saying, 'Euterpe I know. Sappho I know. But Akhmatova?—haven't heard of her.'" The linking of the names was more significant than the self-mockery.

She said that on the train she had woken up in the morning and gone to the window of the carriage: "And I saw a picture postcard of Vesuvius stuck on the window, as big as the window itself. Then I discovered that this was Vesuvius 'in person'." The Vesuvius on the postcard was symbolic of her "new", definitive, and final view: not the fresh inquisitive sharp-sightedness of the foreigner in one of her poems, who, like Adam, names things *in order that* they should have names, but the view from the depths of culture, prepared for any eventuality, in which things exist *because* they have names. And like the whole of this trip, the culture also parodied its fifty-year-old self: the postcard from "the age of the jacket" and "the days of satirical journalism" replaced the canvas from the "Silver Age" depicting that same Italy: "As in ancient faded paintings dim blue skies grow chill," she wrote in a poem at that time. "Banality has beaten me," she said, repeating the words Pasternak had spoken at their last meeting; he said, "Banality has beaten me—abroad, and here."

The same comparison could be made between the party of Russians in Montmartre in 1911 and the delegation with whom she went to receive her prize. "They were good people," she said. "But they didn't drink and so they were absolutely morose. Because if they had had the drinking bout they wanted, everyone would have found out what sort of people they were." But the foreigners who came to Russia to see her were not exclusively Sir Isaiahs either.

The postwoman at Komarovo delivered a telegram from Professor So-and-So in America asking if he might come to see her at a certain time. Akhmatova muttered, "Why don't they stay at home?"—but sank into the armchair by the table at the appointed time. The guest arrived with his own interpreter, and she asked me to stay. The professor was about forty, and had grandiose plans—he was intending to write a comparative history of several countries, including the United States and Russia and, I think, Turkey and Mexico, covering several decades either of the nineteenth or of the twentieth century. He was now collecting material on Russia and he particularly wanted Akhmatova to tell him what the so-called "Russian spirit" was. As he explained, with the bluntness of a wealthy businessman: "They told me back in America that you were very famous, I read some of your things, and I realised that you're the only person who knows what the Russian spirit is." Akhmatova politely but fairly obviously led the conversation round to a different topic. The professor was insistent. She did not oblige him, and every time she began talking about something else, more coldly and more abruptly each time. He continued to press her and even asked me in irritation whether I knew what the Russian spirit was. "We don't know what the Russian spirit is!" said Akhmatova angrily. "But Fyodor Dostoevsky knew!" the American retorted. He was still finishing his sentence when she said, "Dostoevsky knew many things, but not everything. He thought, for example, that if you murder someone you become a Raskolnikov. But now we know that you can murder fifty, a hundred, people—and then go to the theatre in the evening."

When Robert Frost came to Leningrad a meeting between him and Akhmatova was arranged at the home of Alekseev, the authority on English literature. Both their names figured in the list of candidates for the Nobel Prize and the idea of bringing them together seemed an especially felicitous one to the bureaucrats and admirers of literature. After the meeting Akhmatova's recollections were wry: "I can imagine what we looked like to an outsider, complete 'grampas or granmas'." (It was the children's writer Chukovsky who was approached in the street by a child and asked, "Are you a grampa or a granma?") Professor Reeve, who was present during their meeting, saw what had taken place in a different light and wrote about Akhmatova in exalted language: "How grand she was, and how sad she seemed." She read Frost 'The Last Rose': "for some moments we were silent, still". But Akhmatova said that Frost had asked her how profitable it would be to manufacture pencils using the Komarovo pine-trees. She fell in with the tone he had adopted and, just as "businesslike", replied: "The fine here for felling a tree in a recreational area is five hundred roubles." (She disliked Frost as a poet on account of his "farming streak". As an example she quoted a poem in which he said that a person who no longer had anything to sell was in such a bad way that things could get no worse. She was of the opinion that it was not fitting for a poet to reason in this manner.)

In the summer of 1964 Faina Ranevskaya was staying in Komarovo in the Theatrical Society's complex. Her acting ability, intellect and acuteness of mind; her individual powers of perception; her un-constrained behaviour, speech and gestures; and the charm of her tragi-comic exterior, combined to captivate instantly all who found themselves in her presence. It has become a common-place to admit that her artistic gifts were squandered by mediocre directors on roles which did not even remotely measure up to her potential, frittered away on "sketches" and "turns". But regret and lamentations on this score distracted the attention, even among those of her contemporaries who knew her, from something still more distressing: the century accus-tomed to counting people by the million threw away the outstanding giftedness of this unique nature on trivia, and the high calibre of her personality remained quite unappreciated. She and Akhmatova became acquainted in Tashkent and felt a bond of mutual sympathy. When Akhmatova wrote 'No doubt you're someone's spouse ...' she made the following comment on the line "But when by chance you caught that rarest intonation": "An actor is someone who has a command of the rarest intonation, that is—one unlike anyone else's, and this is what makes him an actor; Faina knows all about that, ask her." Ranevskaya's respect for Akhmatova was obvious, and not feigned. Tinging that respect with humour, she addressed her as "rabbi" and "madame". After Mandelstam's widow made her anti-Akhmatova attacks, Ran-evskaya always called her "that Khazina woman", using her maiden name. On reading in one of the series of memoirs which came out in the early 1980s that Akhmatova did not like Chekhov, she telephoned me out of the blue and indignantly declaimed in a sobbing bass, with her typical charming stammer, asking how it could have been that first "this Khazina woman" and now "this ..." had the effrontery to publish vile fabrications about things of which they knew nothing, things that could not have happened, because she revered two people. "A-hannochka Andreevna" and "A-hanton Pavlovich" more than anyone else on earth, she idolised both, both were geniuses, and how could one not like the other when he had written "the whole truth about us all: 'People, lions, eagles and partridges, horned deer, geese ...'" and so on, and she quoted Nina Zarechnaya's monologue from *The Seagull* almost in its entirety, with spellbinding pauses, and in a tragic tone, so that it did indeed come out "cold, cold, cold; empty, empty, empty; terrible, terrible, terrible".

That summer Ranevskaya brought Akhmatova a book by a chemist called Kachalov about glass. "Faina is always reading something differ-ent from the rest of the human race," said A.A. "I asked her to lend it to

Anna Akhmatova with her brother Andrey, *c.* 1895 (*top left*). A rare picture of Akhmatova on the bridge near Slepnyovo, 1910 (*top right*). The house in Slepnyovo (*below*).

With her husband
N. S. Gumilyov and
their son Lev.

Drawing of
Akhmatova by
D. Bouchène, 1914.

With N. N. Punin,
1920s.

A courtyard at the
house on the
Fontanka, 1920s.

Akhmatova, 1920s.

With Olga Glebova-
Sudeykina, 1924.

Ахматова и Ольга Судейкина, 1924.

справа: Ахматова, 1924

me." Perhaps both were specially interested in the author, the husband of the actress Timé", whose fame dated from the 1910s. A few days later we went out for a walk, and when we came back a note was sticking out of the door—I came across it subsequently, when I was re-reading some letters from that time. "Dear A.A.A., madame Rabbi, How annoying—did not catch you. Please, please, tell Tolya I beg him to chain the 'Glass' book to his bike and if I'm not in, drop it in my den." Like Akhmatova, she had touchingly crossed through with a horizontal line all the small *a*s. The "den" was a room on the ground floor of the Actors' Union building; another time she might have called it "an illusion of the emperor's lifestyle", one of those phrases of Ranevskaya's which Akhmatova used often.

At one point when they were in Tashkent she had told Ranevskaya her version of the duel in which Lermontov was killed. Evidently Lermontov had said unacceptable things about Martynov's sister. She was unmarried and her father was dead, and so, according to the code of duelling at that time (which Akhmatova knew inside out because of her work on Pushkin and his duel), her brother defended her honour. "Faina, tell me again what you made up that time," she said to Ranevskaya. "If you'll be Lermontov," she agreed. "Nowadays this quarrel would have looked rather different ... Martynov would have gone up to him and said, 'Did you say'"—here she spoke in a vulgar voice and for some reason a Ukrainian accent—"'that my sister was a whore?'" The word was pronounced with relish. "'Well'"—implying, yes, I did—replied Akhmatova on Lermontov's behalf. "'She is a whore.' 'Give me a cigarette,' Martynov would have said. 'Is that the sort of thing you say in public? That's the sort of thing you say to a young lady in private ...' Now we shan't get by without the trade union meeting to prognosticate." Akhmatova exulted like an impresario who has had it confirmed that the act he chose was a big success. Anyone playing opposite Ranevskaya was doomed to be overshadowed, but Akhmatova played her part with such expressive amateurishness that her unalloyed anti-artistry was a match for her partner's skill. Martynov was master of the situation; Lermontov did not inspire sympathy, but he was clumsy, and thus evoked pity.

This was in the new post-*Requiem* phase of Akhmatova's fame, with its attendant fuss. She remained indifferent to the interest which she aroused, to compliments, etc. She was, though, capable of unexpectedly attaching special significance to some brief item in a European news-paper, and would ask people she knew what they thought of it, and refer to it when talking with people she had just met. "The Swedes are demanding a Nobel for me," she said to Ranevskaya, and unearthed a newspaper cutting from her handbag. "Look, it's in a Stockholm paper." "Stockholm!" Ranevskaya exclaimed. "How provincial!" Akhmatova laughed: "I can show you the same thing in a Paris paper if that's more to your taste." "Paris, New York," Ranevskaya continued bleakly, "it's all, *all* provincial." "What isn't provincial then, Faina?"— the question was put in a mocking voice: she was ridiculing both Paris and her friend's seriousness. "Everything's provincial," Ranevskaya replied, not taking up the invitation to joke, "everything's provincial, except the Bible."

❖   ❖   ❖

Leningrad television had arranged a memorial programme in honour of Aleksandr Blok. They approached Akhmatova, but she categorically refused to be filmed, though she was willing to tape-record her story of the few times she had met Blok. The television people had evidently decided that they would break down her resistance when they arrived, and on the appointed day instead of a reporter and a tape-recorder two buses and several cars showed up in Lake Street in Komarovo. We saw them out of the window and Akhmatova said, "I won't give in," with despair in her voice. She had been feeling unwell and looking ill for several days. A minute later two women with bouquets of roses were coming in, and the electricians were dragging a cable towards the house. Akhmatova said sharply that the camera was out of the question, and that the tape-recorder was the most she would agree to, although because they had not kept to the agreement and had brought so many people even that was now in doubt. The coaxing began: "millions of viewers", "a unique opportunity", and specially "my mother hasn't slept at night, waiting for the moment when she'll see you". She turned to me for support, looking ill and harried. One of the women, a distant acquaintance of mine, looked at me encouragingly, obviously sure that I was on her side. I said that they should leave her alone. The women dragged me out into the corridor and whispered vehemently that she was old, and that history would not forgive us. In the end the two parties agreed, with mutual bad feeling, on the tape-recorder.

She did not have a television, but I made a point of watching the programme, and when we met the next day she asked what I thought of it. When it was time for her contribution the presenter announced that because he had such reverence for her he could not utter her name without standing up, and he rose from his chair. The cameraman had not anticipated this and supplied a fairly prolonged shot of his belly. Akhmatova's voice was heard, and only then did the camera pan slowly towards the face of the upright presenter. In the meantime he had begun to sit down, and disappeared out of shot. For some time Akhmatova's words were played against a picture of an empty wall. Even so my final impression was one of solemnity, mystery and incisiveness. Her absence only enhanced the effect, particularly in comparison to the contribution of the elderly actress Verigina, who recalled, with a noticeable lisp, how much "Al'ksan Al'ksan'ich" had loved her dress at the New Year's fancy-dress ball in nineteen —teen; but it was impossible to imagine, looking at the television screen, that she had ever looked any different, and the bright crêpe paper ball-dress in combination with the decrepit body and wrinkled face made one think what debauched macabre tastes Blok must have had. Akhmatova laughed.

"But all the same, no one believed you really didn't have an affair with him," I said ironically. She continued my line of thought: "All the more so since everyone knows that his mother actually encouraged him to have an affair with me." "No, it's no good, you've cheated the hopes of millions of viewers ..." "It's too late to put things right now—the programme's been broadcast." There were a few more remarks in the same vein and then I said, "But what would it have cost you to make people happy and agree that you'd had an affair?" She replied very gravely, "I have lived my own unique life, and my life lacks nothing; it has no need to borrow from other people." And a little while later: "Why should I invent another life for myself?"

Meanwhile "other lives", "legendary lives", were being created and written for her before her very eyes, not only as a result of memoirists' and critics' ill will or unscrupulousness, but in accordance with the laws of rumour which have their own logic, as they have always had. Akhmatova knew this, and took evasive action, making notes intended to forestall it, but she knew even as she did so that the logic of rumour would resist all her medicaments like a mutating virus and attack her biography from some unanticipated angle. Lydia Chukovskaya's diaries contain Akhmatova's account of the occasion when a friend of hers who had lost her reason said to her, "You know, Anya, Hitler is Feuchtwanger, and Ribbentrop is that gentleman who flirted with me at Tsarskoe—you remember." Ten years after Akhmatova's death an elderly woman approached me and said that she wanted to tell me something that no one else knew: "Akhmatova and I became friends in Tashkent and we were inseparable throughout the war. I want to tell you who saved her from ultimate disaster . . . When Ribbentrop came to Moscow and was driving down Nevsky Prospect with Molotov—they were old school friends (the Ribbentrop family are Petersburg Germans)—he turned to Molotov and asked, 'Vyacheslav, how is the idol of our youth, that poet we worshipped, how is Anna Akhmatova?' 'Well now, she blotted her copybook,' replied Molotov. 'The Central Committee had to pass a resolution about her.' 'Well, see what you can do for her, as a favour to me.' Molotov appealed to Zhdanov, and Akhmatova was saved." I probably could have discovered a few more interesting things if I had not asked thoughtlessly in what year this had happened. "In what year, in what year?" she mimicked. "The year he came, that year," and she looked at me with hostility and suspicion and walked away. This is redolent of Kharms's stories, and the kind of anecdotes about Pushkin and Lermontov, and I even fancied having fun writing a biography of Akhmatova in this vein. There is, for example, a photograph in the Central State Archive of Akhmatova and me sitting on a bench in front of the Cabin, captioned "Akhmatova and Brodsky at Komarovo". That's funny, but one autumn day in 1964 she and I were sitting on a bench—another one, in the copse near the road to Pike Lake—when a young postman rode by on his bicycle and then stopped suddenly and asked me, very embarrassed, "Are you Brodsky?" When he had pedalled away Akhmatova observed, "He very much wanted it to be Brodsky who was with Akhmatova—it's more symmetrical that way." And another time she said that abroad they had married her off to Erenburg: people had come across her name, and who else was still in Russia?—Erenburg; so they must be husband and wife.

This is the reason behind her (often unjustifiably) angry letters, writings, and monologues, and such phrases in her autobiography as "My only son Lev was born on 1 October 1912"—because she had heard of Blok's many children, Mandelstam's daughter and other non-existent relatives. Slamming shut the journal in which she had been reading some memoirs of Mandelstam, she said irritably, "Anna Grigorevna Dostoevskaya said that memoirists brought her much grief, and that every time she heard that new memoirs about her late husband had appeared, her heart sank: 'More exaggeration, another fabrication, more gossip.' And she was rarely mistaken. Most memoirs which are published are a misfortune. Various encounters are rolled into one, one person is passed off as another, dates are carefully mixed up. But they recall who ate what in monstrous detail: Mandelstam had fish, Pasternak had chicken ... If I were publishing memoirs I would take my epigraph from Gogol's *The Government Inspector*: 'Well, how goes it, brother Pushkin?—So-so, brother, just about par for the course ...' The scourge of memoirs is direct speech. In fact we remember very few pieces of dialogue exactly as they were spoken. But they provide a vivid impression of a person that cannot be provided in any other way." She wrote about the same thing in her diary: "Continuity is also a fake. The human memory is so organised that it works like a searchlight, illuminating certain objects but leaving impenetrable darkness all around them. Even someone with a magnificent memory can and should forget some things."

By "someone with a magnificent memory" she meant, of course, herself. She remembered details of events which had taken place sixty years ago as clearly as yesterday's. Her memory for poetry was particularly well developed, as was her visual memory. She remembered, for example, where to look in a book for the phrase she wanted, that is "fairly near the end, at the top of a right-hand page". She once read me a new poem and I immediately repeated it after her from memory. She set great store by this: "I see how it is: reading you a poem once is a bit excessive."

Just before her trip to Italy at the end of 1964 she went to see Erenburg on business. During a conversation with her hosts a lady of about fifty with a beautiful expressive face came into the room, bent down towards Akhmatova's armchair, and said vibrantly, "Anna Andreevna, how glad I am to see you!" Akhmatova said hello, but it was obvious that she did not recognise her. "You must have forgotten me, I'm Ariadna Efron," said the lady: as it happened, that day Erenburg was playing host to the official commission dealing with Tsvetaeva's manuscripts, and one of its members was the poet's daughter. When she had gone, Akhmatova said, "I remember her of course, but how much she's changed." "Yes, she has," Erenburg's wife responded, and she led the conversation on to something else so as to gloss over the embarrassment caused, she thought, by the elderly Akhmatova's forgetfulness. But A.A. made a point of recalling the details and even the date of their last meeting and repeated insistently that "Alya" had changed very much since then. She was annoyed by the polite tone in which they again agreed with her, and she then said, "It's like that episode Sukhotin records when Tolstoy was already well into old age. Tolstoy says to his son over lunch, 'Where are you off to, Lyova?' 'To see my wife.' 'Isn't she here?' 'No! She's staying in Petersburg.' 'And who is that?' 'That's your granddaughter Annochka, Ilya's daughter.' 'Oh. And what is she doing here?' 'I've been here for a week already,' she answered." When we had left the house and were out in the street Akhmatova said, "They're making me out to be an old woman who's lost her faculties— I'm surprised I still remember anything at all."

And if obvious things were convoluted during her lifetime, how much more incapable did she feel of convincing people a hundred years' hence that Hitler was not Feuchtwanger. She saw that the only way of proving that things had been one way and not another was to provide a unique and objective account of the evidence, to summon to the witness-stand at least one eyewitness of the way things had been. She begins her piece on Mandelstam with the words "... And Lozinsky's death seemed to break the thread of my memories. Now I dare not remember things which he can no longer substantiate ..." This was almost a forensic device: the semester she had spent at the Faculty of Law on the Higher Courses for Women in Kiev had acquainted her with the history of law which explained the tragedy of her times in the language of justice, showed that the "new legality" was lawlessness, and was reflected in her conversation in unexpected assertions such as "As a lawyer I can state that ..." Neither in Jewish nor in Roman courts was one witness deemed sufficient: "Two unchallengeable witnesses constitute adequate evidence." Lyric poets bear witness to what happened to them and to those who shared their experiences: to other people, nature, books. Nature and books give their evidence, and the reader, who is the judge, determines to what extent the poet is telling the truth. But relationships with lovers, friends and family are always personal, and poets do not want to rely on the unknown experience of a hypothetical reader. Poets consciously and instinctively seek a partner, another poet who can corroborate their words: Alcaeus for Sappho and Sappho for Alcaeus. Apart from confirming the truth, this saves both from a kind of narcissism, from looking at themselves alone. It is difficult to say whether Akhmatova had this attitude from the very beginning, or whether it arose spontaneously in her youth and then became a necessity, but Gumilyov, Shileyko, Nedobrovo, Anrep, Punin and certain other people to whom she addressed her poems were all poets. In 1914 Blok wrote her a madrigal which challenged her to a correspondence in verse (his 'Beauty's dreadful, they will tell you' and her reply 'Visiting the poet's home'), which he published at the time. At the end of her life Akhmatova wrote some lines which belong to 'Midnight Verses' and to *Prologue*:

Worst of all is that two marvellous books
Will soon emerge, revealing all to all.

In her last years she kept a file which she called "In a Hundred Mirrors". Here she collected the poems which had been dedicated to her during her life, regardless of how good they were or by whom they were written. There were several hundred, and most of them functioned only as "mirrors" reflecting her in one way or another; but a few are pages from "two marvellous books", one written by her, the other by them. This is not to say that it was immaterial to her whose voice she registered, and who registered her voice. The poems which make up the 'Midnight Verses' cycle and *Prologue*, like all her poems which describe the relationships between "you and me" or "me and him", are addressed to a specific person, and she had fairly harsh words for the lines which one poetess had "addressed to two people at once", implying that poetry is unforgiving of such immorality and avenges it with humbling verse. But like any truth, the truth about two specific people becomes the truth about any two; and in order for *that* to become the truth about two specific people, immune to doubts and re-trials, the corroboration of a second person is required—and thus we come full circle.

While the poetry spoke of a witness to, and participant in, a lyric drama, everything was comparatively clear: "But misery lay down upon my life like light eternal, and my voice has cracked," she wrote, addressing Gumilyov, and his poem offers corroboration: "She's silent, just shivering, she can't manage anything, I'm sorry for her—it's her fault." The voice of this witness was later incorporated into Akhmatova's poetry and given the same rights as the other voices quoted, but it has a quite different status: once having introduced the witness's voice, she can refer to their "lyric correspondence". She used this method of alluding to previous "evidence" in *Poem without a Hero*, where she did so to the greatest conceivable extent and to the greatest possible advantage.

Akhmatova began to write the *Poem* when she was fifty, and continued until the end of her life. In every sense this work lies at the centre of her *oeuvre*, her fate, and her biography. It was her only complete book after her first five, i.e. after 1921, though it is not comparable to them and indeed encompasses them and all else that Akhmatova wrote. When she remarked in a letter she wrote in 1960 "I have also lived with constant misfortune on the creative side, and the official misfortune has poss. even partly concealed or taken the edge off the more important thing," it is perfectly possible that she also had in mind the absence (after *Anno Domini*) of books with a single lyric plot, which had enabled *Evening*, *Rosary* and so on to became books, as distinct from collections of poems. She made skilful and definitive divisions within her collections of poems when they were being prepared for the press, or when they had already come out, or happened to come under the knife, and she was master of the art of bringing poems together into cycles. One day when a quirky combination of events had led to a quarrel between us, she said angrily, "As far as the poems are concerned, your cycle is finished, but put the most recently written poem first—that is my advice as a comrade with some experience." But the *Poem* wrote itself—for all the author's strict supervision of its composition—and she was more often obliged to exclude a passage which had merely the guise of the poem than to coax into it a passage which was directly relevant, but bore no formal resemblance.

Akhmatova collected people's opinions of *Poem without a Hero*, wrote about it herself, and was worried about its future fate, fearing that the text was too hermetic, or seemed so. She said that she had a request from one of her female admirers who gave poetry readings on stage: "I hear you've written a poem 'without something'. I'd like to read it." She gave me two different versions of it with a two-year interval in between, and questioned me closely about my impressions. When she was looking for the right place for new stanzas, inserting them, or, conversely, crossing them out, she would not want to know whether her choice seemed natural, persuasive, or unexpected. After one such conversation she suggested I should put everything I had said about the *Poem* into an article. I thought at the time that what was required was a weighty article, and that my observations were only fragmentary, but all the same eighteen months later I collated it all and wrote something, gradually coming up with fresh ideas, but I did not succeed in becoming authoritative. I gave a detailed description of the stanza form of the *Poem*: "Its first line, for example, attracts one's attention and excites one's curiosity; the second carries one away irrevocably; the third is frightening; the fourth leaves one at the edge of the abyss; the fifth bestows the gift of bliss; and the sixth exhausts all remaining potential and concludes the stanza. But the next stanza begins everything afresh, and this is the more striking because Akhmatova is the acknowledged master of the short poem." After her death it became clear that she had written down my observation on the very day of our conversation: "More on the *Poem*. X.Y.Z. said today that the most characteristic thing about the poem is the following: at the very beginning the first line of the stanza evokes, let us say, amazement; the second—the desire to argue; the third lures one away somewhere; the fourth is frightening; the fifth is deeply moving; and the sixth gives ultimate peace or sweet satisfaction—least of all does the reader expect that the next stanza has in store all that has just been enumerated. I have not heard such things said about the poem before. This reveals a new aspect of it."

The *Poem* was for Akhmatova, like *Eugene Onegin* for Pushkin, a compilation of all the themes, plots and principles of her poetry. It is like a catalogue in which one can more or less locate individual lyrics. Having started out as a survey of all Akhmatova had experienced, and therefore written, it immediately assumed the function of a credit and debit ledger—or the electronic memory of a modern computer—in which there were "entries", coded according to a set system, for *Requiem*, 'The Wind of War', 'The Wild Rose in Flower', 'Midnight Verses', and *Prologue*—in short, for all the major cycles and for some of the pieces which stand alone, as well as for all Akhmatova's Pushkiniana. At the same time Akhmatova quite consciously wrote the *Poem* in the spirit of a dispassionate chronicle of events, perhaps carrying out in her idiosyncratic way the mission of the historiographer poet undertaken by Pushkin and Karamzin.

Like a brain which has received sufficient information to generate more "by itself", the *Poem* produced new lines without the author's intervention, as it were:

> All the players required are ready,
> The Summer Garden wafts the heavy
> Scent of Act Five . . .
> A drunken sailor sings . . .

The sailor, the seaman—one of the central figures of the revolution—immediately took up his place in the picture of pre-revolutionary anticipation, either recalled from memory or descending from Tatlin's canvas, or from the latest posters, or coming out of Blok's *The Twelve*. But the positioning of the last line on the page seemed to indicate additional meaning and when the stanza next breathed out, it suddenly ironed out this wrinkle:

> The Summer Garden wafts the heavy
> Scent of Act Five. Tsushima's bloody
> Spectre awaits. A drunken sailor sings ...

One can guess more or less accurately that the appearance of this new line was prompted by Pasternak's 'The Seaman in Moscow':

> The wind was drunk, and slopped the tremors:
> Rowdy on wine.
> The seaman looked (and he was likewise
> Drunk like the wind) ...

towards which a line from the next poem also gravitates:

> January. Tsushima's year.

More important, however, than the inspiration for one or another of the insertions is the structure of the *Poem*, with its many layers, into which new lines, or sometimes a block of new lines, can be inserted if necessary or where they can be discovered. Everything is already contained within it, and though the version from the 1940s differs from the 1960s version in size, it does not differ in completeness: it is like a balloon which is ready to take off and is either half- or fully-inflated. One reader observed that the lines "Or is someone really standing there between the stove and the chest again?" echo the scene in Dostoevsky's *The Possessed* before Kirillov commits suicide, when he hides in the corner between the wall and the cupboard. Akhmatova told many people about this coincidence without specifying whether it was accidental or deliberate, and seemed to be pursuing the goal of revealing the method of the *Poem* to as many of the uninitiated as possible.

The fact that it conceals within itself more than it reveals is one of its main features, but not the only one. In the prose she published about the *Poem*, in the so-called "Second Letter", Akhmatova expresses sincere or feigned bewilderment: "L.Ya. Ginzburg thinks that its magic is a proscribed device—why?" (The last word is in English.) And in her poetry about the *Poem* she herself admits openly:

> I fear neither death nor shame,
> These are secrets, a cryptogram;
> This device is proscribed.

The presence of inconspicuous cryptograms in the *Poem* is given away by those which here and there lie on the surface. An example of this can be found in published material where a stanza was replaced with lines of dots and the footnote "The omission of stanzas is in imitation of Pushkin"; it is devoted to "the women in camps, in exile, in prison" during the terror:

> Clenching our bloodless lips,
> Hecubas driven insane
> And Cassandras from Chukhloma,
> We will thunder in soundless chorus
> (We, who wear the crown of disgrace):
> "We have passed through hell."

The final line of the stanza, *Po tu storonu ada my,* is a grisly word play on a line from Mikhail Kuzmin's jocular hymn to the Stray Dog cabaret, *Tsekh poetov—vse Adamy*: "Poets' Guild—Adams all". These women, particularly those so recently celebrated by poets as the Cassandras and Hecubas "of the year 1913", are separated from the crowds of men on the other side of the camp, most notably from those who celebrated them—the Guild members Mandelstam and Narbut.

123

In the *Poem* the voices of her poetic ancestors who are waiting to speak—that is, to come to life—through her voice, and the voices of the poet-witnesses combine with the anonymous voices, fusing with the murmur of time, or with the crowd, and coming through in dialogue which has been recorded:

> "By St Isaac's at six o'clock sharp, I propose ..."
> "We'll find our way in the dark, never fear—
> We're going on to the 'Dog' from here ..."
> "Where are you going from here?" "God knows!"

They do not fuse into a chorus, but disclose a new quality in which the author's voice manifests itself. During one of her conversations about Blok, Akhmatova remarked, "When I wrote that he was 'the tragic tenor of the age' everyone got very indignant and remonstrated with me: 'He's a great poet, not a prima donna opera singer.' But in Bach's *St Matthew Passion* the tenor sings the Evangelist." Performing in the same capacity in her tragic contralto, Akhmatova sings the parts of all the *Poem*'s guests, the recognisable and the unidentified, and of all those who lent the sound of their own voices to it.

The addressee of the verse is also qualitatively new. The poem opens with three dedications, behind which stand three figures who are as specific as they are generalised and symbolic: a poet from the turn of the century, who died on its threshold; a beautiful woman, also from the turn of the century, a friend of poets, improbable, real, and evanescent; and the guest from the future, to whom the author and her friends raised their glasses at the beginning of the century: as Akhmatova wrote then—"We drink to the health of the man who isn't among us yet." By playing with the grammatical tenses of verbs the *Poem* compels the past to return and the future to appear before its time, so that at the moment when the poetry sounds both are enclosed within it, but they nevertheless attempt, like magnets, to pull the moment into their own domain. The whole *Poem* and every word in it is addressed to time itself and to its swift flight.

At various times Akhmatova showed or gave various people her prose writings about the *Poem*, which she cast in the form of letters: 'Letter to X.Y.', 'A Second Letter'. Their literary style is very close to that of the prose piece entitled 'Instead of a Foreword', which at a certain point became a permanent part of the *Poem*'s text. She gave me a piece called "What to Put into the Second Letter".

1) About Belkinism.[28]
2) About the *Poem*'s excursions into ballet, the cinema, etc. *Meyerkhold*. (Demonic profile)
3) About the shades wh. readers seem to see.
4) "Not with our kind of luck," as they said in Moscow in late December 1916 when they were talking about the rumoured death of Rasputin.
5) ... and I can already hear a voice warning me not to disappear into it, as Pasternak disappeared into his *Zhivago*, which was his downfall, but I reply, "No—I am threatened by something entirely different. I have just read my own poems. (A fair selection.) I thought they seemed incredibly austere (none of the gentleness of the early poems!), naked, destitute, though they also contain no complaints, no self-pity, none of that insufferable stuff. But who needs them? Hand on heart, I would not have read them if they had been written by someone else. They *offer nothing* to the reader. They are like the poems of a man who has spent 20 years in prison. You respect him for what has happened to him, but there is nothing to learn from them, they offer no consolation, they are not so perfect that one can admire them, and it is impossible, I think, to take them as a guide and follow them. The voice is severe and black as coal, and there is neither a gleam of light, nor a ray, nor a drop ... This is the absolute end. P'haps if they are put together with the last book (1961) this will be less obvious or they will create a different impression. I see no grandeur in them at all. They are generally so bare, so direct—so monotonous, even though the theme of unhappy love has gone. 'Faded Pictures' is a little bit brighter, but I am afraid that it will be read as a stylisation—God forbid!—(and this is my earliest Tsarskoe poem, pre-Versailles, pre-Rastrelli). And the rest!—charcoal sketches on tar. God!—is this really poetry? Tragedy itself should not be like this. One feels that people who have come together to read it should murmur to each other, "Let's go and have a drink," or something like that.

> Such a creature the world's never seen:
> Sunk in poverty, lacking all rights.

Anatoly Nayman

I am friends with the winds, and they speak
Through my shutter that's off at the hinge.

How I envy you in that bewitching countryside of yours outside Moscow, and with what oppressive horror I recall Kolomenskoe, without which it is hardly possible to live, and the monastery, wh. was once defended by Prince Dolgoruky-Roshcha (as the plaque over the Gates says), and where one's first glance at the iconostasis tells one that this country would produce both Pushkin and Dostoevsky.

And God alone knows what I have written—a libretto for a ballet, or a scenario for a film. I forgot to ask Alyosha Batalov about it. I will write about this aspect of my work in greater detail elsewhere.

Footnote
The only passage where I mention it in my poems is:

> Or a terrible New Year portrait
> Which has suddenly stepped from its frame ('Cinque', IV)

i.e. I offer to leave it to someone as a memento.

Readers are struck by the fact that when new patches are sewn in the seams are invisible, but I cannot claim the credit for this.

❖   ❖   ❖

It is in *Requiem* that the "voices of others" in Akhmatova's poetry first merge into a chorus, or, to put it another way, that Akhmatova's voice first sings for the chorus. This is not a tragic chorus to which she refers in the *Poem*: "I agree to take on myself The role of a fatal chorus". The difference between the tragedy of *Poem without a Hero* and the tragedy of *Requiem* is the same as that between a murder on stage and a murder in the auditorium. In the former everyone has a role to play, including the role of the classical Greek chorus, and after the end of the fourth act comes the fifth; the latter is a mass for the soul of the departed, and a requiem for the dead and for the self, in which everyone is the audience and everyone is the dramatis personae.

Strictly speaking, *Requiem* is the ideal embodiment of *Soviet poetry* that all the theorists describe. The hero of this poetry is the people. Not a larger or smaller plurality of individuals called "the people" for political, nationalist, or other ideological reasons, but the whole people, every single one of whom participates in what is happening on one side or the other. This is poetry which speaks on behalf of the people, where the poet is of the people and for the people. Its language is almost the simple language of the newspaper; it is accessible to the people; its devices come head on: "I've worked them a funeral shroud from each word of pain that escaped them and I overheard," Akhmatova writes in *Requiem*. And this poetry is full of love for the people.

What differentiates it from, and thus contrasts it to, even ideal Soviet poetry is the fact that it is personal, just as profoundly personal as her early poem 'I clenched my hands beneath my dark veil'. It goes without saying that much else sets it apart from actual Soviet poetry: first its basis in Christian faith, which has the power to counter-balance the tragedy; then its anti-heroic tone; then its sincerity, which knows no bounds; and its calling taboo things by their real names. All these constitute the rejection of such things as the declaration of human self-sufficiency and licence; a grandiosely heroic tone; limitations; and taboos. But the personal attitude is not a rejection of anything; it is an affirmation, which is manifest in every word of *Requiem*. This is what makes *Requiem* poetry—not Soviet poetry, but simply poetry, for Soviet poetry on this theme would have to be state poetry: it could be personal only if it dealt with individuals, their loves, their moods and their selves in accordance with the officially sanctioned formula of "joys and sorrows". When they had Akhmatova on a string over the issue of her visa before she could go to Italy, she said "They think I won't come back," and then continued angrily, "I wish my government more citizens the like of me." The emphasis fell on "citizens" as strongly as on "me". Similarly, in the couplet

And should they once silence my mortified lips,
The one hundred millions for whom my voice speaks ...

the word "my", tucked into the chink between metrical stresses, weighs
just as heavily as the thunderous "one hundred millions". Those who
censured Akhmatova's poetry as the chamber poetry of the boudoir
gave rise, unwittingly, to a tragic piece of word play: it became the
poetry of that other chamber, the prison cell.

When the *Requiem* cycle came to the surface in the early 1960s after
lying on the bottom for a quarter of a century, the impression it made on
the reading public was quite different from the impression Akhmatova's
poetry usually made on its readers. After the documentary revelations of
the "thaw", people wanted literature too to engage in revelations, and
they approached *Requiem* from this point of view. Akhmatova was
aware of this, and thought it legitimate, but did not set these poems,
their artistic devices and principles, apart from the rest. When she was
abroad and talking to someone who went into immoderate raptures
over them as a poetic document of the age, she cooled him down by
saying, "Yes, there is one good passage—the beginning: 'luckless'—
'where my luckless people chanced to be'," reminding him that these
were ultimately poems and not only "blood and tears". In the eighth
poem, 'To Death', for example, the line "Burst in on me, a poisoned
shell" would seem to point again to Shakespeare's *poison'd shot*, the
poisoned shot of slander, i.e. denunciations, and not, say, to the
poison-gas attacks of World War I.

Then, in the 1960s, *Requiem* was listed along with the samizdat
works of camp literature, and not with the semi-official anti-Stalinist
writings. Akhmatova's hatred of Stalin was mixed with scorn. When the
conversation turned one day to a young poet who had earned the
reputation of being a "gadfly" and now spent all his time and energy
keeping up this reputation, she said, "His days are numbered. The
house will come tumbling down in a single moment ... All day Stalin
listened to the 'Hurrahs' and heard what a leading light he was, what a
generalissimo, how much everyone loved him, but in the evening some
little Frenchman on the radio would call him 'that old cockroach'—and
he'd have to start all over again."

One Day in the Life of Ivan Denisovich was given her to read when it
was still in typescript, and still bore the pseudonym Ryazansky. She told
everyone, "Whether one likes it or not is not the point: it should be read

by two hundred million people." A few days after she met Solzhenitsyn she said, "He's forty-four, and has a scar on his forehead near the bridge of his nose. He looks thirty-five. His face is honest and transparent. He's a tranquil person, and doesn't bustle about or behave like a business-man as they do in Moscow. He has enormous dignity and lucidity of spirit. He dislikes Moscow and he's oblivious to Ryazan; the only place he loves is Leningrad. You can imagine how I felt—you know how I feel about this Hero-City stuff—one day others will judge whether it was my fault or its. I read him 'the sisters of '37'.* He said, 'That's not you speaking—it's Russia speaking.' I replied, 'There is temptation in your words.' He objected: 'What do you mean! At your age ...' The Christian concept is not familiar to him. I said, 'In a little while you will be famous the whole world over. That's hard. I have woken up in the morning to find myself a celebrity more than once, and I know.' He replied, 'That won't hurt me. I'll survive.'"

Then, in the 1950s and early 1960s, the "torture, shootings and deaths" of the preceding decades were referred to officially as "the cult of personality" and unofficially as " '37", after the year when the mass repressions reached their peak. Depending on the tone of the conver-sation, Akhmatova might use the one expression or the other, but in serious discussions she always called this time "the terror". For her it began long before and finished long after 1937. She gave (and wrote down) an account which she entitled "Sparks from the Steam Engine" of an August evening in 1921 when she was travelling by train from Tsarskoe to Petrograd and felt a poem taking shape. She went out on to the platform of the carriage, where a group of Red Army soldiers was standing, took out a cigarette, and lit it—to a chorus of approving comments—from the fat sparks flying from the engine and settling on the railings of the platform between the carriages; then to the sound of the train's wheels she composed a poem about the execution of Gumilyov, the lament which later became so famous, 'You are not designed to live'. One day when someone close to her said that her son was a difficult person, she replied sharply, "Don't forget that from the age of nine he was not allowed to enrol at any library because his father had been executed as an enemy of the people." And, recalling the period after the 1946 Resolution, she said, "From that day forth I did not leave home a single time without a man getting up from the steps leading

* The lines "So that I should swab down the blood-stained floor/With the sisters of '37" are from the poem 'They departed and no one returned'.

down to the river to follow me." I was green enough to ask, "How did you know he was following you—did you turn round?" She replied, "When they start following you, you'll know."

In late 1963, at a time which was incomparably more benign than the Stalin years, the Brodsky case got under way. In November a Leningrad newspaper printed a satirical article called "A Paraliterary Drone", which was in the best traditions of slander and persecution. I was then living in Moscow, but someone brought it round the next day and that morning I met Brodsky, who had also come to Moscow not long before, in a café. We were tense, but not upset. In mid-December Akhmatova invited Shostakovich to Ordynka Street: he was the deputy to the Supreme Soviet for the area of Leningrad in which Brodsky lived. She asked me to come in case any information or clarification might be needed: Brodsky himself had already left Moscow. With one or two twitches and in a gabble that required one's full attention, Shostakovich spent most of the time attesting to his profound and sincere respect for Akhmatova; about the case he spoke dejectedly and despondently, asking me only one question: "He didn't have any meetings with foreigners, did he?" I replied that he had, but ... Before I could finish he said like a shot, "Then nothing can be done!"—and he did not touch on the subject again except to say as he was leaving that he would "find out" and do everything he could. In February Brodsky was shoved into a car in the street and taken to a cell at a police station. A few days later he was tried and sent to a lunatic asylum for examination. At the second trial in March he was sentenced to internal exile for parasitism and sent to a village in the region of Archangel. At this time Vigdorova, Chukovskaya and two or three score of others, including Akhmatova, made efforts to save him. It was either Akhmatova or Chukovskaya who said on hearing the news from Leningrad after his arrest, "All over again—'it is permissible to hand in a toothbrush', all over again—trying to find woollen socks and warm underwear, all over again—visits and parcels. Just like it always was."

At the end of April I suddenly fell ill and had to go into hospital. I came out at the end of May in a sorry state, and in June, the night before Akhmatova's birthday, I moved with her and Olshevskaya to Leningrad where, contrary to all the laws of probability, we found Brodsky, who had managed to get three days' leave. I was not even relatively well again until the autumn and when I was walking up to the Cabin one day in late August after a swim, Akhmatova said to Olshevskaya, "Ninochka, do you remember what a wet rag we brought with us from

Moscow in June—not Tolya at all." In the middle of October I set off for the village of Norinskaya in the Konosha district of the Archangel region, where Brodsky was serving his sentence of exile. I was taking food, cigarettes and warm clothing. Our mutual friends kept telephoning and asking me to take letters and various bits and pieces; one of them offered some leather mittens and I went round to pick them up, but the door was opened by the wife, who said that her husband had not realised that their son was using them. On hearing this, Akhmatova said, "What a scoundrel!"—I thought this was on account of his having sent me chasing right across town and having hidden behind his wife's skirts, and I started to defend him, saying that he might not have known that his son had the mittens. "In that case one goes to the shop," she interrupted crossly, "and buys another pair."

Konosha is a big railway station and a small town, and Norinskaya is about thirty kilometres away. I had to make my way there in one of the five or six lorries which passed through daily. Only one of them was reliable, and this was the post lorry which was officially forbidden to convey persons, but which picked travellers up anyway because there was no other means of transport. When I arrived in the town I saw, in the window of the first hut on the left-hand side, a packet of Kent cigarettes. Brodsky was renting the house from his landlords, the Pesterevs, for something like ten roubles a month. Pesterev and his wife lived next door in another wooden hut, but a newer and more solid one. They were kind, sympathetic people, and well disposed towards Brodsky, whom they called Josef-Aleksanych, all in one word. The house was lopsided, and had a long exterior staircase and a smoke stack which had lost half its bricks, with the result that when the stove was lit the iron got hot and glowed in the dark: the Pesterevs lived in constant fear of a fire. Round the village were fields, bare at this time of year, and the squat, damp, wild forest was close by. At the other end of the village there was a little river by which stood the club, alias the primary school, in which we saw a film starring Olshevskaya's son Batalov. One day, when we were walking through the village in the early twilight and the odd snowflake was settling on the ground, a drunken peasant ran out of his house in his felt boots and long johns with a quilted jacket thrown over his shoulders and a rifle in his hand, shouting, "There's a marten! There!" He threw up the rifle, fired into a rowan and a small animal thudded to the ground. We came up at the same moment and saw that it was not a marten but a cat. The hunter spat and went back into the hut. It was so quiet that the sound of an engine could be heard ten minutes before the car came into sight.

It was an isolated and depressing place, but no more depressing or isolated than many others, and only a little more isolated than, for example, Mikhaylovskoe, where Pushkin was exiled. In the evenings the BBC and the Voice of America broadcast various odds and ends, including some items on Brodsky. There was enough to eat, enough firewood, and enough time for poetry too. Letters came, books were sent. It was sometimes possible to telephone Leningrad from the post office in the neighbouring village of Danilovo. I spent one day on my own because Brodsky had been sent to Konosha for a one-day seminar on anti-atomic defence. He came back with a certificate and fantastic ideas about protons and neutrons, as well as about atomic and hydrogen bombs. I gave him a schoolboy's guide to the subject before we went to bed, but he woke me up several times, asking, "A.G., what's the valency of liquid oxygen?" or "Is it right that the H-bomb (he called the hydrogen bomb by its English name) doesn't freeze? Not ever?" In short, everything would have been normal, or even fine sometimes, had he not been in exile, had he not been shut in there, and for five years. When I was leaving he accompanied me as far as Konosha, pressed a rouble into the hand of the driver, a young lad who refused to take money, and said gutturally, and with insistence, "Come on lad, don't make my life a misery!"

The next time I went was in February, with Mikhail Meylakh, who was then still just Misha, aged nineteen. When we arrived I sent Akhmatova a telegram as agreed, to say that we had got there safely. She sent one in return: FROM LENINGRAD 23.02.65 TO DANILOVO FOR NAYMAN C/O BRODSKY STOP THANKS TELEGRAM STOP RECEIVED PROOFS FLIGHT TIME STOP LOVE ALL THREE STOP AKHMATOVA STOP. The frosts were ferocious and water froze in the porches. On Soviet Army Day the chairman of the village council came round with a lot of drink inside him but still vertical and seeing straight. He was wearing his hat with the earflaps up and had not even put on fingerless mittens. I opened a bottle of vodka and poured a glass for him and another for myself— Brodsky's status as an exile did not allow him drink, nor Meylakh's as a juvenile. The chairman asked cheerfully, "You've come to take him away then?" "Will you let him go?" "It's not me that's keeping him here, you can take him away right now if you like." "Well who is keeping him here?" "The powers that be." "Is he a parasite?" I nodded in Brodsky's direction. "I wouldn't say that," the chairman replied seriously. "A spy, perhaps?" "That's about it!" he said promptly, with a laugh. And as he was going, he announced, "In that case, three days' leave."

In May it was Brodsky's twenty-fifth birthday and Reyn and I went to see him. When we reached the house with our heavy rucksacks we found the door locked and at the same moment Pesterev came running towards us, shouting from a distance, "Joseph-Aleksanych has been arrested." He had been taken to Konosha for infringing regulations and sentenced there to seven days in prison. An hour later the lorry to Konosha arrived and I set off on my return journey. The Konosha prison was housed in a long single-storey building constructed out of thick logs. At the very minute I approached it, Brodsky stepped down from the verandah carrying two white buckets, one labelled "Water" and the other labelled "Bread". He explained that it was all up to the judge and that the judge was now in court, an identical building across the road. While I was waiting for the judge, a peasant came up to me and asked for a cigarette. He wondered what I wanted, and when I told him, he said that the judge wasn't busy at the moment, the court was in recess, it was a murder trial, he was the murderer, and they were going to give him eight years, as the prosecution was demanding. He'd attacked his wife with an axe, he'd been drunk, he was from Yartsevo, and they'd be sending him to the camp at Yartsevo, one stop down the line from Konosha. He asked politely for a couple more cigarettes for later and I gave him the packet; then the judge appeared and he disappeared through a door. The judge refused my request, so I went to see the secretary of the Regional Party Committee in the building nearest the court, which had a silver bust of Lenin standing in front of it. The secretary was my age and wore the badge of his old institute on his jacket; he was grave, and listened to me without animosity. He dialled a three-digit number on the telephone and said, "Let Brodsky out for the evening—he can finish his sentence later. It's a big day and his friend's here." He evidently heard out a number of objections, and then repeated, "Let him out for the evening." He put down the receiver and said to me, "You can relax in the station buffet," meaning, celebrate his birthday. I said someone else was waiting in the village, not to mention vodka and snacks—give us twenty-four hours. He thought for a moment and agreed to twenty-four hours. When I was going out of the door he said that he had lived in Leningrad when he was a student, and he asked how many stations the Leningrad underground had now. I ran through them. "Why doesn't he write patriotic poetry?" he asked, and let me go. We could not expect any cars to pass by at this hour, so

Brodsky and I, together with another exile he had got to know there, stepped out smartly in the direction of Norinskaya. Halfway to Norinskaya there was another village, where the brigade-leader who had got Brodsky arrested lived, and we had to go round it. Fortunately, a hundred yards short of it we were overtaken by a lorry which soon took us to the house.

On 11 September I received a telegram from Komarovo: REJOICING STOP ANNA SARRA EMMA STOP. Sarra Yosifovna Arens was keeping house for Akhmatova. Emma Grigorevna Gershteyn was staying with her at the time. The rejoicing was on account of the fact that Brodsky was finally at liberty.* This had been preceded by several false promises of imminent release. In Leningrad in October 1964 I met Vigdorova who had come from Moscow to collect signatures from people who wanted to vouch for Brodsky to the authorities. As she stepped out of the train on to the platform she cried, "Tolya, we've won!" The office of the Procurator of the USSR had told her that he would be released any day. The Writers' Union assured Akhmatova of the self-same thing just before her trip to London in the summer of 1965.

* This is what K. M. Azadovsky, who was then a young man, remembers about that day: "Someone telephoned to say that Osya Brodsky had been released from exile. I do not recall whether they asked me to give Akhmatova the good news or whether I decided that I should do so myself. On the day I received the telephone call Silvana de Vidovich was staying with me. She was an Italian, in Leningrad writing a finals dissertation on Sukhovo-Kobylin. I suggested she should come to Komarovo with me.

"I found Akhmatova's little house by asking people in the street. Of course, Anna Andreevna did not recognise me, so I told her my name and reminded her of my visit in the winter. I introduced her to Silvana. This time too Anna Andreevna had a lady I did not know staying with her—she turned out to be Emma Gershteyn. I explained the reason for our sudden intrusion. Anna Andreevna listened attentively to my news about Joseph but was, I would say, restrained, which somewhat surprised me. (I thought that someone else had already told her.) Nevertheless she said aloud, 'Well, well. That is a great joy. Now we shall rejoice.' And with these words she began laying the table and at the same time turned to Silvana and asked, 'Silvana, do you know what rejoicing is?' Poor Sisi, intimidated enough by meeting Akhmatova, muttered something unintelligible, but it was clear that she did not really understand the meaning of the word. At this point Akhmatova, glancing at the blushing Sisi, said magnanimously, 'Cheer up, Silvana, truth to tell we don't know what it is ourselves.' And then she explained in detail how the verb 'to rejoice' arose and came into use in Russia (on great feast days when they carry an icon out of the church the crowd falls to its knees before the face [*lik*] of the icon and rejoices [*likuet*]). Then we sat down at the table and began 'rejoicing' (I think we even drank vodka). I do not remember exactly what we talked about. Anna Andreevna asked what Silvana was studying and spoke most approvingly of Sukhovo-Kobylin, calling him an important writer. She said something about Osya, rather about practicalities: about his return, residence permit, getting settled, etc." [This explanation of the verb "to rejoice" does not coincide with the generally accepted one; Azadovsky quotes it as he remembers it.]

It goes without saying that when compared with "'37", "the Brodsky case" was "a battle between butterflies" as Akhmatova liked to say. It meant suffering, poetry and fame for him, and Akhmatova, while doing what could be done to help him, spoke approvingly of the biography they were "making for our Ginger". *Requiem* began to circulate clandestinely at approximately the same time, in the same circles and in the same number of copies as Vigdorova's transcript of Brodsky's trial. Public opinion unconsciously made a link between these two things, though not one which could be named openly: the poet defends the right to be a poet and not to have any other occupation so that he or she should be able when necessary to speak on everyone's behalf. The transcript of the poet's trial sounded like poetry on the most profound themes of public concern; and *Requiem*, poetry on the most profound themes of public concern, sounded like a transcript of the repressions, a kind of martyrology, a record of acts of self-sacrifice and martyrdom.

The war-time poems in the cycle 'The Wind of War', which earned Akhmatova official recognition and official transfer from the category of "poetesses of intimate emotions" to "poets of public resonance", were written in the same manner, albeit somewhat etiolated, as *Requiem*. In the interval between *Requiem* and 'The Wind of War' she wrote poems which belonged thematically to each. The Winter War of

1939–40 against Finland is superimposed on the arrests and the queues of anxious friends and relatives outside the prisons from the preceding years, and the poem 'New Year's greeting, New Year's grieving' is in the same tone as *Requiem*:

> And what was the fate he apportioned
> To those who escaped the torture?
> They went to the field to die.

The poem 'Did I not know insomnia' is about the same thing: considerations of censorship mean that Finland has to be hidden behind Normandy, but it gives itself away in the line about someone else's mirrors:

> I go into empty houses,
> Into someone's recent warmth.
> No sound, only snow-white shadows
> Swim in the mirrors' depth.

The "empty houses" and someone else's mirrors revealed their Finnish connotations when they came into focus in the late poem 'And some are on holiday still in the south' in the line about Finland's empty mirrors, which had to be replaced with another line for reasons of censorship. Instead of

> Where mirrors at evening's most languorous hour
> Keep something mysterious all to themselves,—

Akhmatova originally had

> A furtive Suomi's affectionate glances
> In mirrors where emptiness reigns,—

just as "an ancient jagged knife" replaced "a jagged Finnish knife". The ending of the poem 'Did I not know insomnia' is transparent:

> And what is out there in the mist?
> Is it Normandy, Denmark, or just
> A place where I've been before?
> And is this a mere second edition
> Of moments forever forgotten?

If Normandy is in fact Finland, then the snow-white shadows are not only the ski-mounted infantry in their white camouflage suits (the most common image of that war) but also the ghosts of moments forever forgotten:

—of Tsarskoe Selo, formerly Sarskoe Selo, from its Finnish name Saari-mojs;

—of the Gumilyovs' estate at Slepnyovo, which Akhmatova calls "the quiet Karelian land" (in her poem 'That August'): resettled Karelians made up a substantial part of the population of the Bezhetsk area;

—of the sanatorium at Hyvinkaa near Helsinki, where she "visited white-robed death" (as she writes in 'As a bride I'm given');

—and, finally, of the whole of turn-of-the-century Scandinavia, with its Symbolist culture, including the "then major influence Knut Hamsun" and "the other major influence Ibsen" as she wrote in her memoirs many years later.

These "familiar friends, my faithful Northlands" form a clear contrast to the hostile West, East and South on the map of Akhmatova's poetry:

> The West was pleased to utter bare-faced slander,
> The East luxuriated in betrayals.
> The South dispensed me air in tiny doses,
> And simpered from behind its jaunty verses.

In short, the North is, as she wrote, "this land, though not my native land" which is "ever present to the mind"; it gave her shelter at the end of her life beneath the Komarovo pine-trees, and laid her ashes to rest beneath them too.

A few more words about one of the substitutions which were forced upon her. One evening the editor of her book *The Flight of Time* telephoned to suggest that she should alter the line "A crucified city" in 'The Way of All Earth':

> The meeting will be
> A hundred times worse
> Than all that befell me
> In times now long past.
> A crucified city
> Now leads to my home,—

this was no way to speak of Leningrad. Brodsky and Samoylov were visiting her at the time, as well as myself. She told us, "All right, I'll change it." Comparatively quickly I thought up "Another misfortune Dispatches me home" and straightaway she said, "Agreed." Brodsky and Samoylov snorted and expressed their dissatisfaction, but made no specific counter-proposal, and she just laughed. The new version was nothing more than an exploitation of Akhmatova's own method. The whole episode, together with other thefts committed by the censor and the whole fate of her poetry in general is described in the lines from 'Drinking Song' in which she addresses her own poems:

> Mauled and maimed by gossip,
> Beaten with a flail.
> Branded with the stigma
> Of those condemned to jail.

Clumsily and naïvely she attached a quatrain to her essay 'A Word about Pushkin' with the transparent phrase "they might have heard the poet say ...", but the quatrain did not refer to Pushkin, and it was included with the sole aim of publishing lines which the censor had banned:

> You won't answer for your tender mercies,
> Wring from this what respite you may take.

Remembering Anna Akhmatova

Might is right. It is your children's curses
That will execrate you for my sake.

❖ ❖ ❖

At the beginning of 1962 I began to carry out the duties of literary secretary to Akhmatova. At first when the need arose, and then regularly. My duties were not onerous: answering routine letters, making telephone calls, and, less often, going on errands, typing out new poems or old ones she had just remembered, or editing her prose—mostly her memoirs—in a minor way, usually by rearranging certain passages. This required one visit every few days and took only a short while on each occasion. Whenever I suggested we should not postpone this and that but do them now, she would proclaim majestically, "Remember, one thing each day."

Every day brought a number of letters from readers, for the most part wildly complimentary. "I am sixty-seven, and I love your poems as much today as I have all my life ..." When I had read the letter thus far she suddenly asked, "How old?" "Sixty-seven." "Naughty girl," she said playfully. She dictated her, invariably brief, replies to some of the letters. Generally speaking, all Akhmatova's personal letters are short. Someone wrote to say that he had found consolation in her poems at difficult times in his life. She dictated immediately: "... But I have never been consoled by my poems. And so I live inconsolate. Akhmatova."

From time to time letters came from the labour camps: "You do not know me, but ..." and sometimes if the person was pouring out his heart to her the letter would be a long one. One day a man who had just been released from imprisonment in Siberia, wrote from Tomsk or perhaps Irkutsk: he had already told her about himself when he was still captive and now he was asking her for help. She immediately asked me to telegraph him some money.

The first letter I received from her was when I was in Moscow and she had moved from the Leningrad flat to Komarovo. It began with a quatrain: it looked as if she had written the poem and then decided to use the same sheet of paper for her letter.

I've come out from beneath death's dark arches
So that I can, perhaps, once again,

139

Late at night or when morning is starting,
Conjure magic beneath the green moon.

I came back to the Cabin today. In my absence autumn has well and truly got in and its breath has pervaded everything. But the poppies were waiting for me.

The room has become unsociable and I had to bring it to its senses with Bach's *Chaconne*, Stravinsky's *Symphony of Psalms*, a red-hot stove, flowers, and your telegram.

Now almost everything is right. The candles are lit, and a silent mysterious Marina is drawing me. When I go to town I shall expect a call from Moscow, from Nina at least.

A.

21 September 1963

Instead of "well and truly" she had first written "irrevocably".

Marina Basmanova was an artist and at that time Brodsky's fiancée. She was making some drawings of Akhmatova on a small pad the size of a man's palm, not only in silence, but biting her lips, as it were.

The poppies in the middle of the little lawn which had been sown very late in the year beneath her window had suddenly come into flower when autumn had already arrived.

Her housekeeper at the Cabin in Komarovo, Sarra Yosifovna Arens, was a little old lady of nearly seventy, who wore a pinafore from morning to night and always had a smile on her small wrinkled face, and sad eyes. Quiet, affectionate, obliging and selfless, she was afraid of Akhmatova, but could not restrain her ineradicable desire to report on expenses; she would find a moment to mutter something about the rising price of curd cheese, to which Akhmatova would immediately respond with fury: "Sarra, I've forbidden you to talk to me about curd cheese!" She was even more afraid of her husband than of Akhmatova and her love and respect for him were boundless. Lev Evgenevich Arens, the brother of Punin's first wife, was also short, with an eccentric's expressive animated face, lively laughing eyes, and a long white beard which blew in the wind when he rode his bicycle, which he did mainly when he was going swimming in Pike Lake. He was a botanist, and had a degree, I think; he knew the names and properties of a multitude of plants. He was a religious man, Russian Orthodox, and often took the electric train to go to church at Shuvalovo. He had, in his time, fallen victim to the repressions and had answered the interrogator's question "How is it that an enlightened man like you believes in God?" with "It is because I am an enlightened man that I believe." He wrote poetry exclusively for his own satisfaction, and when Akhmatova, Ranevskaya and a dozen or so other guests, mainly young people, were celebrating his birthday on the verandah, and a friend of his son's who had had a few drinks said, with emotion, "Uncle Lyova, please recite some of your poems," he roared, "Be quiet! Think whose presence you are in!" That birthday was a noisy occasion in more ways than one. The object of the celebrations was anxious to accompany Ranevskaya back to the Actors' Union building, but she put on a frightened face and whispered to the people sitting next to her, "A right couple we shall be when we appear on the doorstep! They'll all say I'm making people laugh on purpose." One of the guests, an actor with the Contemporary Theatre, stood up, glass in hand, to propose a toast to Ranevskaya, but had forgotten her patronymic and instead of "Faina Grigorievna" said, "Allow me, my magnificent Faina Abramovna ..." after which he could get no further, staggered, and in the twinkling of an eye was being carried to a mattress behind the sofa in the arms of his friends. Coming out of her room for breakfast the next morning, Akhmatova asked, "And where's the someone who collapsed?" His confusion of the patronymics reminded her that when the Moscow Art Theatre put on *Anna Karenina*, a production everyone praised to the skies, she had criticised and mocked it, and a fellow guest on that occasion, a woman who was a great admirer of the MAT, got upset and protested, "You are being unfair, my dear Anna Arkadevna ..." bestowing Karenina's patronymic on Akhmatova.

In the mornings she came to breakfast quite fresh and with a kind of abruptness, giving the impression that in the interval between yesterday's "Good night" and today's "Good morning" she had contrived to spend some time in a place where she had seen things worth talking about, and that she was pleased to meet her friends again after such a long absence.

Stretching along Akhmatova's side of the fence there was a rutted cart track overgrown with grass and from time to time a horse and cart would pass down it. The cart was driven by a "woman groom" who lived diagonally across the road from the Cabin, and with whom Akhmatova was on decidedly friendly terms even though it was only a nodding acquaintance. She would break off the conversation, translation work, or whatever else she was doing as soon as she heard the cart, and greet her acquaintance with a wave of the hand. The latter replied happily in kind and Akhmatova admitted—it was impossible to tell whether she was serious or joking—that she was afraid of what her neighbour might think, and tried just a little to ingratiate herself with her.

Another of her neighbours was Viktor Maksimovich Zhirmunsky, who was by this time an academician, but who had known Akhmatova in the 1910s when he was still a junior lecturer. Whenever he had a glass or two he recalled the time when he had obtained his junior lectureship and he seemed to set greater store by this than by his present seat in the Academy of Sciences, perhaps because that had been a wonderful time, when he was young. One day Akhmatova was visited by an English Slavist who was married to a woman who had emigrated from Russia shortly after the revolution. As he was also due to visit Zhirmunsky, whose *dacha* was three minutes' walk away, Akhmatova asked me to show him the way. The Zhirmunskys had already sat down to dinner and invited us both to join them. It was during the White Nights and rain had just cleared. The Englishman passed on greetings from his mother-in-law, the widow of a man who had taught Zhirmunsky when he was a student. Zhirmunsky thanked him: "He not only taught me, he was also my friend, though he was rather older than me. I did course work for him in ethics, aesthetics and mathematics." Then he asked suddenly, "How old is your wife? They left in 1920 and she was this tall, about ten years old. So how old must she be now?" Both Zhirmunsky's wife and I realised that she was considerably older than her husband, who was very embarrassed, and kept saying, "No, no, that can't be right." Zhirmunsky's wife led the conversation on to something else, but our host, who seemed not to have considered his guest's age or to have noticed his discomfiture, returned to the original topic and asked me, since I had had a technical education, to calculate how old she must be now if in 1920 . . . and so on. I knew that this was just the story to tell Akhmatova and when I got back I began straightaway. She listened avidly and even leaned slowly towards me as the story progressed. "It came out that she must be at least fifty-five," I summed up. She leaned back into the armchair and said, in the tone of a person who had been present at the birth, emphasising the first word, "*Sixty*-five, if not seventy . . . Over there they all took ten years off their age." She said the same thing in the same tone about Balzac: "Women deceived him. His fading lady of 'thirty' was, of course, forty or fifty. She kept insisting she was thirty, counting on the great writer's gullibility. But a woman of thirty—you can see for yourself—is no fading lady. She's a blossoming young woman. She hasn't changed in half a century. So one must assume that our fine Madame Hanska had made great efforts."

With great reluctance she took a walk once a day, although her doctors were insistent that she should take two or three. As a rule the route was as far as Lake Street and back again, along a path through the pine forest. A few yards before Lake Street there was a small low bench where she would sit down for a little while and, while continuing the conversation, would sweep the end of her stick across the ground to left and right, so that she soon cleared the debris of pine-needles, leaving a segment of clean damp earth. There was something mesmeric in the way that this thin brown stick skimmed the black earth like the swinging hand of a metronome and gradually cleared it as if it were a slate ready to be written upon, leaving a rim of yellow needles. I caught myself thinking that this had become oddly more important and interesting than the conversation, and that, given the shuffling sound and the tracing of the arc, it mattered not a jot what the conversation was about.

One day we set off in the opposite direction, towards the Zhirmunskys' in fact. It was a sunny August day but the heat had gone out of the sun and there was an autumnal chill. The soldiers who had been detailed to dig a trench to take some pipes down the street were having a break, and many of them had dropped to the ground where they stood and were now asleep. She said, "The reason that the Russian army is invincible is that they can sleep like that." A few paces further one of her stockings began to slip down. I pretended not to notice, and she asked me to walk on in front and then wait for her. She soon caught me up, but her stocking slipped down again and the scene was repeated. And again, two or three more times. The Zhirmunskys' cleaning lady answered the bell and said, "They're asleep." Everyone except us proved to be asleep and we turned back; Akhmatova was quite out of sorts. However, a sleepy Zhirmunsky appeared half an hour later with his apologies, and a week later when Akhmatova began talking about something she had remarked in passing, "That day—you remember—when my clothes kept falling off ..."

Of her neighbours on the same plot she was friendly with the Gitoviches and was on what may be called neighbourly terms with another writer and his wife. He had been injured in the war and it was a miracle that he had survived his dreadful wounds: Akhmatova repeated

143

what she had heard, apparently from his wife: that there was only 40 per cent of him left—the rest was artificial. When I came back to Komarovo after a month's absence she told me, amongst other pieces of news, that her neighbour had gone off with another woman, causing a great hullabaloo: "Just think, two women fighting over 40 per cent."

Not far from her little house was a *dacha* belonging to a literary critic who had done well for himself in the late 1940s by persecuting Akhmatova. When she passed his two-storey villa she used to say, "It's built on my bones." One day we were walking slowly along the road to the lake when the owner of the *dacha* appeared, striding towards us with his young daughter. He took off his beret and said hello respectfully to Akhmatova. She did not reply, possibly because he might have thought she had not seen him. Then he overtook us by cutting through the forest, got in front of us, and greeted her again in the same way. She bowed. After a few minutes I asked why she had done that and whether she had recognised him. She replied, "When you are seventy-five and your heart has as many holes in it as mine, you'll understand that it's easier to say hello than not to say hello." Her comment on two famous women writers from Leningrad was: "They write enormous novels and they're building themselves enormous *dachas*."

Another time we were sitting on the bench when a breeze was blowing from the Gulf of Finland, and the pines were swaying and making a lot of noise. She said, "They're talking incessantly." She was silent, then added, "X, who belongs to the Writers' Union, describes 'the brass chimes of the pine-trees'. Well, they talk, whisper, argue, moan—whatever you like. But where does he get the brass chimes from? Wherever did he hear that?" "It's a flight of fancy!" I began defending him ironically. "Or the costs of inspiration! Or an original perception! He is a poet after all." "Yes," she said in a flat voice. "A poet. A billiard game." It is not impossible that the barbs were aimed at a much more important figure than some Soviet lyric poet from Leningrad, namely the peasant poet Nikolay Klyuev ("He's the one who taught Blok to write 'My Russia, my wife'," said Akhmatova) whose book of poems called *The Pealing of the Pine-trees* was reviewed by Gumilyov ... In general her relationship with trees combined the affection of an older sister and the respect of a younger one, and in the course of a conversation about pantheism she responded to something I had said with the opening lines of Gumilyov's poem from *The Pyre*: "I know the grandeur of a perfect life is granted to the trees and not to us", which she advanced as part of the argument without reciting them as verse, so that

In Punin's
apartment, 1920s.

With Osip
Mandelstam, 1930s.

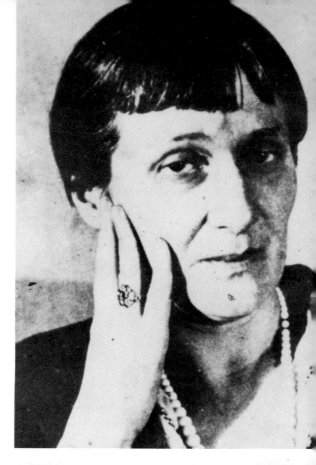

Akhmatova in 1936.

With Boris
Pasternak, 1946
(*photo L. Polyakov*).

With Anatoly
Nayman at the
house in Komarovo,
1964.

Akhmatova's desk
in the house in
Komarovo, 1960s
(inscription in her
own hand "Poem",
i.e. *Poem without
a Hero*).

Akhmatova in 1964.

Her funeral, 1966. Left to right: E. Reyn, Anatoly Nayman (*leaning forward*), E. Korobova (*with hat*), D. Bobyshev, Joseph Brodsky. (*Photos B. Shvartsman*).

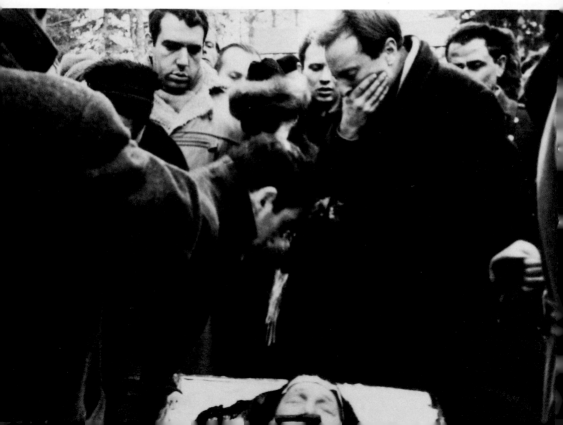

at first I did not hear them as such. And a moment later she intoned, now as verse, and for her own pleasure, the lines:

> Amongst the oaks are veritable Moses,
> And Marys 'midst the palms ...

If she saw a mosquito on her arm she did not swat it but blew it away. She was against the bloodthirsty old spider in the children's story who enticed the fly into his den, and was of the opinion that "Children don't need to know that." She called Gluck, the enormous *dacha* cat who used to jump off the branch of the pine-tree on to the roof of the house with a great crash, "a cat and a half", and one day she commented on Brodsky: "Don't you think Joseph is a typical cat and a half?" When Punina's husband was stung by a wasp and he came down like a ton of bricks on the little boy next door who was interested in insects, accusing him indignantly and at length of "making the wasps a nest in a dwelling house", she retorted imperturbably, "No one made them anything; they make their nests themselves, wherever they want."

The windows of her room looked out into a little pine-wood, full of "green air" in summer, which she showed visitors most willingly and with a certain pride in nature. A couple of times a week dry branches, pine-cones and pine-needle debris were burnt on a fire in front of the house. She liked these occasions very much: roaring flames, dying red embers. But if the person in charge lacked experience she would issue a warning: "My bonfire is one of the cunningest creatures in the world." And she made sure that they covered it carefully with earth before night came: once, she said, she had been woken during the night by flames blazing higher than the pine-trees: "But the previous evening it was pretending to be a meek little bonfire. You don't know it like I do."

She liked summer and winter for their constancy and clear definition, but disliked spring and autumn for their fickleness and "transience", although she always had a soft spot for hot dirty Moscow springs which unleashed themselves on the city all at one go.

She liked collecting mushrooms from around the house and along the road to the lake, and preparing them. An unexpected visitor arrived, Sarra Yosifovna announced him, and she said loudly and irritably, "Say that I'm peeling mushrooms." Five minutes later a young man knocked, put his head around the door, and introduced himself as an admirer of and expert on the works and personality of Voloshin. She replied sharply, "Can't you see I'm peeling mushrooms?" The reason for her anger was probably Voloshin rather than his unceremonious devotee. "I am the last inhabitant of Chersonesus," she often said, repeating the phrase insistently, so that *her* Crimea should not be confused with *Voloshin's*—the Koktebel area. She did not like Voloshin as a person, could not forgive him for his violent resentment of Gumilyov in the Cherubina de Gabriac episode, thought nothing of him as a poet, and was of the opinion that he was a hollow man who had had incredible strokes of luck in memoir literature: "First Tsvetaeva writes about him—she's in love with him. Then Erenburg, who's rehabilitating everyone, presents him in an entirely favourable light." She thought the whole "Koktebel institution" and all its devices and gestures quite disreputable.

The little card-table which stood next to the window in her room did duty both as a desk and as a dining-table. This dual role is described in 'Drinking Song': "Underneath the tablecloth the desk is hidden from view". The song goes on to speak of poems—that is, of what was created on it when it functioned as a desk. The room would suddenly be transformed from a sitting-room into a dining-room. When dinner-time came, a little cloth would be thrown over the table and the places set. Akhmatova might say, "*L'eau-de-vie*, perhaps? And a little something to go with it?" as if the idea had only just entered her head, and she would get a ten-rouble note out of her old purse. I or one of the young guests would cycle to the little shop near the station. *L'eau-de-vie* did not absolutely have to be vodka: cognac was also approved of, and "a little something to go with it" meant ham, smoked sprats or other tinned fish, such as "gudgeon in tomato"—these were the cheapest sort at the time and the shelves held stacks of them. A friend who once saw me buying them said understandingly when he found out who they were for, "I expect they remind her of her childhood in Odessa." Sarra Yosifovna's speciality was boiled lentils, which Akhmatova would start with a saying derived from Esau's words in Genesis: "Let me swallow some of that red broth," and she finished with the compliment, "I am ready to sell my birthright." She drank her vodka in the same way as wine: in little sips, and if someone spoke to her at that moment she would lower the glass from her lips, reply, and then finish drinking as slowly as before.

In her room, opposite the wooden bookshelf with its assorted books, from the newly published volume which she had been given (and which she usually hastened to give to someone else) to Parny in French, or Horace in Latin, there stood an old "Record", a valve wireless with two bands, medium and long wave. She said it looked as if it needed the obligatory picture of Comrade Stalin hanging on the wall above it: in the 1940s magazines published pictures of cosy rooms and smiling families with an abundance on the table, a fig-plant, a picture of Stalin in the icon corner, and beneath him—a "Record". We once got a broadcast from Radio Liberty on it in broad daylight: the speaker, completely unjammed, was reading something tooth-grinding from Abram Terts' *Lyubimov Town*. Terts (Sinyavsky) and Arzhak (Daniel) had already been arrested, and Akhmatova had shown me Sinyavsky's name in the list she had made the previous month of the hundred people to whom she intended to give her *The Flight of Time* when it came out. Sinyavsky's name had been placed next to one of the round numbers. When the programme finished, she said, "I don't like this prancing about on people's bones. But as far as theft is concerned, we were taught in our law course that theft in Russia is to be explained by a diminished sense of private property stemming from the Slavs' original communal systems. And what drunkenness is can be seen by looking out of the window—never mind law courses."

At the head of the truckle-bed was a low table with an electric record-player: either I had hired it locally or someone had brought it from town. She listened to music frequently and for long periods; she listened to various kinds of music, but sometimes she would be especially interested in a particular piece or pieces for a certain time. In the summer of 1963 it was the Beethoven sonatas, in the autumn—Vivaldi; in the summer of 1964—Shostakovich's Eighth Quartet; in the spring of 1965—Pergolesi's *Stabat Mater*, and in the summer and autumn—Monteverdi's *L'incoronazione di Poppea* and, specially often, Purcell's *Dido and Aeneas* in the British recording with Schwarz-kopf. She liked listening to Beethoven's *Bagatelles*, much of Chopin (played by Sofronitsky), *The Four Seasons* and other Vivaldi concertos, and also Bach, Mozart, Haydn, and Handel. As we know, Vivaldi's *Adagio* appears in 'Midnight Verses': "We shall meet again in music, in Vivaldi's bold *Adagio*." The little record was entitled "Vivaldi's *Adagio*" with no indication of the specific opus number. It was a piece for violin, hence:

> But the bow will not ask how you entered
> This, my midnight house.

147

One French translator translated these lines with something like: "But the dog will not bark when you enter", thinking that Bow was a dog's name.

One day she asked me to find some music on the radio for a change. I began moving the needle along the dial and observed aloud that it was all light music. Akhmatova replied, "Who needs that?" "Ah, here's some opera." "Operas aren't always bad." "When aren't they bad?" "When they're *Khovanshchina*. Or *Kitezh Town*." Suddenly we heard part of *The Queen of Spades*: "I am now ready to perform a feat heroic in your name ..." "Well, well. And what does that mean?" she said, as if she were hearing this for the first time. "Incidentally, *The Queen* is always good. *Onegin*'s a horror."

It would not be correct to say of Akhmatova that "she wrote poetry": in fact, she wrote poetry down. She would open a notebook and write down the lines which had already formed in her head. She often replaced a non-existent line, one which had not yet come, with dots and then carried on, filling in the omitted lines afterwards, sometimes several days later. By the way, the last two lines of the quatrain in the letter quoted above were written in over two lines of dots which she had crossed out. Some poems she seemed to find: they already existed, but as yet were unknown to anyone in the whole wide world, and she succeeded in discovering them—as discrete entities, at a stroke, without subsequent emendations. They were usually quatrains. For example:

> Your eyes so uncontrolled and wild,
> Your icy turns of speech,
> Your declaration of your love
> Before we'd chanced to meet.

When she was "composing poetry" the process never let up for a moment: suddenly, while someone was speaking to her, or she was reading a book, or writing a letter, or eating, she would half-sing, half-mutter, "hum" the almost unrecognisable vowels and consonants of the incipient lines, which had already found their rhythm. This humming was her outward expression of the constant vibration of poetry which the ordinary ear cannot detect. Or, it was the transformation of chaos into poetic cosmos. In Akhmatova's case, as the years went by, this process grew: her famous irregular metres gave way to classically regular ones, the three- and four-stanza poems gravitated towards the sonnet, and approximate assonances were edged out by exquisite rhymes. She said that Lozinsky had said of truncated rhymes such as cold/soul or speak/see: "Only you succeed in using such rhymes and making them sound good." And when she dictated to me the little song which she later bestowed on *Poem without a Hero*:

> For you I paid the price in full,
>   In ready cash,
> I walked exactly ten whole years
>   At pistol-point.
> And not to left nor yet to right
>   Did I once look,
> But ill fame rustled in my wake
>   At every step,—

she remarked, "I like rhyming voiced consonants with unvoiced: *zaplatila/khodila* and *glyadela/shelestela*."

She was insistent that commas and punctuation marks in general should be few in poetry, but she made frequent use of a punctuation mark she called "her own": the comma followed by a dash, and she quoted Lozinsky again as saying to her, "Generally speaking there is no such punctuation mark, but you can use it." When I once pointed out to her a particular place in a manuscript and said, "There should be a comma here," the answer was, "I felt myself that there already was something comma-ly there." When she became tired and was not watching what she was doing quite so closely she would write some words using the archaic letters which were dropped from the alphabet in 1917, or misspell the genitive case ending. These little slips gave her words still greater expressiveness and lent charm to her handwriting.

Poetry did not leave her even when she was ill, and she wrote many of her well-known poems in hospitals, and even when she was in an isolation ward delirious with typhus she composed:

> Here comes night, a Sleeping Beauty,
> Starry, frosty, all in white.
> What a poor head, what a poor head,
> Typhus drags me into night,—

and so on—a poem which, she said, a certain eminent professor cited to medical students as documentary evidence of the hallucinations which typhus cases suffer.

Sometimes she dreamt poems, but she was distrustful of these and subjected them to strict checks when she was her sober daytime self.

❖   ❖   ❖

I received the following letter six months later. This was an appendix to one of those conversations which she initiated more and more often at that time, and which I could neither join in nor put a stop to: conversations about her imminent death. The conversation mentioned in the letter was one which I broke off abruptly, but even after this the subject did not entirely go away. When she came back from Italy she gave me a miniature edition of the *Divina Commedia* published in Milan in 1941 and wrote in it *"Era a me morte, ed a lei fama rea ... Petrarca."* In Petrarch's *Canzoniere* he begs the Virgin Mary to intercede because the aid which his earthly lady might render him would be death for him and infamy for her: "... *ch'ogni altra sua voglia Era a me morte, ed a lei fama rea*" (CCCLXVI). The gift and inscription coincided with the appearance of the following quatrain:

> It's dawn—this is the Judgment Day,
> And meeting is more pain than parting.
> And deathly fame will come to take
> Me—from your hands and from the living.

in which "deathly fame" drew together the semantics and phonetics of Petrarch's line.

The letter was given to me by her, from her hands directly into mine.

Moscow
31 March 1964

Your distress today was so unexpected and profound that I am utterly dismayed. I have often talked to you about this, and began

150

doing so long ago, and you have always listened to my words with complete self-possession.

I beg you to believe me: today too they contained nothing but the wish for your good. I am now finally convinced that all conversations on this subject are destructive and I promise *never* to begin one again.

We shall simply live like Lear and Cordelia in a cage, translate Leopardi and Tagore, and trust each other.

Anna

After "the wish for your good" she had crossed out "in the best sense of this word".

The contract for the translation of Leopardi's lyrics—"Akhmatova Anna Andreevna and Nayman Anatoly Genrikhovich, acting co-operatively and called henceforth The Author"—which stated that we were to deliver the translation to the publishing house in May 1965 was only signed in the late summer of 1964, but we had got down to it the previous winter. The book, *Giacomo Leopardi, Lyrics* was brought out by the State Literary Publishing House a year after her death. Tagore, whose poems had to be translated at short notice for his multivolume collected works, unexpectedly cut into Leopardi that spring. In the autumn of 1965, shortly before Akhmatova's last illness, we were given a contract, like that for the translation of Leopardi, for a translation of poems by the Greek communist Rita Bume Papa, whom A.A., enjoying the assonance, immediately began to call Papa Grisha. The editor of the Progress Publishing House chivvied us politely to submit the manuscript quickly, explaining that the book's publication was "planned for International Women's Day, 8 March".

Akhmatova regarded translation as necessary but burdensome work and harnessed herself to this cart like a creature rather less glorious than Pushkin's "post-horse of enlightenment": like an obedient cart-horse which will work for any master. Whatever respect or sympathy the poets she was translating might inspire, they were torturers and they demanded that she compose Russian verse, invariably in large quantities, because translations constituted her main source of income. She wrote her own poems as and when she wanted: sometimes several close together, sometimes none at all for six months; but she translated every day from morning to lunchtime. She preferred, therefore, to take on the

151

work of poets to whom she was indifferent, and she was still more willing to take on the work of run-of-the-mill poets: she declined to participate in a volume of Baudelaire and refused to do Verlaine.

This is not to imply that she worked unwillingly: these were poems, after all, and she was Akhmatova. The quality of the work which she submitted to the editor was impeccable: she called herself, almost publicly, a professional translator and a pupil of Lozinsky. Amongst her translations she singled out the Serbian epics ("following Pushkin"), some works of classical Korean poetry, 'The Wanderer' by the Romanian Alexandru Toma:

> Each time a guest arrives outside your tent
> Meet him with kindness: give him bread and salt,
> And save him pain—pour water on his wounds.
> But do not ever dare to question him
> Or ask where he is bound for, whence he comes,—

and 'Autumn' by Perets Markish:

> The leaves here whisper not in unexplained alarm,
> But hunch themselves, lie still, and dream in autumn's gale,
> Though one awakes from sleep and trails off down the road,
> A golden mouse that seeks the shelter of its hole.

She could recite these last lines when appropriate: "But do not ever dare to question him ..." or say, "Markish has a wonderful image: a dried-up leaf is a golden mouse."

She translated Nerval, whom she called "a perfumery", Hugo, whom she simply disliked, Tagore, whom she came to appreciate when she had finished, and many others. She accused those critics who reproached translators for using cribs, of ignorance, or of settling personal scores, etc. "We all translate from cribs: even people who know the original language see a crib before them at one point." She was indignant when she read in Etkind's book that Diakonov's translation of *The Epic of Gilgamesh* was more exact than Gumilyov's: "Kolya was a *Kulturträger* pure and simple. He was translating from the French—how can one make comparisons?"

Her remarks about the material she was translating were nearly always ironic. "Blank verse?" she said, starting on one author. "Well, that's noble of him." She was a complete master of blank verse, but rhyme, although it disciplined the translator, was a struggle. As soon as we were deep into Leopardi she started to feel sorry for him: he was a great poet, he wrote magnificent poetry and so on, but he was seriously ill, he was short, the Aspasias and the Nerinas—the heroines of his poems—disliked him, and he died young. When she became tired, her iambic pentameters were capable of becoming hexameters without her noticing. Once they changed completely into trochees, and I said, "Now we've got Haiawatha." From that day on, whenever she was reading a new section she would ask humorously, "No Haiawatha yet?" Another time, when I had read my section—we were actually by then on Tagore—she stopped listening in the middle of the reading, and asked with exaggerated politeness, "Is this the translation, or is it still the crib?" In the same connection she asked one day, "Is this us writing or them writing for us?" And she explained, "That's probably one of Karamzin's stories. A scribe is reporting news to the governor; the latter, wrapped in a huge fur coat, sits and listens in all his dignity, and finally asks this question: 'Is this us writing, or them writing to us?'"

"Oh dear, 'con*trov*ersy' and 'contro*ver*sy'!" she bemoaned in jest. "There has always been two of everything in my life: two wars, two devastations, two famines, two resolutions—but I shan't survive two different stresses."

A few days after the last translations of Tagore were finished, she said for the first time, "He was hanging over me like a debt … But he's a great poet, I can see that now. It's not only a matter of individual lines which have real genius, or individual poems such as 'Let me go', but that mighty flow of poetry which takes its strength from Hinduism as from the Ganges, and is called Rabindranath Tagore." She had begun speaking in an ordinary voice but finished like an orator, making this statement not to me but to a third person while I stood by, as if counter-balancing her irritation with Tagore, and the caustic gibes she had made about him while working on the translation, with this majestic aphorism. Hitherto she was between the shafts, but now she was sitting in an armchair as she spoke. Hitherto she spoke from the heart; but now "as was mete and right so to do".

It is difficult to decide whether Akhmatova's translations should be published alongside her poems, since many are not her own unaided work. For example, the translations of Leopardi undertaken by one hand were invariably corrected by another, and the attribution to the one or the other name in the book is very arbitrary. I know the extent of the assistance given to Akhmatova, and the degree of participation in her labours, by Khardzhiev, the art historian and literary scholar, and Petrovykh. No one who was involved in this work of hers would vouch for Akhmatova's authorship of any specific translation. The best thing to do would be to respect the wish which she expressed more than once and to a number of people: after she was dead not to reprint the translations in her books. This was a tangled and cheerless matter, and a task forced upon her, and an eminent academic, to whom I told the remark about Lear and Cordelia living in a cage and translating Leopardi and Tagore, observed very accurately, "It sounds to the ear as if it's a leopard and a tiger in a cage, not Leopardi and Tagore."

At the end of April 1964 I went into hospital with a diagnosis of "micro-infarct". This was then a rarity amongst young people and the doctors descended upon me with apprehension and enthusiasm. I did not understand the seriousness of my condition, got out of bed, contrary to doctor's orders, and asked to be discharged on my own responsibility. Akhmatova visited me several times and regularly asked my other visitors to bring me short letters and little bunches of flowers.

Maundy Thursday

Dear Tolya,

This is all nonsense. The main thing is that you should get quite well and lucid.

Correct breathing is the way to tame the heart, and faith in one's friends is the way to control black thoughts. Partings, separations and absences are simply not real—I became convinced of this quite recently and had cause to confirm the truth of it virtually within the last few days. I freely share my new discovery with you.

Yesterday I spoke with "home". Irina sends her regards. Nika has arranged the letter about Leopardi for you. Send Tagore—we will type him out and give him to the young Turk. Boris says very important things about your play.

I am sure that you had the same thing in 1963, but you got through the whole illness without a doctor.

Don't get depressed!

A.

Remembering Anna Akhmatova

The issue of *Youth* with my poems in it came out today.

... and do not forget that hospital has its own charm, not unlike a monastery, as M. L. Lozinsky once told me in one of his letters.

Friday
During the night

Dear Tolya,

Today has been a vast empty day without even a telephone call or the slightest hint of an "Akhmatovka". For some reason I slept nearly all the time. I was pleased when Sasha Nilin said that you had recognised the biblical narcissi. Please thank the friend who telephoned me on your behalf.

How much cosier it would be if it was I who was in hospital and you who visited me, as you did when I was in the Harbour Hospital. Lida Ch. has found an epigraph for all my poems:

> But I stand on calamity's scaffold
> As if throned 'midst the courtiers' homage.

But I think there are some which it does not fit?!

Ranevskaya came round this evening. Aleksey has invited her to see his picture, *The Three Fat Men*.

Tomorrow I'm expecting Nika.

If Tagore is tiring you, leave him alone and, most important, have a break at the first sign of tiredness: we will go and see the birches and Pike Lake again.

Good night!

A.

Will write often.

In the first letter "home" is put in quotes. In the three-room flat at 34 Lenin Street there lived, apart from Akhmatova, Irina Nikolaevna Punina (Punin's daughter) and her husband, and her daughter Anna Kaminskaya and her husband. Both Punina and Kaminskaya were, of course, respectful to Akhmatova, but their respect had a touch of crossness—minor crossness, the reasons for which were never

155

explained. There were times of greater intimacy and affection but they gave way to cooler relations and arguments. A certain antagonism and a certain intimacy, as witnessed to by their calling Akhmatova "Akuma", were not subject to such vacillations and were in a separate category. Akhmatova once said of Punina in her best phase, "Ira is a pacified highlander." "Home" tried to get Akhmatova a place at the Writers' Union's House of Creativity in Komarovo for when she returned from Moscow in the winter; when she left the Cabin in the autumn they put her things together and sent her off to Moscow, often within days.

Her room, a long one with a window looking on to the street, was next to the kitchen. Over the bed hung Modigliani's drawing and near the wall opposite stood the trunk or *credenza*, which she pronounced distinctly as *cradenza*, containing papers. Perhaps, because of this pronunciation, the *credenza*, together with the little table with the revolving top under which letters and papers were kept; the little picture of the stag, which stood on the table and looked like a tapestry, but was in fact a blotting pad and also held letters; the oval mirror, the cracked scent-bottle, flower vases, and all the other antique pieces which looked like Akhmatova's own and as if they had nothing to do with her, have become merged in my mind with the description in *Poem without a Hero* of the bedroom belonging to Olga Sudeykina, the "heroine", which ends with the line: "These are half-stolen goods." "Half-stolen", *polukradeno*, seemed to echo *cradenza*. One day a young man fresh from an Oxford college who was working on "The Folk Sources of Akhmatova's Poetry" came to see her and recited with a slight accent her stylised lines "It's best if I shout rhymes out with a whoop and a call, and you wheeze out a tune on that accordian of yours" so as to explain what he understood by folk sources. In a little while the conversation touched on Modigliani; she asked me to show him the drawing and I went up to the bed and beckoned. He did not get up from his seat. Concluding that there was something he had not understood, I explained that this was it, the drawing, and, tugging the visitor by the sleeve, I began to urge him forward. He took one frightened glance at the portrait and immediately returned to his place. When he had gone, Akhmatova said, "Over there they're not accustomed to seeing old ladies' beds. He looked dreadful when you dragged him to the edge of the abyss." Then, "They can't believe that we live like this. Nor can they understand how we write at all in these conditions." And after another pause: "He might have thought up something wittier than rhymes and a squeeze-box on Akhmatova and folk culture."

Punina's husband, Roman Albertovich Rubinshteyn (whom Akhmatova also called behind his back, in Zoshchenko's phrase, "the drama artiste") was a literary recitalist who gave readings of Smelyakov's narrative poem 'Harsh Love' in libraries, clubs, and such unexpected places as, for example, the house-surgeons' rooms in hospitals—at eight in the morning, when the day and night doctors were changing over. He was "a devotee of beauty", such as, apparently, no longer walked the earth, and would begin impassioned conversations in the corridor about the fact that "one should not underestimate" or "one should not overestimate" the poetry of Such-and-Such among the young generation, and So-and-So amongst the older, and since Akhmatova remained stonily silent, he addressed himself to her visitors. On 5 March 1963 Akhmatova invited Brodsky and me to celebrate the tenth anniversary of Stalin's death. We had some decent cognac and at about one in the morning we got up to go. Roman Albertovich appeared unexpectedly by the coat-stand. He asked me whether I agreed that one should not underestimate Voznesensky and Surkov—I could not summon up the strength to reply. He addressed the same question to Brodsky, who caught Roman drunkenly in his field of vision and said very loudly, "It's all right Roman!" Akhmatova's comment on him was: "I value him highly. In his stead we might have a person who would admonish me with 'Mother, you've left the bathroom light on again.'"

She did not like staying at the House of Creativity: there was no getting away from people, who were not of her choosing moreover, there was "reveille" and "lights out" as if it were a barracks, the bath was shared, and breakfast/lunch/dinner was also communal, but she accepted it as inevitable. One of the guests started to complain to her that a friend of hers, a writer worthy of the greatest respect, had been given a little two-roomed cottage in Maleevka, while the untalented secretary of the Union had a luxurious five-roomed cottage. When the door had closed behind her, Akhmatova asked, "Why did she tell me that? I've written every one of my poems on a window-sill or the edge of something or other." When we were together at the House of Creativity in Komarovo, the neighbouring table in the dining-room was occupied by a group of middle-aged writers who talked about the same thing at every meal and with ever increasing passion: you put out crumbs for the doves, and the sparrows fly down and peck them up straightaway. With each passing

157

meal the doves became more and more open-hearted and defenceless and the sparrows more and more cunning and predatory, so that they soon seemed not to be doves and sparrows but entirely different creatures, some of whom the speakers wanted to do favours for, some of whom they wanted to tear to pieces. Akhmatova sat with her back to this table. One lunchtime they opened a bottle of champagne and one of the writers, a big round-faced man in exactly the same Finnish sweater as his big round-faced wife, approached Akhmatova with two champagne glasses, asking her to have some on the occasion of his birthday. Interrupting him, she announced very sharply that her doctor had forbidden her to drink. He was embarrassed and, stumbling over the phrases, reminded her of a reading they had given together at the NKVD in 1936 or 1937. "You're off your head," she said. "You simply don't know who I am."

On another occasion when she was staying there we were sitting on a bench near the entrance when a fine-looking old man, a well-known poet from Leningrad, appeared, carrying a small suitcase. He had been born in Tsarskoe Selo, a fact which he liked to broadcast, into the family of a priest, a fact which he tried to keep quiet. "He's the very image of his father," Akhmatova said in an undertone, "when he was on his way to officiate at a rite." An hour later it was revealed that the poet was in exile. A sleazy den had been discovered in Leningrad and he turned out to have been one of the clients. His wife declared in court that after this she could no longer share a bath with him, and he was exiled to the House of Creativity for a few months. Akhmatova exclaimed, "And do I want to share a bath with him?!"

She found Kaminskaya's husband, the artist Leonid Zykov, sympathetic, and she made efforts to help him when he got into difficulties with the Military Registration and Enlistment Office. One day she found herself in an ambiguous situation because of him. She was visited in Leningrad by Chagall's daughter, who told her, sentimentally and pompously, how much her parents loved her poetry. Then she asked what she could send her from Paris—what perfume, or books, or medicines ... "No, I don't need anything, thank you." "Please, do let me send you something, whatever you like, it will be no trouble, it will be a pleasure." And at this point Akhmatova remembered that they had recently been wondering where to get pastels for Leonid's work, and she asked her to send some. A month later someone brought a message from France: Chagall wanted to know which pastels, early ones, or perhaps Akhmatova had particular pictures of his in mind? The confusion was sorted out and at last a little box of pastels arrived in Moscow. The episode upset Akhmatova. She had never in her life asked anyone for anything and she thought of Chagall as a great artist and contemporary. She said dispiritedly, "So much for 'I shall describe you as Chagall did his Vitebsk'!" quoting her ode to Tsarskoe Selo. (Chagall's daughter was accompanied by a famous art connoisseur who was a distant acquaintance of Akhmatova's. At the end of the conversation he said to her, "Why don't you deposit anything with the archives? The Central State Literary Archive would be glad to have something. Even your autograph is worth having." After they had gone she said, "Nature has taken care to imprint all his vices on his face. But the man himself doesn't see.")

Leonid's brother Vladimir Zykov was a perspicacious, calm, handsome man, who was then embarking on a technical career. Akhmatova said, "He's a typical Russian junior engineer. People like him suddenly appeared in Russia after Alexander II's reforms—doctors, judges, engineers, people active in the work of the district councils. In a few years they transformed the face of the country and by the mid-sixties you could find them wherever you looked."

In the meantime, ripples continued to fan out from the Brodsky case, which had ended a month before with his being sent to Konosha, and they now reached his friends and defenders. The charge of parasitism on the same grounds as in his case was a real threat hanging over the heads of several young people who had no official status as writers, myself in particular, especially since I had obtained a statement from one of the publishing houses to the effect that Brodsky was working there as a translator. The statement figured in court and I was described as a swindler, *provocateur*, etc., and the editor-in-chief who had issued the statement was reprimanded as an accessory to swindling, provocation, etc. Moreover, the man who had instigated the whole case was club leader at the Institute where I had been a student and knew me personally, having published a denunciation of me five years earlier. The situation alarmed Akhmatova, especially after the Ionisyan saga.

In the winter of 1963–4 there were several vicious murders in Moscow, all identical in almost every detail. In the middle of the day a bell would ring and when asked, "Who is it?" the murderer would reply, "Moscow Gas". He would come in, take an axe from his briefcase, and murder those present, for the most part old women on their own or old women and little girls, and take some stupid thing, such as an old television, which he would then haul to the taxi rank. The murderer would then disappear. He was not furtive about this, with the result that many people subsequently remembered what he looked like and the police put together a "verbal portrait". The inhabitants of Moscow were pretty terrorised and pretty excited and fascinated by the course of events. They sought mystical explanations for his simultaneous appearances in various parts of the city: at 12 noon he was proclaiming "Moscow Gas" in Troparevo in the south-west, at 12.05 he was in Beskudnikovo in the north. Then a rumour went round that one morning Khrushchev had gone to see the Procurator General without warning and without his bodyguard, and had announced that he was giving him three days to catch the murderer. They caught him by the end of the second twenty-four hours, at night, when a taxi in which I was going from Ordynka Street to Peace Prospect, where I was renting a room, was stopped every hundred or two hundred yards by police patrols who checked my documents and the driver's under the streetlights. He was tried instantaneously, sentenced to be shot, and the sentence was carried out immediately.

A few days later my landlady told me that a divisional inspector had come while I was out, made a search of my room, and left a summons for me to appear at the police station. I was interviewed there by the superintendent, who blandly brushed aside my protest about the search, leafed through the books containing my translations which I had brought with me, and said, not without smugness, "So you're a writer. So what? He was an artist too." He burrowed in the desk drawer and threw down in front of me an Identikit picture of Ionisyan, small and difficult to make out, and explained, "That's the joker." It turned out that the criminal had been discovered virtually on his patch; in any case the story had given him the opportunity to check on all doubtful characters, in which category the concierge or some vigilant neighbour had, naturally, included me.

All this took place before Akhmatova's very eyes. I had been renting this randomly-found room for some months when A.A. told me that Nina Leontevna Shengeli had invited her to stay, and she asked me to help her move. We set off in the taxi and she asked the driver to stop—outside my block of flats. I was struck dumb for a few moments and then told her why, and it was her turn to be amazed. I lived on the first floor, Shengeli on the sixth.

When I came back from the police station I went up to see Akhmatova. She listened to my story, was silent for a little while, and then said, "*You* could have been Ionisyan instead of him. The probability is exactly the same. So thank your lucky stars. They could have given me a winning role too: the old woman who used to tip him off and then act as the fence. As you know, I'm also living here without a residence permit. Aren't there too many of us to one staircase?" I did not take what had happened seriously and soon went to live in my friends' flat. But she took it all too much to heart, I thought then: she tried to persuade me several times, without a hint of jocularity, that I had escaped from mortal danger—real, not imagined, danger—and she told the story to many of the people who visited her at the time. She therefore hurried the publishing house into giving me a letter of intent before the Leopardi contract was signed, just in case the security forces should set about me more decisively.

Nika—Nika Nikolaevna Glen—was an editor with the State Literary Publishing House, where she worked on Bulgarian literature, and as a result A.A., who always spoke of her affectionately and with deference, called her "the Queen of Bulgaria". She enjoyed Akhmatova's exceptional confidence, put at her disposal one of the two small rooms in the communal flat where she lived with her mother, came to Komarovo to look after her, and carried out secretarial duties for her for a while before 1963. She did what was demanded of her quietly, and spoke rarely and briefly. Her silence during conversation gave the impression that she was not really there, and she seemed to come into being only when she was needed, and always with considered and clearly-formulated views. So unassumingly did she combine highly professional editorial abilities, a gift for literature, and a precise knowledge of special subjects that to call this modesty would be an exaggeration. At that time a number of first-class editors, genuine specialists, scholars and intellectuals had congregated at the State Literary Publishing House. Akhmatova knew their worth and, generally speaking, felt well disposed towards the whole place. When she went to collect her fees, it was rather like stepping into a painting of a "minor processing of the cross in the province of Tver": everyone came out to meet her—those she knew and those she did not, accountants, proof-readers, and managers. She recounted what Pasternak had said at the time he was being persecuted over *Zhivago*. Whenever he appeared in any room in a publishing house in connection with his fees, the poor female editors would bury themselves in their papers and whisper, "We're very fond of you, Boris Leonidovich, we're very fond of you." The male editors, however, were different—at least the one whom Akhmatova called "the young Turk"

on account of the sum total of his character, appearance, and behaviour
...

That year I was either beginning or ending a love affair with the
Contemporary Theatre. I had written a play with three characters. The
theatre—that is the director, some of the principal actors, and the Head
of Literature—were interested in it, and it was convenient to put it on.
At some point the thing foundered, but I was hardly upset because I was
already writing another play. The plot of this involved lottery ticket
winnings which had remained on the ticket-seller's hands unsold and
were then claimed by a group of people who gave the appearance of
having rights to them, who had bought a certain number of tickets, and
of whom the ticket-seller was, by force of circumstances, himself a
member. The two main antagonists were to be played by one single
actor and, similarly, their wives by one actress. It was about this play
that Boris, the youngest of the "Ardov lads" had said "very important
words" to Akhmatova, and that Akhmatova, who had "peered" into the
plot, wrote "the crux of the matter is your play", in one of her
subsequent letters. She thought that the play contained improper allusions: the very concept of the doubles was taken by her as an attempt to
present in disguised form a situation which had some relevance to her
or, more exactly, to something she was then writing. I had inadvertently
given grounds for this by introducing into the action a character who
had an overly obvious resemblance to someone from her circle. There
followed: an unpleasant explanation, a disagreement, and then a reconciliation.

"Lida Ch."—Lydia Korneevna Chukovskaya—has exhaustively
detailed the many years of her relationship with Akhmatova with
insurpassable completeness in the three volumes of her *Notes about
Anna Akhmatova*: her name will for ever be associated with Akhmatova's. These were people born in different times, with different casts
of mind, different tastes and ideas, and now, when history makes
Chukovskaya almost the same age as Akhmatova, this should be
emphasised. Akhmatova appreciated to the full, I thought then, not
only her generally acknowledged virtues—honesty, fearlessness,
straightforwardness—but also her rarer ones: her naïvety and even
simple-mindedness, at which she was capable of chaffing behind her
back, though never to the detriment of her constant respect for this
loyalty to ideals. This was especially attractive when contrasted to the
artfully stultifying minds and compromising inventiveness which the
majority of people displayed. The epigraph which she suggested for all

Akhmatova's poetry comes from the opening quatrain of the cycle 'Fragments of Pottery':

> I'm deprived both of fire and of water,
> My only-born son is wrenched from me.
> But I stand on calamity's scaffold
> As if throned 'midst the courtiers' homage.

"But I think there are some which it does not fit?!"—a necessary, artful and subtle qualification. This is an epigraph to the image of Akhmatova in Chukovskaya's *Notes*, rather than to Akhmatova's poetry. The relationship between them began in the nightmare years of the 1930s which set the tone for its further development. But Akhmatova was both like this, and not like this, and, as she liked to say, different again. Diaries are unique documents, but conversations which are oriented, albeit unconsciously, towards the record, are bereft of the illogicality, disconnectedness, and often the meaninglessness which make them genuinely alive. Moreover, Akhmatova suspected that people were recording her words—it is true that I did not hear Chukovskaya's name amongst the supposed Eckermanns to her Goethe—and she sometimes spoke for the record, to be remembered, for posterity, turning from Anna Andreevna into Aereperennius Pyramidaltius. When she was with Chukovskaya, Akhmatova was entirely different from when she was with Ranevskaya, for example—not better or worse, not more exalted or more mundane, simply different.

As far as the reference in her letter to me to Aleksey Batalov and *The Three Fat Men* is concerned—shortly before this he had made his first film, *The Overcoat*, and he was getting ready to make his second, based on Olesha's political tale. He was fabulously popular as an actor—after making *The Rumyantsev Affair*—and a favourite of cinema-goers of both sexes and all ages. One day Olshevskaya was in a taxi talking to the director who was taking her son Boris into his company. When she got out of the taxi the driver called out after her, nastily and aggressively: "Obviously you can't get on the stage unless you know the right people. Only Batalov did." She said, "He's also my son."

Akhmatova made play of lamenting that visitors who knew that she was friends with the family invariably asked her, "Do you know what Batalov is doing at the moment?" He consoled her, "Whatever club I'm visiting, wherever I meet audiences, the first thing they always ask me is how is Smoktunovsky?" Smoktunovsky was also a famous film actor at the time, less so than Batalov, but his popularity was at its peak. Once, when everyone was sitting over lunch, a telegram arrived from an admirer he had met in Spain: USELESS WRITING. Those present gave full credit to this Spanish girl and her ability to put everything into two words. Akhmatova smiled and said, "That's beautiful ... Oh, what rubbishy telegrams I've sent in my time ..." Ranevskaya agreed to be in the film and went to Peterhof for some screen tests, but in the end Auntie Ganymede was played by Rina Zelyonaya, with whom he found it easier to communicate as a director.

❖   ❖   ❖

It is possible that I have not arranged the following letters in the exact order in which I received them, although there are fairly weighty arguments in favour of this sequence.

Dear Tolya,
    Anyuta has accidentally taken the volume of Mistral and my poems. Please ask Tanya to put them back in their place.
    Yesterday Karpushkin and Marusya came to see me. They are in a great hurry for Tagore, and we must send him in by 1 June.

Akhm.
    Please don't think of telephoning me. I know you are not allowed to get out of bed.

Dear Tolya,
    The crux of the matter is your play. I will explain this in more detail when we meet. Please do believe me. Everything else is as it was. Look after yourself. Write me a few words if you can—I still don't believe I have talked to you.
    Well, today certainly had some morning!—Ravings.

A.

164

Ordynka Street
2 May, 9 p.m.

Dear Tolya,

Natasha Gorbanevskaya brought me *Poland*. There are some poems in it which will remind you of one or two things. We sat Natasha's son on a big white horse and he screwed up his face. I asked, "Are you frightened?" He replied, "No, it's the horse that's frightened."

N.A. complains that you are very hard. Tolya, please don't behave like a maniac. [...] I cannot say that I enjoyed hearing this ... Humiliation is a very complex thing. It looks as if I have brought down evil by my own prophecies, as usual. Remember how often I said that Nature is kinder than human beings and rarely interferes in our affairs. She probably overheard and reminded us politely of her existence.

Please give me your word that you won't leave hospital in the face of the facts. This would only mean that you want to go in again very soon and on different grounds. I know all about hospitals. But that's enough about hospitals—we'll consider them a closed chapter already. The main thing, as Joseph says, is the grandeur of the conception.

Sasha will tell you what I have been doing. In fact I am drowsy and vacant. I have begun to find people a bit tiring. I don't make any telephone calls. The recital will be on 23 May.

Please write me a really kind letter.

Is it true that you've written some poetry?

Anna

3 May

Dear Tolya,

Thank you for your kind letter. Today was another grey, empty, and sad day. I heard the end of the Russian mass from London on Misha's new radio. A choir of angels. The very first sounds reduced me to tears. That happens to me so rarely. Koma came yesterday—he brought some flowers, and Nika brought the contents page of my Bulgarian book—she has arranged it very

165

elegantly. I also had a visitor from Leningrad—Zhenya Berkovskaya.

Please don't tire yourself with Tagore.

Write and tell me about yourself.

Nina says categorically that I cannot get to see you, but I recall Shengeli's flat on the sixth floor!—You remember.

Tomorrow I shall get my summer coat and start going out.

Good night!

A.

Today Ira is sowing the Moorish lawn which you brought, near the Cabin, the bonfire is drying out, the cuckoo is saying something like cu-ckoo, and I'm interested to hear what your poplar is doing.

5 May

Dear Tolya,

Galya Kornilova is coming today, and I will give her this note. My 'Shade' will be performed on the 7th at the Moscow Khaykins'. Perhaps we'll go together.

It gets more difficult to write as the time for meeting gets close. I am completely alone at home. There is a deafening silence round about and the local poplar (near the dining-room window) is also ready to come into leaf.

Yesterday the Slonims and Ilina were here, and today Muravyov is bringing my summer coat and the mail from Leningrad. However, you know all this already.

Goodbye,

A.

My dear Tolya,

I am obviously fated to write to you every day. The thing is that Ibragimov himself has just telephoned—he is giving you a contract, but doesn't know your address. You obviously need to tell him your Leningrad address, that is what I do.

Rest really quietly in bed.

You can see that everything is all right.

I have received Reeve's book, where he demands the Nobel Prize for me.

If you can, send a couple of words and *your address* to Ibragimov.

A.

The first two notes were the result of a mix-up and soon lost their importance once everything had been explained, and there is now no sense in stirring up the trifles which have remained in my memory. The painter Anyuta Shervinskaya was the elder daughter of the translator and classical scholar Sergey Shervinsky and had first met Akhmatova as a little girl: in the summer of 1936 she stayed at their home near Kolomna. The poetess and translator Tanya Makarova, the daughter of Margarita Aliger, was also one of the children who had "been born to friends" of Akhmatova's. Of the various stories about these children she liked to tell the following. One day when she was at Peredelkino she met the critic Zelinsky in the street and he invited her to step into his *dacha* for a minute to look at his son. "A young woman came to the gate with a twelve-month-old angel in her arms: blue eyes, golden curls and so on. Twenty years later in the street in Tashkent Zelinsky invited me to step into his house for a minute to see his son. It was too awkward to remind him that I had already met him. A young woman came to the gate with a twelve-month-old angel in her arms: blue eyes, and golden curls. Both the woman and the angel were new, but the whole thing was like a bad dream."

In 1963 a collection of poems by Gabriela Mistral came out in a translation by Savich, and for a time this little book was Akhmatova's main source of reading. They were born in the same year, and Mistral first came to prominence in 1914. Her favourite authors were Russians. It turned out that she had received the Nobel Prize and had died very recently. Her poetry is unexpectedly Acmeist and its tone, especially in the section called 'Pain' is surprisingly close to Akhmatova's. There are almost word-for-word parallels and coincidences:

The wild rose stood beside us
When we had no more words,—

167

Anatoly Nayman

(Akhmatova has: "The wild rose smelled so very sweet—it even turned into a word".) Or the poem 'Fern' with its refrain

> Pick it and give it away
> On Midsummer Night before dawn.

Akhmatova said, almost with delight, "That redskin's overtaken me." Mistral was a South American Indian. She asked to have 'The Fountain' read aloud to her several times, had her visitors read it, and demanded that they tell her immediately what they thought of it.

> I am exactly like a dried-up fountain.
> Though dead, it hears its own departed drone:
> the noise from yesterday, still vital, slumbers,
> and even now alarms its lips of stone.
>
> Fate, I believe, has not as yet made public
> its dreadful sentence, and although I grieve,
> I have not yet lost anything that matters:
> if I stretch out my arms I'll touch your cheek.
>
> I am a silent fountain; in the garden
> another's song, another's triumph flows;
> the fountain, maddened by its thirst, imagines
> that distant song it hears is in its soul;
>
> that it can toss the splashing streams of droplets
> into the blue—but it is long since choked;
> it thinks its breast drinks living water's kisses—
> but that is water which is poured by God.

In Akhmatova's poetry "living water" is an indication and a characteristic of Tsarskoe Selo and of that part of her life and Russian history, and also of the person through whom, she felt, Tsarskoe Selo expressed itself most completely and exaltedly. It is an image which, once Pushkin had started the ball rolling, became inseparable from the place, as Akhmatova's poem demonstrates:

168

Remembering Anna Akhmatova

I listen still to freedom's vital summons,
I feel that liberty is my domain,
And yet "these living waters" can be heard still
Where long ago young Pushkin first declaimed.

It was very striking to come unexpectedly on "living water" in the work of a Latin American poet whose existence she knew of only by hearsay. Not to mention the fact that the syntax, composition, rhythm and rhyme in the second stanza—perhaps not without the translator's involvement—are directly, concretely, "patently" Akhmatova's, a calque on her poetry. There was a stanza from 'The Pine Forest' about which she never said a word, and which seemed to have escaped her attention:

At dawn there was a hill,
like a rosy land,
but the pine-trees covered it
with black.

But using her favourite device—developed to the point of virtuosity— she included it in some lines which she wrote soon after:

The rosy body of the pines
Is bared when sunset's hour is come.

('This land, though not my native land')

Poland, the magazine which Gorbanevskaya had brought, contained a poem by the Pole Wislawa Szymborska translated by Akhmatova. Natasha Gorbanevskaya was a Polonophile; she quoted Polish poetry from memory, and had a special respect for Norwid. She lived in Moscow, but made frequent appearances in Leningrad, travelling there on lorries which were going her way. Akhmatova announced in fun, "Natasha rang—she got here in cars going the opposite way." She was immediately recognised as a poetess by Akhmatova, who valued her poetry and made no allowances for age, unfavourable circumstances and so on. Akhmatova singled out two of her poems as "shock workers": 'Listen, Bartok, what have you composed here' and 'Like a soldier in Anders' army', with its wonderful lines:

> The fight goes on without us. We're betrayed.
> And Anders' shoulder straps are like a dancer's buckles,
> Like high-heeled shoes and other bits and pieces.
> And this instead of military spares.

Of course, Anders' army reminded Akhmatova of her meetings in Tashkent with Józef Czapski, to whom she addressed the poem 'That night we went out of our minds when we met'. She also liked one short poem very much:

> "Leave me alone!" I cry, addressing
> those who don't notice I exist.
> And cursing other people's rooms,
> I slump in other people's lobbies.
> But how am I to breach the wall?
> And who will offer me their hand?
> I burn upon a sluggish fire.

Gorbanevskaya used to type her poems out on small pieces of paper, put them inside a cover, and give these thin little notebooks to her friends, in particular to Akhmatova. One day A.A. asked me to find a manuscript she needed from amongst her papers, explaining where it would probably be, and what it looked like. I went through several files, but could not find the manuscript. I looked in another place, and in a third, and said that no, I could not see it. Nothing that looks like it? No. "What about Gorbanevskaya's poems?" she asked suddenly. I laughed, and said that I had not come across them. She said fatalistically, "Before one could at least find her poems, but now they've got lost too."

Outside the window of my hospital ward there was a tall poplar. During the time I had been there, its swelling buds had begun to open and it had turned pale green. It stood in the sun, but the one which grew in the middle of the courtyard at Ordynka Street was in the shade, and was a few days behind. We had a kind of game, boasting about our poplars. The ward was on the second floor but latterly she found all staircases as difficult to climb as Shengeli's. On the occasion Akhmatova mentioned, I had been seeing her home after having people round, but when we got to the lift we found it wasn't working. It was seven long flights up to Shengeli's flat and the time was 1 a.m. I started thinking of various solutions: I suggested getting a taxi and going to X's, or Y's—no one would refuse her a bed, that went without saying; or finding a mechanic to mend the lift . . . She said our sole salvation was to start going up the stairs without delay. We took more than half an hour to conquer the staircase: whatever means I found of making the climb easier she rejected categorically and without wasting words. She adopted her normal method of putting both feet in turn on each step and taking five or six deep measured breaths on the landings between the flights of stairs ("correct breathing is the way to tame the heart"). This she called "yoga breathing", but Nina Antonovna, mimicking the well-known actress Birman as the nurse in a play that was popular at the time, called this way of climbing stairs "A step! And—rest!" She twice sat down on the steps. When she got into the flat she asked her hostess to give her some drops of Valocordine and before I left she said that now she was like that grandmother or aunt in Proust to whom they kept singing the praises of the weather and the air in the Champs Elysées, trying to tempt her out for a walk. She would agree, appointing the next Sunday for the excursion, but they all knew that she would never leave the house, because she was convinced that she simply could not. However, when the house caught fire, the old lady got down the fire escape, apparently without even holding on to the rail. Shengeli's stairs gave her confidence and experience: there was a long marble staircase with steep steps in Italy in the palace where they were to award the prize to her, and she said that she remembered this nocturnal climb and went on up without giving it a second thought.

"Koma" who brought the flowers was Vyacheslav Vsevolodovich Ivanov, an academic specialising in linguistics and literature, and whose nickname this was. And "Sasha" was Aleksandr Nilin, Aleksandr Pavlovich Nilin, a close friend of the "Ardov lads". "Marusya"— Mariya Sergeevna Petrovykh—also took part in the Tagore enterprise. Karpushkin was the executive editor of the translation. The fuss which blew up around it seemed necessary and important: one person was holding up the signing of the contract, and another was pushing it along; but once the translation had appeared no one could remember what this had all been about or why it had concentrated everyone's attention. The same alarm and anxiety, of which not a trace was shortly to be found, recurred many times later, always with equal force and intensity. When my usual difficulties had started on the scenario-writing course and I was upset and depressed, Akhmatova comforted me: "Two weeks after you've finished it you'll have forgotten what cinema is, once and for all." (She was out by a few days.)

The "visitor from Leningrad" was Zhenya Berkovskaya, Evgeniya Mikhaylovna Berkovskaya, one of those sixty-year-old women who had been worn out by life but made no claims upon it, who never complained, and of whom there were several in Akhmatova's circle. She came from a very well-to-do Petersburg family and had suffered accordingly. She was now living in corners of other people's flats and earning her living by knitting and typing manuscripts, for Akhmatova in particular. Akhmatova was unfailingly affectionate to her and gave her much support, psychological above all; when she lost Akhmatova, Berkovskaya was finally orphaned: she somehow lost all her strength at once, and very soon died. As a rule Akhmatova's friends from Leningrad and Moscow who travelled between the two capitals brought her things she had left behind, or mail, or, if she was staying on for a long time, clothing appropriate to the season, as did, for example, Vladimir Sergeevich Muravyov, who is mentioned in the letter of 5 May.

The poem 'The Shade' was dedicated to Salomeya Andronikova, about whom Akhmatova wrote in her diary before her trip to England: "We have not seen each other for forty-nine years, nor shall we do so, for she has gone blind"; it had been set to music by Arthur Lourié and the score sent to Moscow. The Khaykins were Ardov's cousins, but 'The Shade' was performed not at the home of Boris Emmanuilovich Khaykin, the famous conductor, and not at the home of his brother, the famous physicist, but at the home of the physicist's son, who was married to a musician. A tape-recording of the evening has survived in which the romance is sung twice, followed by Akhmatova's poems, which she recited willingly after the music.

Ilya Lvovich Slonim was one of the few sculptors who see with their eyes and feel with their fingers the lines, planes, and volumes which space exudes, and do not produce phantoms which resemble the human form—blown up to twice or ten times the proper size. He was married to Tatyana Maksimovna Litvinova, the writer and artist. He did a head of Akhmatova, for which she came to his studio in Maslovka Street several times, but the portrait was not entirely successful, as is often the case when the subject is too "sculptural". In the course of her life

Akhmatova sat for several dozen artists and she felt at ease in artists' studios and was very professional during sittings. At about this time she said, "I would like to see your Tselkov, please." Oleg Tselkov and I had been friends since our childhood in Leningrad and we met frequently in Moscow. I took Akhmatova to his room in Tushino, which also served as his studio. He put a chair near one wall, invited her to sit down, and began propping up one canvas after another against the opposite wall, at intervals of one to two minutes. I thought she had been expecting to see something more superficial, less serious and less accomplished. Once when I had told her about the collages at an exhibition of Pop-Art, which was then *le dernier cri*, she had counted silently, moving her lips, and then said, "That's the fifth time in my memory", and she may have been about to say something similar now. While he showed her his pictures Tselkov chatted with me, and from time to time she made polite remarks, at which he smiled, pausing in the conversation. When 'Group Portrait with Agaves' appeared she asked, "What flowers are they?" He replied straightaway, "The same as the people". She studied him, and he her, before we had a cup of tea and left. A few days later she said, "Please thank your friend again." On the first page of a manuscript she liked to draw with a quick flourish the sign or letter "α", and this was the sole piece of graphic art by her hand—if her handwriting is to be discounted. Once when I went to Ordynka Street she pointed to Nina Antonovna's eight-year-old granddaughter, who was playing in the next room, and said that the little girl had asked her to draw something. "When she was very little I used to draw things for her on a piece of paper when she asked. But after today's artistry she asked politely, 'Have you forgotten how to draw?' She can do it now."

Reeve's book "in which he demands the Nobel Prize" for Akhmatova would seem to be the same one, *Robert Frost in Russia*, in which he describes their meeting at Komarovo.

I was kept in hospital several days more and there received this last note:

Moscow
12 May 1964

Dear Tolya,

I am now leaving "the Legendary Ordynka". I have given Nina the Leopardi for you—I have another one, a present from Lida Chukovskaya.

173

Anatoly Nayman

Nina will tell you why everything is just right, and I think that

> For fragrant flowering May
> In hundred-headed Moscow
> I'll give up flocks of stars
> With all their shining glory ...

A.

❖   ❖   ❖

At the end of that year Akhmatova travelled to Rome and from there to Sicily, to Taormina (she was not sure whether the name of the town was Taormin, Taormino or Taormina), and then the literary prize was awarded to her in Catania. She was supposed to be accompanied by Nina Antonovna, who went off to Minsk while the documents were being processed, to put on a play at the theatre there. In September Nina Antonovna suffered a sudden stroke. Akhmatova took this misfortune very hard and felt it deeply; she immediately asked me to fly to Minsk and I telephoned her from there to tell her how the patient was. Her illness dragged on, and Punina went to Italy in Olshevskaya's place. While Akhmatova was away I received seven letters (mostly postcards sent in envelopes) and a telegram, and I also spoke to her on the telephone. Earlier, when we had been at Komarovo, the post was brought as usual, and I said of a letter from abroad which had been in the mail almost two months, "It walked every step of the way." "And we don't know who's been holding its hand," commented Akhmatova, attaching these words as an epigraph, so to speak, to all correspondence of this kind.

[From Rome to Leningrad, envelope postmarked 7.12.64. Postcard of the Piazza di Spagna.]

This is what it is like, this Rome. Like this, or even better. Very warm. Latterly came through a dazzling pink and scarlet autumn, but beyond Minsk there were snowstorms dancing and I thought of Nina.

174

On Tuesday we are going to Taormino. They hope to arrange a poetry reading.

Please give my regards to your parents [...]

A. Akhmatova

[From Rome to Leningrad, postmark illegible. Postcard of the Piazza dell'Esedra.]

Have you returned to Leningrad? On Wednesday we are going to Taormino. Today we spent a half day looking round Rome and saw much of it from the outside, but none of it was more beautiful than that rosy day on Suvorov. Both well. Akhm.

[Postscript, written at the top:] Regards to friends in Leningrad.

[From Rome to Leningrad, postmark 9.12.64. Postcard of the Pantheon.]

Waiting for the Embassy doctor. He will be able to say whether I can go [to] Taormin, etc. Such grim and terrifying dreams that what Trauberg's daughter said in Vilnius would seem to be true.

Where are you now?

We do not yet know the date of the prize ceremony.

Please ring Anya. Remember me to everyone.

Akhm.

[From Rome to Leningrad, postmark 9.12.64. Postcard of Trevi fountain.]

Today was a very special day—we drove down the via Appia— the Romans' most ancient cemetery. A hot rusty summer and graves and more graves all around us.

Then went on to Raphael's grave. It seems as if he were buried yesterday. (In the Pantheon.)

Going to Taormin tomorrow. Ira spoke to Anya on the telephone two nights running.

Akhm.

175

[From Taormina to Leningrad, postmark 10.12.64; the letter arrived in spite of being incorrectly addressed: instead of Karl Marx Prospect, Akhmatova had written Lenin Prospect. Postcard of the Pantheon at night.]

"Taormin, en route"

We have been in Taorminina [*sic*] since this morning. Everything I have just told you about is here. Dozed all day. Al-ey Aleks. has just come in to see me. He is cheerful and very solicitous. He said that Signora Manzoni wants to do my lit. portrait. So he asked me to see her.

A.

[Postscript written above:] bibliography required. Obviously she should work with Zhenya. I knew you would outstay your welcome in Moscow. Love to my Nina in Moscow. Regards to your family.

[From Taormin to Leningrad, postmark 11.12.64. Postcard of an engraving by A. P. Ostroumova-Lebedeva, 'The Kryukov Canal'.]

"Taormin, en route, Akhmatova"

And here is our Leningrad. I am as good as in Africa. Everything around me is flowering, shining, and smelling sweet. The sea is radiant. The reading is tomorrow. Shall read from *Prologue*. Everyone reads in their own language. Journalists have already been. Television threatened.

I'm writing to Nina.

I think about her. Regards to all.

Akhm.

[Postscript written at the top:] Ira says, "We will telephone when we get back to Rome."

[Postscript written down the side:] Buy *Unità* on Sunday.

176

[From Taormina to Leningrad, postmark 12.12.64]

A letter instead of a postcard today for a change.

Poetry concert in the hotel this evening. Everyone will read in their own language. I have decided to read three sections from *Prologue* in the *New World* text, which I think I've told you already.

Tomorrow the award of the prize in a solemn ceremony—in Catania, then Rome again and ... home.

It's all like a dream. For some reason writing letters is not at all difficult. Someone has probably hypnotised me. The doctor has given me some wonderful medicine and I felt better straightaway. How is my Nina? What would comfort her ...

I must think.—You are now in Leningrad. Please give my regards to your family. Have just been to see the ancient Graeco-Roman theatre at the top of the hill.

Please telephone Anya and say that Ira and I are getting on well together and she feels well.

We will telephone from Rome.

A.

[Telegram:] FROM CATANIA 14.12.64 TO LENINGRAD STOP TOUT VA BIEN DEMAIN PARTONS POUR ROME STOP AKHMATOVA STOP

Akhmatova once asked me to take a letter to Surkov. I telephoned him beforehand and he turned out to be abroad. "Well, that means he'll soon be back," said Akhmatova. "In the past people went abroad for long periods but now it's two weeks and back again." Her trip was like that too.

It was preceded by a meeting in Moscow with Giancarlo Vigorelli, the chairman of the European Literary Society, which he seemed to have set up himself. Akhmatova received him at Ordynka Street. At a meeting of the Ordynka Council it was decided that it would be most convenient and impressive to do this in the "nursery", reclining on the couch. She put on her kimono, powdered her face, and lay down on her side, supporting herself on her arm—this was the classical pose of the women who presided over the European salons, Mme Récamier et al., and was calculated to be reminiscent of something of the kind. Plus an unexpected resemblance to the Modigliani drawing, which leapt to the eye immediately. The kimono was a new one, perhaps the one her brother Viktor in America had sent her; apart from this her wardrobe contained one or two old, not to say delapidated, dresses of ancient origin for wear at home, although they were at the same time too formal for home wear. It may be that this style began with Punin and his trip to Japan. She made brief mention of having visits from Japanese translators—but one of them had made a real impression on her. He was the translator of Tolstoy's complete works, and when she asked him out of sheer courtesy whether he had translated any other Russian authors, he replied, "Yes, all of Dostoevsky."

I looked out of the window and saw two little fat men stamping about in the empty courtyard looking at the numbers on the doors. I went downstairs, asked them in French who they were looking for, and showed them the way. One radiated pleasure, the other looked me over in an unfriendly manner—he was not a foreigner but the escort from the Writers' Union. Vigorelli went into the room, stopped in the doorway, stepped picturesquely back, spread his arms picturesquely wide, and exclaimed, "Anna!" She raised her small hand, waved it slightly in the air, and said, with a certain gravity, "Hello, hello." He kissed her hand, sat on the chair, and began speaking straightaway in a businesslike tone.

Sr Vigorelli's literary enterprise was pro-Soviet, if not indeed Communist. The Writers' Union, headed by Surkov at the time, was seeking ways to establish friendly relations—without sacrificing its own dignity—with "realistically minded" literary people in the West. The recent Pasternak affair had made this rapprochement, desirable on both sides, rather more difficult. Although Akhmatova drew reproaches from the one party (she was not left-wing, not a revolutionary, in Pasolini's terms) and from the other (she was not Soviet and so on), she turned out to be the ideal focal point (*Requiem*, her persecution, and her general un-Soviet stance suited them; her patriotism and un-counterrevolutionary stance suited us; and her prestige, authority, and reputation suited everyone). However, the fact that "Al-ey Aleks." (Aleksey Aleksandrovich Surkov) was "very solicitous" did not in the least mean that he was merely interested in keeping the goods he had brought with him in the best possible condition—and no more. He and Akhmatova were linked by the long-standing and far from schematic relationship of supervisor and subordinate. He had printed the cycle of dutifully loyal poems 'In

Praise of Peace' which she had written in hopes of getting her son released, after the Resolution and her son's second arrest. And he sought her approval for his own poetry, saying of himself, "I am the last of the Acmeists." After an interval of many years he published the first book of her poems to appear since the Resolution; it acquired the nickname "Communist Party Manifesto" on account of its deep-red binding and "official" typeface. It was an obnoxious book, containing her poems about peace (over which she pasted autographs of other poems when she gave people the book as a present) and very many of her faceless translations—but he published it, which was what mattered. He was a person whom she could ask to help people, to instigate the process for getting someone housed; he was her manager, and he suited her nicely. From time to time she would call him "Surkover" behind his back, an indulgently affectionate nickname of less than clear domestic origin. She wrote in her letter that he was "cheerful" [*bodr*], but when I read it the first time I read "kind" [*dobr*], and that seemed quite natural.

The trip was a short one. Rome did not have time to block out Leningrad, or the Appian Way the Kryukov Canal, or the Pantheon Suvorov Prospect. The rhyme "Rome and . . . home", to which attention is drawn in her letter by the aposiopesis, is not only a joke of Akhmatova's (in Rome/at home) and *Urbis*/*Orbis* turned inside out, but it reveals, as it were, knowledge obtained from experience and communicated to an addressee whom life has not yet made wise: this was the knowledge that home, at any rate at the end of one's life, not to mention one's last home, includes in itself all Romes and the whole world.

She travelled to Italy by train as she did six months later when she went to England. In general she liked travelling by train—partly because its character and its very essence had hardly changed since the early years of the century, when she had travelled a great deal and without difficulty, except that speeds were now somewhat greater. She remembered returning to Petrograd from the south (I imagined this was in the very early 1920s, but it may have been in 1916) via Moscow: "I arrived in Moscow in the morning and was due to leave in the evening. I did not want to see anyone, and I got a cab from the station to go to pray at the Iversk icon. Then I walked through the streets all day. It was so good to be a nobody." This recollection, like all the others of the same kind, betrays no hint of the trials travelling involved for her, which not only always attracted colourful descriptions from those who witnessed them, but which genuinely constituted virtually the whole content of her journeys at that time and afterwards. "What could be nicer than a trip through Finland in winter in a comfortable Russian railway carriage! The very image of well-being," she said one miserable frosty day in Komarovo when the grey damp cold was freezing her to the marrow. In her last years, however, moving from place to place became increasingly difficult, mainly because of her heart trouble. An hour before she had to leave the house she would get symptoms of *Reisefieber*, travel fever, and sometimes her heart would act up. She would only travel with a female companion—some close acquaintance or a relative. They would arrive at the terminus long before the train came into the station. Once, when she was sitting in the waiting-room of the Moscow Station in Leningrad, Bolshintsova-Stenich, who was travelling with her, remembered what had happened when she and her husband were seeing Mandelstam off and they too had arrived early: in the waiting-room there was a palm-tree in a tub, and Mandelstam had hung his little bundle of things on it and said, "Lone traveller in the desert." One of the young people would be put in charge of Akhmatova's luggage and someone was always at her side with nitroglycerine for her heart condition to hand—another bottle of nitroglycerine was always kept in her handbag. She would walk slowly to the carriage, leaning on someone's arm, and stopping to rest from time to time. I was often the person who saw her off or met her—the main thing was to walk without hurrying. Once, in the summer of 1965, we decided to travel together from Moscow to Leningrad by the day train, not the sleeper. Several people came to see her off, one of whom was Nadezhda Yakovlevna Mandelstam. She kept running on ahead, then getting left behind, and made sarcastic remarks about the proceedings. Towards the end, when we were inside the carriage, she surveyed the cluster of people saying goodbye to Akhmatova and observed casually, "When I left Pskov, there were two hundred people standing on the platform." Akhmatova heard nothing of this as she was by then hard of hearing. We arrived in Leningrad in cheerful mood, the reception party was running along the platform outside the window, and at its head came, flying an inch or two above the ground and clutching a sumptuous bouquet of flowers to his chest, Roman Albertovich, artiste from the Leningrad Concert-Management Agency.

She had read Einstein and understood the theory of relativity, but her enthusiasm for the achievements of technology was fairly muted. She was hostile to lifts, but tolerated them; she could not bear typewriters, especially in conjunction with carbon paper. She remembered some physicists and astronomers making fun of her in 1929 in the Crimea: "Don't give Anna Andreevna the binoculars to hold, they might explode." Only the automobile met with her unreserved approval. Once a taxi in which we were travelling drew up at a petrol station next to a shining new Mercedes and I said, "It's a handsome beast, don't you think?" She replied with disdain: "Do you really like it? You've got bourgeois tastes. It's probably one of these modern talking ones: 'Time to put some petrol in, it's getting low!', 'Please reduce speed, don't orphan your children!' Grr-!" It gave her pleasure when even car-owners she did not know well offered to take her out for a ride; she fairly often found a reason for telephoning for a taxi to go somewhere to do something, and sometimes she would telephone for no reason at all: "Let's go out for a ride." In one of her postcards she refers to just such a pleasure-trip down Suvorov Prospect one rosy day—though my memory recalls a greenish-pink summer evening. "Do you know the trick with the Smolny Cathedral? If you drive slowly down the square and past it, it begins to revolve, and the angle of vision stays the same. I'll just show you," she said and asked the driver to turn off Nevsky Prospect into Suvorov Prospect. And when she wrote in her letter to me in hospital, "We will go to see the birches and Pike Lake again", she was reminding me of other car trips we had made.

One day Natalya Yosifovna Ilina invited Akhmatova, and Akhmatova invited me, for an hour's drive outside Moscow. It was an overcast day in late autumn and Ilina drove out along the Rublyov Highway, and stopped on the edge of a birch grove, which was leafless, dazzlingly white, and full of tall trunks, apparently spaced out according to some plan. The brightness was softened and dulled by the whitish sky and air, which was tinted by the day's direct light, and the shadow from the birches. It was warm and incredibly quiet. We took a walk through the fallen leaves, and drove back into the city. I suspect that Akhmatova's prose passage about birch trees being "huge, mighty, and ancient as druids" and "like the altar of Pergamon" came into being after this walk. We went to Pike Lake, two miles from her house at Komarovo, several times, at least once with Ilina: that time Bobyshev made up a foursome. He and I swam, Akhmatova sat on a log, and Ilina strolled along the bank, then we all piled into the car, N.I. began to reverse, and Bobyshev began speaking in a generally uncharacteristic almost courteous manner, hesitantly and putting on an accent. He said that, without permitting himself even to contemplate intervening and so on, and so on, he only wished to direct the kind attention of the driver to the fact that the back wheel, over which he was sitting, was apparently approaching a ... She hit the brake a second before I shouted, "A crater!" All three of us jumped out of the car: one wheel was hanging over a three-foot drop, the other had stopped on the very edge. We pushed the car back from the crater with great caution—Akhmatova sat inside, untroubled and dignified. When it was all over I asked Bobyshev why he had been so long-winded, and Akhmatova replied, "What kind of a question is that? The man's made that way." Another time she told me laughingly that Bobyshev had heard her say complimentary things about my latest poem and had said morosely and with meaning, " 'I could present Tolya with a number of criticisms.' And with that he fell forever silent. That reminded me of a little boy, Valya Smirnov: he lived in the flat next door to Punin's and he died in the siege. He put his head round the door of my room and said, 'There'll be cinema tonight'. This had no relation to anything at all—absolutely nothing: it was simply part of a game he was playing." Then she added, "Apart from that he said one other wonderful thing. I was doing some French with him, teaching him: '*Le singe*, the monkey, repeat after me.' He ran out of the room, then stuck his head round the door and asked, '*Lesanych*—will that do?' and ran away again." (When she had read a newly written poem to one of her visitors and heard his or her rapturous mumbling she was capable of saying suddenly, "Generally speaking, *lesanych*—will it do?")

She and I once found ourselves in a really serious fix, in broad daylight, in Pea Street. She wanted to get to the savings bank and time was running short: it was the beginning of the "Akhmatova hour"—this was her name for the lunch-break at official institutions, which always started for some inexplicable reason at the very moment when her taxi was approaching the door. The driver, a nice young lad, wanted to help and drove like a desperado, although the streets were narrow and crammed full of traffic. We overtook a queue of lorries and trolleybuses, leapt out on to the steep little bridge over the Moyka—and came face to face with a heavy lorry going in the opposite direction. Our driver wrenched the wheel to the left and we flew on to the pavement on *the left-hand side*, which was empty, fortunately, and then he immediately turned sharply right and we tucked ourselves into our own lane again. The manoeuvre was performed at high speed, so that we were a little slow to register the details, but once we had indeed taken them in we instantly felt weak at the knees. "We" was the driver and I: Akhmatova frowned because of the jolting and then again sat upright and imperturbable, looking straight ahead. Our car was immediately encircled by others, whose drivers had seen us swerve. Their faces were contorted with the fear that had shot through them, and indignation, and they all shouted in unison that our driver was drunk. I tried to defend him and they retorted, "You thank God you're still alive." They decided to take our car—and us with it—to the nearest police station. Only at this point did Akhmatova stir, turn towards them, look out of the window and say: "In that case our journey is pointless." Her appearance was so commanding, and her tone so unexpectedly tranquil and persuasive that the traffic jam started to disperse: we made it at the very last moment.

Amongst all those people in Leningrad who gave Akhmatova rides in their cars, Olga Aleksandrovna Ladyzhenskaya had a special place. She was a famous mathematician, whom Akhmatova commended to her occasional visitors as the Sofya Kovalevskaya of our time[29] and to those close to her as a "dog mathematician", in a parody of "a woman mathematician". She dedicated her poem 'In Vyborg' to her. The poem came about as a result of an amusing concatenation of circumstances. The usual route for her car rides was along the Gulf of Finland, no further than the Black River, where Leonid Andreev was buried, and one such trip is celebrated by Akhmatova in 'This land, though not my native land'. But she would more often ask the driver to stop on the Coastal Highway between the thirty-five- and forty-mile markers, where there was a wild deserted beach sown with enormous granite boulders. One day it turned out that this isolation, silence, and stillness were an illusion. Akhmatova and I had got out of the car and were moving slowly along, next to a hedge consisting almost entirely of wild roses. Ladyzhenskaya locked the car doors and came after us. At that moment a middle-aged lady stepped out from a narrow pathway between the bushes, gasped, and said, "Good day, Anna Andreevna. And tell me, how is Lev Nikolaevich?" Akhmatova had by then not seen her son, who was living in Leningrad, for several years. "He is in excellent health, thank you!" she rapped out, then she turned sharply round and walked towards the car as quickly as she could ... However, Ladyzhenskaya was not the person who took her to Vyborg. I had a visit from a Moscow friend who was driving through Leningrad and I asked Akhmatova if she would like to go for a ride. We chose a pretty road which ran from the Coastal Highway to the Vyborg Highway and were driving along in a leisurely way when suddenly one of us had the idea of going to Vyborg. She agreed, and then we threw ourselves into a race against time, because she was shortly expecting a visitor and Vyborg was more than seventy-five miles away. We hurtled to the town at sixty miles an hour or more, spun round alongside the park and the quay, without getting out, had an Eskimo ice-cream each and returned with equal speed. All she said was, "A moderately impressive populated point . . ." A few days later Ladyzhenskaya visited Akhmatova and told her that she had been to Vyborg, what a splendid place it was, and what a great impression the granite monolith whose steps went down into the water had made upon her. Akhmatova looked at me with mock distress and pique and told her visitor that we had not seen anything of the kind. Two days later, if not the next day, she wrote her poem which begins 'Enormous underwater steps' and so on, and dedicated it to Ladyzhenskaya.

The last time we went for a drive round Moscow was in February 1966, soon after she was discharged from hospital and about ten days before her death. It was frosty and the sun was setting. We asked the driver to take us to the Saviour-Andronikov monastery. The taxi was old, and it rattled and stank of petrol. The street leading to the monastery turned out to be strewn with large chunks of ice which apparently had been recently chipped off the road, and the taxi began to jolt. Akhmatova frowned, and clutched her heart with her hand; I told the driver to turn back to Ordynka Street. She sucked a little nitro-glycerine, and the driver began to drive round alongside the white wall of the monastery. Still pressing her hand to her breast, she said, "Massive masonry, built to last for centuries." But on one of our first trips round Moscow we had turned off after crossing the Great Stone Bridge, and the car had come level with the three dreadful tall black blocks of flats for government members near the Stakhanovite Cinema. Many of the residents had been shot during the terror. "And don't you think the architect should be shot too for making people look at those ugly things every day?" asked Akhmatova.

On 3 March 1966 Akhmatova and Olshevskaya set off for the sanatorium at Domodedovo just outside Moscow. We took two cars and asked a nurse from the ward where Akhmatova had been to accompany us. In spite of the comparatively long journey and a breakdown on the way, Akhmatova's heart did not trouble her. The sanatorium was for the privileged and had a conservatory, carpets, and trained staff. Wide semi-circular steps led up to a yellow building and then into a white colonnade. We went up them slowly, she looked around and murmured, *"L'année dernière à Marienbad"*. Robbe-

Grillet's *L'année dernière à Marienbad* was more or less the last book she read.

There are frequent references in the letters she wrote from Italy and also from Moscow to the fact that she was sleeping: "I am sleepy and vacant", "such grim dreams", "dozed all day". Of course this can be put down to her age and state of health, but not to that alone. At this time her eye fell upon ... —here I must digress a little: at this time I was reading Yeats ... —and a small further digression: at this time someone gave me a book of Yeats's poems ... —and as a result of the coincidence of these apparently random circumstances, she came across his poem which begins "When you are old and grey and full of sleep," which I was then trying to translate. From then on every remark about sleepiness became an allusion to this poem. But apart from that, almost every sleep which she mentioned (at least, I think every one) involved a dream, and "dozing" in conjunction with "such grim and terrible dreams" was more like dreaming than sleeping. And "What Trauberg's daughter [Natalya Leonidovna Trauberg] said in Vilnius" was then a commonplace in the conversation of those young people who were inclined to link their ideas of heaven and hell with morality, in particular with the morality of their friends and acquaintances, who were, quite unbeknown to themselves, identified as angels or devils.

❖ ❖ ❖

Dear Tolya,
My Moscow winter has come to an end. It was hard and murky. I have not managed to do anything at all and that is very boring.
Now I think of nothing but home. Time to go!
I must pay for the Cabin and collect my pension.
The "White Nights from the sea" are already roaming through Komarovo, the cuckoo is calling and the pine-trees rustling. Perhaps the book about Pushkin is waiting for me there.
Regards to all,

Anna Akhmatova.

The letter is not dated and my memory of receiving it has become confused with a later recollection: of re-reading it for the first time several years after her death, noticing its close connection to 'Seaside Sonnet', and therefore reading a new valedictory content into the words "home" and "time to go!", and guessing that she had intentionally written "wise" [*mudroy*] instead of "murky" [*mutnoy*]—that is, the winter had again taught her something—and that she had then corrected it, or that "murky" was just a slip of the pen. There is sufficient evidence that the letter was written in the spring of 1964, or 1963, or 1965—there are arguments for and against each of these dates.

These three winters were more alike than different: moving from one place to another, two cardboard suitcases of manuscripts, telephone calls from editorial offices suggesting changes in her texts, the production of *The Flight of Time* which dragged on inordinately, indisposition, illness and: visitors; callers; less often—official visitors; less often still—visits to other people. It is not for us to judge how genteel the genteel ladies of the 1910s, whom she recalled without enthusiasm, would have thought Akhmatova, but in our eyes her good manners were impeccable, and in the eyes of the ladies of the 1960s they were even excessive, to the detriment of sincerity. In fact good manners are the very instrument which measures out doses of sincerity and, likewise, all other reactions to what is going on, and it is just as much a vice as a virtue to be invariably sincere. It is quite a different thing that good manners—in the form of ritualised behaviour, outward appearance and affectation—could lead to almost entirely artificial behaviour, and when Akhmatova spoke of a certain desiccation amongst the ladies of Petersburg who were still dressing after the fashion of twenty years before, she contrasted them to the big, solid, coarse-featured maids-of-honour at court, who were quite unlike the beautiful shapely young ladies which Hollywood films imagined them to be. When she had expressed the wish to meet my parents and they had visited her at Komarovo I was surprised to hear her utter, when some two or three weeks had elapsed, a phrase which embarrassed me by its old-fashionedness: "Please ask your parents when I can return their call." I asked, and brought her to see them; she was again obliged to walk up five flights, there being no lift, she sat briefly at the table, and we left. When they went to see her, my father asked me on the way whether she liked Esenin's poetry and also Lev Tolstoy's comparison of poetry to a ploughman who bobs every two or three steps. Having in both cases received the reply no, she did not, he announced, almost as soon as he entered the *dacha*, that his favourite poet was Esenin, who wrote 'You are still alive, my dear old lady', from which poem he then recited several stanzas, and that he agreed with Tolstoy that poetry was ploughing and bobbing every two or three steps. To both challenges she replied simply, "Yes, yes, I know" and after I had seen them to the station and come back she said, "Your father is a charming person."

People who came to see her for the first time were generally openly terrified of crossing the threshold of her room. Out in the corridor my friends would beg me in whispers not to leave them alone with her—this amused and angered her. Over many years the pattern of receiving more or less casual visitors had become fixed. "Please see to the flowers," she would say to someone from the household, freeing the visitor from the bouquet, and to the visitor she would say, "Thank you." Then: "Please feel free to smoke, I have no objection—I smoked myself for more than thirty years." When visitors thought that the visit was coming to an end and they prepared to leave, she would ask, "And what is the time?" and, depending on the answer, she would indicate how much time remained—on hearing, for example, that it was a quarter to eight, she would say, "Do stay just until eight." And when she decided that the visit was over she would hold out her hand without warning, thank the visitor, see him or her to the door and say, "Don't forget us." Her parting words for the young people she knew well were: "Well, off you run then." It was impossible to have a conversation with her on the telephone for she would always interrupt what you were saying with: "Come and see me," and the receiver would be hung up.

In conversation she was always herself. She spoke in a tranquil tone, extremely clearly and laconically, was not afraid of silences, and did not, as is the custom, make meaningless remarks to put visitors at ease. She was reconciled to the fact that people came to see her out of curiosity or vanity, considering it inevitable, and she was pleased if something unexpectedly interesting emerged from such a visit. Some people made up their minds to come and see her simply to share their sorrows, almost treating her as a confessor—and they left comforted, although she said little. When she was in hospital and people found out who she was, they came to her for advice—patients from the ward, nurses. All of them began in the same way: "Well, I haven't been living with my husband for the last three months"—the only difference would be the length of time. As a rule all the endings were similar: "Do you think she, that other woman, will ever feel as terrible as I do now?" And

Akhmatova would reply: "That I can guarantee—you need have no doubt about that."

Humour is a rarity in her poetry, but she often joked in conversation, especially when talking to people she felt close to. Sometimes she would give deliberately exaggerated descriptions of an event or of something she was doing. If a solution to a problem was proposed to her she would say, "Don't try to console me, I'm inconsolable." When something had made her angry and people were trying to talk her out of it, this was known as "rendering first aid". If someone gave her unacceptable advice she would say ironically, "I will give your suggestion cordial consideration." Olshevskaya complained to me that she sat at home for many days without going out and getting any fresh air, and she defended herself good-naturedly: "That's a dirty slander on a pure me."

She would laugh at jokes, sometimes out loud, sometimes chuckling. She would drop the key phrase from a joke into conversation, but without alluding to the joke itself. "And as our comrade from the strait-jacket section of the lunatic asylum rightly points out ..." "Lessons first, dwinks later ..." "Either this one or that one, granddad, otherwise I'm going to wash my hair ..." But she could not bear vulgarity and one day she said indignantly, "After all, there are some things which are unforgiveable. For example, 'Dad's asleep, the mirror water's silent' as some people recently had the temerity to joke in my hearing." This was a play on some lines of poetry which everyone learned at school: "The rushes sleep, the mirror water's silent". "And today," she continued, "my hosts had a playful visitor who said, 'Why is X bald—contemplation or copulation?'" Nor could she bear puns, though she made an exception of one with a universally known content. She said one day, "All my life I have been such an anti-anti-Semite that when someone started telling a Jewish joke, X, who was there, exclaimed, 'You're off your head. How can you, when Anna Andreevna is listening?'" I once had occasion to quote the following joke to her: one drunk says to another drunk, "Do you know Marx?" "No." "Engels?" "No." "What about Feuerbach?" "Oh, leave me alone, will you. You've got your friends and I've got mine." She was amused. A few days later I came to Komarovo and she said that Azarov (an old and boring poet) had brought another (younger) poet, Sosnora, to see her. I promptly responded, "You've got your friends and I've got mine". She burst out laughing, and then made a quick parry with "Oh yes? And who are your friends then?"

She loved the humorous writing of Kozma Prutkov and knew it very well. Not the overworked aphorisms, but, for example: "He said in an undertone, 'I'm leaving for the farm,' and announced to the drawing-room at large, 'Let's go to the mezzanine!'" "Let's go to the mezzanine," Akhmatova would say whenever she wanted to speak to one of her female friends in private. She declared her love of the nineteenth-century poet A. K. Tolstoy's verse; this was not only a tender affection for 'The Bride of Corinth', which she had loved from her earliest youth, and the first stanza of which she recited from memory in a child's "piping" voice:

Our young man who left his native Athens
Came to columned Corinth quite unknown.
There a kindly townsman gave his father
Bread and salt these many years ago.
 When their children two
 Flourished, played and grew
They declared that they were now betrothed ...

It was with the affectionate feelings of a standard reader that she also liked 'The Ballad of Delarue the Chamberlain' and 'Popov's Dream', and she would declaim as if it were a tongue-twister:

The villain plunged his knife in his left side
 And made him stagger.
Said Delarue, "That is, I must confide,
 A handsome dagger!"

and with solemnity:

It was not I betrayed Madame Grinevich!
Strazhenko's safe; the brothers Shulakov
Were to my shame not put in irons by me!

It is commonly thought that satire is alien to Akhmatova's poetry, although in the 1930s she composed a number of variations on the

well-known Russian verse theme 'Where are those islands', one stanza
of which I remember:

> Where Yagoda[30] the blackguard
> Would not put people's backs
>   To the wall,
> And Aleksey Tolstoy
> Would not with patent joy
>   Rob us all.

(This was, of course, about Akhmatova's contemporary, the novelist
A. N. Tolstoy, and not about the poet A. K. Tolstoy.)

In practice she frequently had a habit of pronouncing aloud—
anything from declaiming to murmuring—well-known lines of poetry
which had, as a rule, some paradoxical relevance to the situation at
hand. For example, when she had mislaid her handbag and was looking
for it she might quote from a favourite poem, 'Uncle Vlas', though
altering Nekrasov's intonation: "Who whipped off the ploughman's
shirt? Stole the beggar's bundle too?" (Nekrasov has: "Vlas feels bad. He
calls the sorcerer. Will you help that very person who whipped off the
ploughman's shirt—stole the beggar's bundle too?") In so doing she
encouraged a utilitarian and even proprietorial attitude towards poetry,
rather than a timid approach, as if to a sacred text. Nekrasov was
commonly used in such cases, especially: "They did not sew there very
much and sewing was not their strong point" from 'The Poor Girl and
the Elegant'. She would also enunciate pitifully, mimicking the aged
manservant, "You've forgotten Firs, you've left a person behind!" from
her unfavourite *The Cherry Orchard*. When she was getting ready to go
somewhere, the driver of the taxi she had ordered would already be
ringing the doorbell, chaos would be descending, the people who were
seeing her off would be concentrating on whether she had got everything: nitroglycerine, handbag, suitcase if necessary, and she, already
dressed in her coat and headscarf, stick in hand, would sit down on a
chair in the corridor and say: "You've forgotten Firs." The Nekrasov
who found his way into her poems was a different, public, campaigning
poet whom she had read after reaching "the age of discretion" and
whose "Muse lashed with the knout" Akhmatova turned into her own
"my Muse was flogged to death"; but this Nekrasov, the one she knew

in childhood through her mother's voice, was for domestic purposes: the members of the Poets' Guild amused themselves by reading his 'The merchant Sevenfingers' servants do not observe the fasts' in their own Latin translation: *Heptadactylus mercator servos semper nutrit carne*. She extended this easy-going and light-hearted approach to her own poems too: having changed before the arrival of some visitors, she brought her everyday kimono out of her room and thrust it into the hands of one of the household, saying, "Oh, where can I conceal you, sweet evidence of crime?" (In her poem: "He gave me three carnations, but did not raise his eyes: oh, where can I conceal you, sweet evidence of crime?")

She made abundant jokes, and what made one laugh or smile was their unexpectedness, the contrasts they set up, their paradoxicality and, even more, her acute observation, but never their absurdness, even though the latter had by this time become the fashion. She could make subtle—sometimes also esoteric—jokes if that was appropriate; or coarse or vulgar jokes if that was appropriate; some of her jokes were recherché, but they were more usually on her partner's level. She never lost herself entirely in her jokes, she did not give herself up to them, and did not "kill off" a joke if she saw that it was not making an impression; part of her always observed the joke and herself from the outside. She literally roared with laughter one day at the comedian Raykin's line "Then they put me into a perfume factory and I began making a scent called 'Here Come the Soldiers'". This was the title of an officially inspired ditty which was popular at the time. She told me later, with some feeling, that Raykin, who was in England when she was honoured by Oxford University, had either come to congratulate her or sent a telegram. She was pleased at his consideration, but as she told the story the fact that he was a celebrity receded into the background, and the foreground was taken up by the fact that this was a kingdom, and here we had a queen and the queen's jester ... But she immediately deflated what she had said with: "And Voznesensky also emerged from somewhere in deepest England and sent me one of his books to mark the occasion: 'To my much respected ...' and so on, and then he had inserted 'and dear'. He's a complete Karamazov: 'and to my chicken'." This was Fyodor Karamazov's inscription to Grushenka on a packet of banknotes.

Her general attitude towards all practical routine matters was similar: between "routine existence" and "things to be done" on the one hand and "the grandeur of the conception" on the other she maintained an unstable and fragile equilibrium. Sometimes the needle shifted in the direction of "routine existence"—and life would become "hard and murky" and "very boring"—and sometimes it shifted in the direction of "grandeur"—and it became lucid, constructing itself out of a multitude of scattered observations, like "the book about Pushkin", and everything, from the piercing squeak of the gate at the well to the knock at the door which she did not answer because she could not hear it, turned out to be poetry, 'Midnight Verses', lines from *Prologue*, or poems from cycles and books begun many years earlier. Here are two notes which she gave me listing things which she wanted me to do—the first when I was making my next visit to Leningrad, the second when I was going to Moscow.

I.   The Leningrad *Poet's Day*, 1963 (the one which has my Poem) and the whole of the Poem from home.
II.   Find out up to which day my place at the House of Creat. has been paid for.
III.   L-e-t-t-e-r-s.
IV.   How does Anya know about Emma?
V.   Bring letters wh. Admoni wrote (Ger.) for me to sign.
VI.   My radio.
VII.   Let me know who will come when?
VIII.   Regards to Fausto.

Anya is Anya Kaminskaya, Emma is Emma Gershteyn. Admoni is Vladimir Grigorevich Admoni, one of Akhmatova's close friends, an authority on German language and literature, and a poet; she quoted me some lines from one of his poems: "I can hear my blood course, as do all who are left tête-à-tête with the darkness", and she said, "That is where poetry is now—he's a professor with an international reputation." Fausto is Fausto Malcovati from Milan, who was at the beginning of his career in those days, and later became a well-known literary scholar who specialised in Vyacheslav Ivanov and Soviet theatre of the 1920s.

To Tolya for Moscow

1. Katsnelson. Leopardi to *The Week* (Etkind—foreword) . . .
2. I asked you to find out the Egypt. translations.

. . . .

2. My book of translations, *The Voices of Friends*. When fees?
Money to Ordynka. Nika has details of Sav. Bank bk.

. . . .

Asia Africa Today. Check.

. . . .

Modigliani. Borrow Khardzhiev's text for "Modi"

. . . .

Youth both on yourself and on me (Pushkin?)

. . . .

Lida to find out what —— wrote to Korney about me
Pass on three pictures of me for Konovalov

. . . .

Perfume for Nina

. . . .

Regards and love
                    to our Galya
          Marusya and Arisha
                    Lyubochka
          Nika, Yuliya, Olya
                    Fedya
          R. to the idiot

Katsnelson was the executive editor of *Egyptian Lyrics*. Leopardi did
not go to *The Week* either with or without Efim Grigorevich Etkind's
foreword. Nikolay Ivanovich Khardzhiev, the remarkable art scholar
and literary historian, had been a friend of Akhmatova's since the
1930s. Lida is Lydia Chukovskaya and Korney is Korney Ivanovich Chukovsky, her father. Konovalov is a well-known Slavist, a professor at
Oxford University, and the person denoted by the dashes is Isaiah
Berlin. Nina is Nina Olshevskaya; Galya is Galina Mikhaylovna Narin-
skaya, later my wife; Marusya is Mariya Petrovykh and Arisha is her
daughter; Nika is Nika Glen, Yuliya is Yuliya Markovna Zhivova, the
Polish literature editor at the State Literary Publishing House, Olya is
Olga Dmitrievna Kutasova, the Yugoslav literature editor at the same
place, Fedya is her new-born son. R—in Latin script, not Cyrillic—
meant *Requiem* and the idiot is the person who sent her his copy (either
a samizdat typescript or the edition published in Munich without the
permission either of the authorities or of Akhmatova)—through the
post—and asked her to autograph it.

A note about payment for staying at the House of Creativity stands side by side in her diary with the lines about the "most precious cedar" beneath its windows, and the two counter-balanced each other in her real life. In the same way 'Chamberlain Delarue', which she remembered during a merry evening we spent round the table, and the intentional flatness of her delivery, designed to amuse her guests ("The villain plunged his knife in his left side"), counter-balanced a remark she singled out for emphasis, when she commented on the particular importance in her poetry of the poem 'He marked in charcoal on my left side the place at which to shoot'. She established just such a natural and easy balance between the true value of a person or work of art and their official reputation, and she also showed how the two complemented each other. She knew all too well what wheels turn within wheels, hidden from public view, to make someone's good or bad reputation, including her own, and she did not, therefore, labour under any delusions about the award of degrees or prizes. When I opened the newspaper and asked, rhetorically for the most part, why So-and-So had been given the Lenin prize for literature she growled, "For the sum total," and when I remarked with the passion of youth that this was "scandalous, all the same", she cut me short fairly sharply: "Shame on you—it's their prize and they give it to each other." And if she served up her Italian "Etna-Taormina" and her Oxford "mortar-board and tassel" with some seriousness, this implied much less vanity or other pardonable shortcomings than the conviction that other people—not herself—who believed in justice needed "justice to triumph" and "Akhmatova to receive her just deserts". "After the war when Allied Command were giving receptions for each other," she said, "Zhukov rode into the Western zone of Berlin on horseback, and Montgomery and Eisenhower, who were on foot, took his horse by the bridle and led it down the street. That was the end of him, because Stalin had imagined that *he* would ride in on a white steed and they would walk at *his* side." In her eyes the "Nobel" was this same white steed, belonging to the true victor in a fifty-year war of attrition.

❖   ❖   ❖

Akhmatova brought her times into ours. She was one of the founders of her own age and defined its aesthetics and character to no small degree.

The concept of "her times" sums up the expanse of time between the 1910s and the 1960s, which she sewed and quilted with the lines of her fate and poems. Exactly the same thing can be said of Pasternak, with allowances for the content of his biography and poetry. His death in 1960 and hers in 1966 completed the history of Russian culture in the first half of the twentieth century: while they were still alive it was impossible not to keep looking at them over one's shoulder, and it was impossible to say and do things which became possible only a month or two after Akhmatova's funeral.

She often spoke about the beginning of the century and later wrote this down: "The twentieth century began in the autumn of 1914, together with the war, just as the nineteenth began with the Congress of Vienna. Calendar dates have no meaning. Symbolism is indisputably a nineteenth-century phenomenon. Our revolt against Symbolism was completely legitimate because we felt ourselves to be people of the twentieth century and we did not wish to remain in the preceding one ..." Her poem 'We aged by a hundred years' not only bears witness to the horrors of World War I, the tragedy of which imparted to young people the experience of old men: it is also a literal transition from one century to another. It can also be said of the twentieth century that there is a discrepancy of a decade and a half between the real middle of the century and its actual calendar date.

Neither she nor Pasternak were required to march in step with time, even had they intended to do so; the pace which is demanded of time in true poetry is always greater than the momentum of the age, and this sets the poet's oeuvre outside the bounds of time. The futile expectation of wonders from Dzhek Altauzen in the 1920s was transferred to other names by poetry fans in the 1950s. But Akhmatova and Pasternak, to quote criticism not given to joking, "were unable to die in time", and the simple fact of their presence on the roll—albeit amongst those who were pushed to the side of the road, in conjunction with their non-participation in the race—spoiled the pleasure to be had in the expectation itself and ultimately brought the wonders proclaimed to naught, or at best reduced them to stunts. In spite of their radically different aesthetic positions—Akhmatova wrote in such a way that posterity should "shudder in surprise and read the names on the enigmatic burial vault" and Pasternak wrote in such a way that at the moment the line was read the ink could still be seen drying beneath his hand—the dividers for measuring the scale of her "monumentalness" and his "momentariness" were opened so wide that they were of no use for assessing the size of other talents, and those from whom wonders were expected clearly lost by comparison with them. After their deaths everything changed radically: the scale, the method of measurement, and finally the dividers themselves. The atmosphere changed.

Evening, the end of the day, the end of the year, and the end of the century, presuppose a decline in activity, a dying down—and putting off one's affairs, thoughts, and life itself—until the beginning of the next day, year, or century. When a half of a day, year or century ends or begins all this happens less clearly and is expressed more mutedly, but all the same it is distinctly perceptible. By the mid-1960s the tiredness which had been growing for half a century and whose cataclysms increased it, and which weighed still more heavily after the relief afforded by the death of Stalin, made itself felt in the most varied of fields. The energy which was gathering at the beginning of the second half of the century could not contend with it, although it attempted to do so: poetry in particular began to give way to literature, journalism, dissidence (in the wide definition of the term which goes from Yevtushenko to Solzhenitsyn), prose, and, on the narrowly literary plane, to the analysis of poems written previously. But the signs of decay were also to be observed earlier—in the "thaw" and even in "the upsurge of a new interest in poetry", as Akhmatova said at the beginning of the 1960s. And she herself managed to show these signs of decay, by degrees and unobtrusively, but indisputably.

"She's an old dog now," she used to say from time to time, not by any means complaining: referring not only to the physical weight of the years she had lived through, but also to the impossibility of ignoring what she knew. She recalled the note referring to the days of his youth which the poet Vyazemsky left when he had read *War and Peace*, i.e. when he was an old man. He said that "the late Emperor", as he called Alexander I, could be reproached with many things, but one quality which he entirely lacked was vulgarity: he had been brought up impeccably and could not have thrown money to the people as young Count Tolstoy describes. Not that Akhmatova was on Vyazemsky's side: when I said one day that I agreed with every word he said about Pushkin's poem 'To the Slanderers of Russia' she retorted angrily, "But I don't. True or not, the one said what he wanted for all to hear and the other said it in his diary, and much good that was." Nor was her remark a dig at Tolstoy, whom she affected to curse roundly as a "rubbishy old man" for his notoriously untruthful treatment of Anna Karenina and generally for his damaging devotion to ideas. But such contrasts formed themselves, nearly always without her wishing it, into clear parallels: then and now. Not a grumbling "things used to be better and now they've got worse" but: it used to be like this and now it's different, and which is preferable is a matter of taste. She told a story about Stravinsky's wife Vera, a dazzlingly beautiful woman whom Petersburg connoisseurs of beauty called Byaka, babytalk for "bad". When she emigrated she lived in Paris and had a business making and selling hats. Clients would try on the hats in front of the mirror and if they hesitated Byaka would put the hat on herself and say, "Well, how does it look?" after which they would immediately agree that the hat was amazingly chic, and pay up. "She was a really beautiful woman," said Akhmatova, "and it's so rarely the case. There's that Georgian woman, married to that splendid poet of ours—you've seen her. Her beauty can't be faulted, but God preserve us from beauty like that."

Another time she remembered a story about a well-known actress, the painter Korovin's mistress, which made the rounds in the 1910s if not a year or two earlier. She was entertaining him when Lamanova, her dressmaker, showed up unexpectedly. "It's as if Dior himself had called," she said, naming if not Dior then another Paris fashion house; "or even someone more important": Lamanova was in a class of her own. The lady of the house did not give Korovin a second thought but threw on some piece of clothing and ran out of the room to meet her, explaining that the doctor was there and had been examining her that very minute. The fitting dragged on for a long time and Korovin, tired of waiting, suddenly came in with some of his shirt-buttons undone and his laces untied. "Doctor! What do you mean by this!" the actress exclaimed resourcefully. Shortly before or after telling this story Akhmatova asked me whether I had heard the one about the powder-compact. In the late 1950s or early 1960s a genteel lady from Moscow, a writer, used to go out visiting, preferably to larger gatherings, where she would take her compact out of her handbag, powder her face, and leave the compact open in the middle of the table. Different people who told the story supplied different details: instead of leaving it open she would keep opening it every other minute and powder her face; or it was not in the middle of the table but, on the contrary, concealed somewhere. Finally someone noticed this, suspected foul play, and dropped the compact on the floor, apparently accidentally—it turned out to contain a miniature tape-recorder. "And do you know who the lady was?" asked Akhmatova with pleasurable anticipation, and she named one of her acquaintances, who came to see her regularly and whom she made welcome, albeit insincerely. This was so improbable that it was not even interesting. The only point of moment was the comparison which begged to be made between what constituted a sensation then and what did now.

My friend Yakov Gordin was at that time a patriot of the village of Mikhaylovskoe and he asked me to find out whether Akhmatova would sign a letter defending Pushkin's place of exile against the onslaughts of the builders who had it in mind to put a tall hotel block there. I passed the request on to Akhmatova and began explaining what he had explained to me, but she interrupted: "Do give me the letter. Although I should warn you that asking me is a mistake. The people has its favourite signatories. You know how they boast in Moscow: 'Yesterday our visitors included Shostakovich, Ulanova, academician Kapitsa, the Patriarch of All Russia and Yury Gagarin.'" I said that Gordin wanted to bring the letter himself. She suddenly laughed and recited:

> Arise, brother members, applaud him!
> Our literary order's ambition—
> A volume by Vladimir Gordin—
> Is out in a second edition.

I passed an invitation on to Yakov Gordin, and quoted the epigram; it turned out that Vladimir Gordin was one of his forefathers. Half a century later the butt of a harmless and stylish literary joke appeared before Akhmatova in the person of a supporter of a campaign to preserve a national literary monument.

During one of our comparatively early meetings I relayed to her the content of a monologue I had heard the day before from a mutual acquaintance. He asserted that art had already created a sufficiency to satisfy the needs of today; that the twentieth century had not offered anything genuinely new, and that if it had at first skimmed the cream from preceding centuries there was now no question even of that; that this situation was familiar from history—Rome had long made use of the art of Greece, and there was a multitude of other well-known examples; that there was nothing disparaging in this point of view because art was being replaced by life, which was free and outside its framework, let us say the yowl of a live cat in a symphony of concrete music; and that if there was anything still worth having it was at best a single frame from a film or a single line from a poem. "And it's not snobbery," I said, "as you know, he's a highly educated man who has surpassed everyone—" "Yes, yes. Unprepossessing but very talented, as they say of people like him," she intervened. "But it is snobbery, precisely because he is an educated man. I remember, in the 1910s one extremely educated young man returned from abroad and claimed that one could not say that there was nothing at all to see in the Louvre: he had found one thing. No, not painting—sculpture, and not even a complete sculpture but a fragment from an archaeological dig; in short, a bust, with no head, no arms—but what stone!"

It was as if she had a bottomless sack crammed full of her past and she could extract from it various things which she or the person she was talking to had need of: facts, episodes, or phrases; these were, if necessary, provided with punctilious notes on dates, places and circumstances, but they usually came without any indication of their origin. One day a mutual friend invited us separately to dinner and we came from different directions. I was quarter of an hour late and found nothing better by way of apology than to start explaining that I had been having a bath when they had switched the hot water off and so on—which was true. Akhmatova, already seated at the table, gave me an icy glare and as soon as I had finished said through clenched teeth, "Hygiene and morality": this was a slogan or title—the imprint of the age, as she had at some point remarked. On another occasion I received a fee I was not expecting and wanted to invite all the Ordynka Street crowd out to a restaurant, but she suggested instead that I buy a bucket of beer and a bucket of crayfish and turn up at the Ardovs', buckets in hand. This I did: I bought the buckets in a hardware shop, the crayfish in Sretenka Street and the beer at the Kadashevsky Baths, and everyone noisily did justice to the idea and its execution, gnawing the last claws and scooping the last of the beer from the bottom after one or more extra trips to the same baths. With the same heavy red face as the rest, but without their gusto or verbosity, she said, " 'God grant the same for Easter,' as our nurse's soldier used to say".

Some things recalled the 1910s, some the 1930s. When I was leaving after one of my first visits and putting on my coat in the hall, she helped me to get my arm into the sleeve. I was embarrassed, and almost pulled it out of her hand, muttering, "No, no!" She replied, "When a post-graduate student was leaving his house, academician Pavlov began helping him into his coat. He also grabbed it: 'you? helping me? that's not right!' And Pavlov said, 'Believe me, young man, I have no reason to ingratiate myself with you.'" And also—apropos of departures in general: "Mandelstam said that the most dreadful miscalculation in the world is the look in the host's eye which replaces the smile on his face a fraction of a second before the guest going out of the door has stopped looking at him." And in connection with the conversation about miscalculations, untimely actions and so on, she said that when Gumilyov was in Africa she stayed at home and hardly ever went out. Only once did she sleep at a girl friend's house. That night he came home. She came back in the morning, saw him, and, caught unawares, said that that was just the sort of thing that would have to happen—the first time in months she had spent the night away from home, and it had to be that day. Apparently her father was there, and either he or her husband commented when she fell silent: "That's how all you women get caught!"

After Sosnora visited her she said, "He read me a poem about the different ways people get drunk. A dreadful, absolutely obscene poem, but it will be popular. It has no mystery in it. He asked whether I knew that people were turning my 'Grey-Eyed King' into a song. I replied, 'God, how antiquated!' Even back in '47 they were singing 'All glory to thee, inescapable woe, they've taken the King of Romania's throne'."

She liked to refer to Mandelstam in the course of conversation and to quote various witty sayings of his. One of the undateable ones was: "Poles don't know how to fight wars, but rev-o-olts! ...", a somewhat cynical commentary on his poem 'Poles! I see no sense in desperate feats of arms'. One of the dateable ones was about Abram Efros. When André Gide came to Moscow, Efros was invited or instructed to act as guide to the famous writer. When Gide returned to France he wrote things about the Soviet Union which were not quite what had been expected and Efros was sent into exile, but "these were still vegetarian times" and he got off lightly. He was sent to Rostov the Great, comparatively close, and Mandelstam said, "It's not Rostov the Great, it's Abram the Great". Efros was the editor of *Rubens's Letters*, translated by Akhmatova. When the book was published he took her out to dinner to celebrate the event. The writers Kataev and Shklovsky happened to be in the same room in the restaurant and were a bit tight. They came up to the table, kissed Akhmatova's hand, asked ceremoniously for permission to sit down for a moment, made a few kind remarks, then took their leave, but before going Shklovsky decided to give himself a little pleasure and said, "Abram can invite a Russian woman to a restaurant and she'll still be on good terms with him afterwards" in a rephrasing of Babel's famous aphorism "Benya can invite a Russian woman to his bed and she'll still be on good terms with him afterwards."

The phrase "*Youth*, both on yourself and on me" in her note refers to the proposed publication in that journal of several of my poems. As they passed through each stage of the editorial process their number decreased by a factor of two or three until only one poem remained, and it too was thrown out at the last minute. She said, "I went through all that with Mandelstam. 'Let us have fifteen to choose eight from.' Out of those eight, the chief found three contained allusions, two were untimely, three could be printed. Rather, not three but two, for lack of space. And just in case, bring another one as a replacement ... This was sometimes the only one that got through." When her poems were printed in *Literary Russia* or, as it used to be called, *Literature and Life*, the "progressive intelligentsia" gave her to understand via subordinate clauses that she should not have consented to publish in that newspaper, so *reactionary* compared to *The Literary Gazette*, and that by so doing she had played into the hands of the opponents of progress. After one such conversation she said irritably, "They're all alike when it comes to *not* publishing me. Why should I go looking for microscopic differences when they do publish me?"

She was not taken in by superficial resemblances: "When NEP began, everything started to look as it had before—restaurants, smart cabmen, beautiful young women in furs and diamonds. But it was all 'like'—it was only pretending to be like it had been before, it was spurious. The past had disappeared irrevocably, its spirit, its people—the new was only an imitation of them. It was the same kind of difference as between the Association for Real Art and us."

"Why does everyone get so upset about what has happened to the Moscow Art Theatre? I disagree," she said, when this theatre was in its death throes as a theatre and still more so as the Moscow Art Theatre. "It had a beginning and it must have an end. It's not the *Comédie Française* or our Maly—they've been playing Ostrovsky there for a hundred years and will for a hundred more . . . Stanislavsky's breakthrough amounted to showing how Chekhov should be staged. He realised that this was a new kind of drama, and that it needed staging with new phrasing and with all those famous pauses. And after a grandiose flop at the Alexandrina Theatre he made the public flock to his *Seagull*. I recall, at that time, not going to the MAT was considered bad form, and teachers and doctors used to come up to Moscow from the provinces specially to see it. And after that everything that was similar to Chekhov or could be made similar to Chekhov became one of the theatre's successes and everything else was a failure. Then there was a war between the mice and the frogs because some people treated Stanislavsky's system as something like a faultless miracle-working icon, and other people could not forgive them for it. That's all. The beginning was then, the end is now."

She had lived through so many events that, for instance, a story about something which had happened in the 1950s might call up an echo from the 1920s. "When Roman Jakobson came to Moscow for the first time after the death of Stalin he was already a great man, a Slavist with a world-wide reputation. He was met at the airport, at the bottom of the steps from the plane, by the Academy of Sciences—all very solemn. Suddenly Lilya Brik burst through the barrier and ran to meet him, shouting 'Roma, don't give it away!'" A pause, then, with a little vengeful chuckle: "But Roma did." What she had in mind was Mayakovsky's love affair in Paris and his poems to the *émigrée* Tatyana Yakovleva, which the Briks had kept secret all those years.

I had the impression that, to quote Akhmatova's quotation of T. S. Eliot, "in my beginning is my end"—this is not only the perpetual shadow cast by death on to birth, and not only the roots of the future, concealed within a present so provocatively unlike what is to come; the end is the necessary complement of the beginning, and the beginning has no validity without the end. Her life seemed longer than the life of any other woman who was born and died at the same time because, of course, it was so eventful; because it did not simply include several historical epochs—it also expressed them; and because it seemed to brake, to linger, in order to witness the close of one more episode which had begun several decades earlier, and of yet another, in order to confirm one more supposition or one more observation; to see the end of each of her beginnings and thus the End of her Beginning, the completion of her destiny; to reach the point where she could say of all that was happening: *this* is like *that*, and say it, moreover, in such a way that "this is like that" became the sole true definition of what was happening. Not a comparison of two things based on the likeness or contrast of their attributes, not an arbitrary juxtaposition, but a necessary and natural union of the end and the beginning and, therefore, the incontrovertible truth about incontrovertible reality.

Two months before her death when she was already in hospital she read a slim volume of poems by Alice Meynell who was born a few years before Akhmatova and died in 1922. She chose two lines from it as an epigraph for her own poems:

> ... none dare
> Hope for a part in thy despair.

They remained unused, but one day similar words appeared at the head of Akhmatova's poems: "Don't lose despair"—a phrase of Punin's, either from a letter to her or from a conversation with her.

Even if a specific "this is like that" turned out to be erroneous, it did not destroy the truth of the principle itself or her general rightness. At the time when the newspapers were reporting the fanatical devotion of the Chinese to Mao-Zedong she said, "The Chinese devote themselves to one single idea for ten thousand years. I know—a top China specialist explained it to me. They follow Confucius for ten thousand years, then he vanishes like magic and something new appears, then that's there for another ten thousand years." The top China specialist could only have been V. M. Alekseev, but he would hardly have given this kind of explanation. She bestowed the name "the sage of China" on the poet Semyon Lipkin, known at that time as a translator, mainly of oriental poetry, and it looks as if this phrase came from the same popular source as the "ten thousand years". The Chinese love of Mao did not last that long, but Akhmatova's story about the Chinese was more convincing than the change of ideas which soon ensued, and it gave the impression that it was true, or at least should have been, even in the face of evidence to the contrary.

One October day in 1964 we were driving across the Kirov bridge in a taxi. The sky over the Neva was filled with low storm clouds with fluid outlines, but suddenly a pillar of light rose up from behind the Old Stock Exchange, vertically into the sky, and a red flush passed swiftly across it; if one was inclined to think there was something behind it, it was rather frightening. Then something like a cross-beam appeared towards the apex, and the clouds round that point dispersed for good, the sun came out, and the vision disappeared. Later we heard that Khrushchev had been ousted on that day. Akhmatova commented, "It's Lermontov's doing. Something awesome always happens on his anniversaries. The centenary of his birth, 1914, was the First World War; the centenary of his death, 1941, was the Great Fatherland War.

One hundred and fifty years is not such an important date and the event is watered down a little. But even so it comes with a sign from the heavens ..." She said: "I'm a Khrushchevite," on account of his having released people from Stalin's camps and officially revealed the fact of the terror. Her mention of Lermontov prompted her to recall a trip she had taken half a century before in a cab "so old that it could even have had Lermontov for a passenger"; Akhmatova's fifty years, and the cabman's nearly one hundred, and Lermontov's hundred and fifty, and her very personal and affectionate attitude towards him (as if she were his friend from a guild of poets, his older sister, or his "grandmama Arseneva") were all so intertwined that in some mysterious way they extended her own life to almost twice its length, and at the same time removed the fall of Khrushchev from the present moment and placed it in a series of generally dynamic events, such as the Decembrist revolt, other revolts, palace coups, etc. "One could say 'he's my favourite poet' of Lermontov *ad infinitum*," she remarked one day. "But to say it about Pushkin is like saying 'I am finishing my letter and Jupiter, my husband's favourite planet, is looking in at the window,' to quote what Shchepkina-Kupernik came out with when she wrote to Ranevskaya."

The context of her biography recast everything which came into her orbit "in its own image"—even peripheral phenomena, and even those which were alien to her. "In Tashkent," she recalled, "the flat below was taken by some anti-Fascists who had escaped from Hitler's Reich at one time. They swore at one another and fought so much that I thought, if anti-Fascists are like this, what are Fascists like!" In her remark one suddenly saw a Mussolini, a dunce in an early romantic aura, come peeping out from behind the swear-word "Fascist", the symbol, the animal. Equally "Akhmatovan" was her description of phoney, spurious people, books and ideas as "inflated/stuffed", a phrase she had acquired from a manufacturer's list of assorted products: "inflated/ stuffed toy". Also the phrase "the aspirations of the people", acquired from the newspapers and used for wish-fulfilment dreams.

When we could not agree and each of us stuck to our own point of view, especially if it was some practical matter, she would frequently declare with mock aplomb, "Who is the mother of Zoya Kosmodemyanskaya, you or me?" The first time I heard this I asked her where it came from. She said that after the war they were choosing a site in Stalingrad to build a new tractor factory in place of one which had been destroyed, and a member of the committee, one of the representatives from official organisations, was the mother of Zoya Kosmodemyanskaya. Zoya was famous for her exploits as a partisan and had been hung by the Germans at the beginning of the war. To everyone's surprise she suddenly announced in a tone which brooked no contradiction that it should not be built on the site favoured by the experts but right here, and when they tried politely to make her see reason she asked this rhetorical, classically killing question: "Who is the mother of Zoya Kosmodemyanskaya, you or me?"

She made other writers' material her own with such ease that it was as if she were taking back what she had lent, and if one looks into the process a little more deeply one sees that this is indeed what happened. When I returned from my visit to Brodsky I told her how cosy it was there in the evenings with the stove banked up, listening to the radio, which gradually filled the Vologda darkness outside the windows with the ghosts of Paris, Leningrad and London. I also told her that we had heard a programme about a dinner given in Priestley's honour by some society or club, and that we had both been moved by the incisive conclusion of his speech of thanks in which he quoted Edgar's words from *King Lear* on man's powerlessness to choose the moment of his arrival in the world and departure from it, ending with the famous "Ripeness is all." Brodsky later used the whole of this speech of Edgar's as an epigraph for one of his books, and Akhmatova noted in her diary immediately after I had spoken to her "K.L.—is all", as if attaching no great importance to it. At about the same time she met a woman, a writer from Leningrad, who had served during the war as something like an able seaman in either the Baltic or the Northern Fleet, and was now very active in defending justice and trying to liberate "that young shaver Brodsky" from "those parasites". She insisted on having an interview with Akhmatova, partly out of strategic considerations and partly out of curiosity, but when she left the room afterwards she was disappointed: "She's hard of hearing and we need A1 people." When I went in, Akhmatova, by contrast, looked pleased: she had liked the visitor and to my "Well, how was it?" she replied approvingly, "The marines." Brodsky soon conjoined both themes—exile and the military—and resolved them: when he was released, he came to Komarovo, and immediately began digging Akhmatova a shelter under the Cabin. When I came back from the forest I found him up to his shoulders in the pit and her standing at the window, smiling, but a little perplexed: "He says it's in case they drop atom bombs." I could hear a question in her voice and replied, "He's got a diploma—he's an expert on anti-atomic defence."

❖ ❖ ❖

In one conversation I said that I had noticed that people who were compelled to keep retreating from one position to another compensated for it with a desire to make something within themselves so impregnable that it could also withstand their own weakness; and that something was often resentment. She responded sharply: "In no circumstances should one nourish that monster. Let it die of hunger. Resentment has terrible results: look at Gorodetsky." And a little while later: "When someone has lived as long as I have they get certain final ideas . . . It is just as difficult to do good as it is easy to do evil. One must force oneself to do good." "She's such a good person," she would say joyfully, meaning her brother Viktor's first wife, the selfless obliging Khanna Gorenko, who would come from Riga as soon as she was asked. Even when she was angry with her, tenderness could be heard in her words: "Khanna presumed".

I brought a poem for her to see which I had dedicated to her and which, to judge by various signs, seemed to be to her taste. The next day she talked about it in some detail and then went on to something else, and then she suddenly interrupted herself as if she had just remembered something: "Oh yes. You've got one foot too many in one of the lines, you should put that right." I counted the feet in my head, then when I had left the room I counted on my fingers, and when I got home I jotted down a diagram—there was no extra foot. Next time we met I told her this but she did not listen: "There *is* one too many, there's no need to check, I'm not mistaken. I've spent fifty years plying my trade." Her obstinacy annoyed me and only in retrospect did I realise what it meant: the foot was not superfluous to the metre but to the musical rhythm; the line needed to be shortened and broken up; its length made it weak. This was one more case of her being right in contradiction to the rules, one of the most obvious cases, not one of the most profound ones. It was a truth which she could advocate by referring to the fact that she had been in the trade for fifty years.

❖ ❖ ❖

Of the several dozen portraits of Akhmatova, Altman's was particularly appreciated, although she liked Tyshler's and Tyrsa's better. Perhaps this was because Altman had painted her in her life's happy days, or the sittings had taken place in a specially friendly and intimate atmosphere and were associated with something which was pleasant to recall in retrospect, or because this was her first "famous" portrait. Speaking of Altman, she said that after they had met frequently in the 1910s he had disappeared for almost thirty years and then suddenly telephoned: "Anna Andreevna, are you busy just now?" "No." "Shall I come round then?" "Yes." "And he came round, exactly as if that was how it ought to be, and we talked as easily as if we had seen each other the previous day." "When he was painting me, some foreigner used to come up to his studio, look at the picture, and say, 'That ... will be ... a great ... *zmyaz*!'" From time to time she would repeat this Pythian sentence but she never explained what this mysterious word meant. I thought it derived from *smekh*, "laugh", and was something like the noun *smeyas*, "laughing"—which conveyed too the grandeur of the thing, of the event. The phrase turned out to be more or less universal and was suited to almost everything that happened to Akhmatova. "That will be a great *zmyaz*" applied to her visit to England to get her academic gown, Brodsky's trial, her plan to have her coat remodelled, and *Requiem* coming out abroad ...

There were a number of such sayings, halfway between puns and prophecies. One of the letters she wrote to me in hospital mentions an illness which I had "got through without a doctor" a year earlier. That was at the end of the summer and when she heard about it she "dispatched" Brodsky from Leningrad to visit me, just as she dispatched me to see Olshevskaya shortly after. She gave him a new poem for me. This was 'Thirteen Lines', copied out in his hand and certified with her signature.

> At last you spoke the word—and to my ears
> Not like that lot ... the kneelers down ... you sounded,
> But like a captive broken free who bounded
> Towards sheltering sacred shades of birch, and peers
> Across a rainbow film of tears.
> Around you then the silence turned to song,
> And through the dusk the purest sunlight glistened,
> The world transformed itself for just an instant,
> And wine was strangely altered on the tongue.
> And even I, who was to be the knife
> By which the godly word would meet its slaughter,

Fell reverently still, lest I make shorter,
When I would yet draw out, its blessed life.

However, it was only twelve lines long, apparently on purpose, since he
had overlooked one and she had not noticed. In the first conversation
we had about the poem I began to object to "was to be": "And even I,
who was to be the knife by which the godly word would meet its
slaughter"—because if this "was to be", then "I" and "you" do not have
equal status in the poem. The hero is in the heroine's power; he only
plays out the role of participant in the drama, and does not have an
independent part in it. She agreed with the argument, but defended the
poem, gently—mainly on the grounds that "it has come out well". A
year or eighteen months later, after a similar but more vociferous
argument about a quatrain in *Prologue*, she took a rubber and rubbed
out the pencil-written lines in her notebook. But that time she laughed
and said, "You remind me of Kolya. He said that all my poetry was
summed up in the Ukrainian folk song

> I poured it out myself,
>   Oh, why not?
> I drunk it up myself—
>   Oh, my God!"

And she continued without pausing: "But to make up for it, when he
came back from Abyssinia they sang him 'Where were you in the
demons' arms? We'd have married you off at home!' That's good too,
even though it's not as apt."

Her acute ear ("a dog's ear", "like a borzoi's", if one may use remarks
she made about others) would listen to ordinary conversation, radio
programmes, or poems she read, and pick up a few words which, in her
voice and emphasised and removed from their original context,
acquired a new sense, aspect, and weight. "I will steal into here as a
shadow", she picked out one of my lines. "It will serve as an epigraph. It
has an incorrect stress—it's a good line." Another time I was reading
Suetonius, who had just been re-published, and I came across a wonderful remark: "Virgil had no lack of denigrators," and she responded: "A
first-class epigraph." And of the book itself she said one day, "In any

case it's useful to read Suetonius, Plutarch, Tacitus and the rest. Something remains with one all one's life. I know from my own experience: I remember some writers from my school days, and others from my 'great insomnia' when I read masses of books ... The 'soldier Caesars' are more appealing than their predecessors, except for Caius Julius perhaps. I can't forgive 'the divine Augustus' for sending Ovid into exile. Even if it was a shady business, it's another case of a tsar destroying a poet." And also: "We know as much about Rome as we know little about Athens," that is—Roman civilisation is the foundation of European civilisation in general, but the state, culture, and life of ancient Greece do not resemble anything else.

On one of the Pushkin anniversaries (125 years since his death?) *The Literary Gazette* printed a short article which claimed that, judging by the ricochet of the bullet, d'Anthès had probably worn mail when he fought the duel in which the poet was killed. "Who wrote it?" she almost bellowed in rage. I said I thought it was Gessen. "It's Gessen who would have gone to the duel wearing mail!"—it was as if she too fired again. "You know how fond of d'Anthès *I* am, but he was in the Horse Guards, he was the son of an ambassador, a man of the world, and he could never have thought of such a thing: death would have been a blessing for anyone who went out to fight and took precautions of that kind!" "In general that's typical of jubilee revelations. Once every ten or twenty years they unearth completely new cast-iron proof of the fact that Pushkin was murdered by d'Anthès, Salieri poisoned Mozart, Boyan wrote *The Lay of Igor's Host* and that the *Iliad* and the *Odyssey* were not written by Homer but by some other old man, who was also blind."

One hot summer evening in 1963 we went to visit Mariya Petrovykh. Akhmatova was then staying at Ordynka Street. At about midnight I was sent to get a taxi and went as usual to the petrol-station in Begovaya Street: they came there at that time to fill up, one after the other. I got in and started showing the driver the way: it was only a few yards, but down narrow winding branching avenues, thick with greenery moreover, and past identical little houses, scattered erratically over a wide area. It was soon obvious that we had got lost. At this point a mighty female figure in a nightshirt appeared at the open dark window of the nearest house, attracted by the noise of the car. I got out and asked where no. 2 was, and she asked who I was looking for. I observed for her edification that that didn't matter, I was just looking for no. 2. She leant on the window-sill and objected yet more edifyingly that everything mattered to public-spirited people. At that moment a policeman, a man in civilian clothes, and a woman came out of the bushes smelling of alcohol. The policeman enquired what the matter was and demanded to see my "document". Hardly had I got it out when the man in civilian clothes put my identity card in his pocket without looking at it, and dived on to the back seat of the taxi, whence he ordered everyone to come to the police station. I climbed in to retrieve my "document" but the policeman gave me an adroit push, and squeezed himself in, so that I found myself sitting between them. The woman got in the front and the doors slammed. The driver did not like this at all, and said rudely that he wasn't going anywhere until he was paid. The civilian showed him *his* identity card, threatened him with reprisals, and we moved off slowly. At that very second I saw no. 2 with a brightly lit window on the first floor and shouted, "Stop!"—the car stopped. The policeman agreed to get out, though the other man resisted with all his might. We went up the stairs together and I rang the bell. Mariya Sergeevna opened the door and we tumbled in. The policeman was embarrassed, but pointed at me and said, "Do you know this citizen?" Akhmatova was sitting at the table, almost with her back to the door; she did not turn round, but simply turned her head a few degrees in our direction to show that she could see us, and said slowly, "Yes, he's our friend . . . " and gave my first name, patronymic and surname. They gave me back my identity card, and the guardians of law and order departed. We went downstairs and drove off. On the way I told Akhmatova what had happened and the driver added a few embellishments to my story, such as "tattered old bivouacker" for the woman who had been sitting next to him. Akhmatova listened to the very end, and then quoted a line by the eighteenth-century poet Feofan Prokopovich: "What is it, Russes, that we do?" I saw her to the Ardovs' flat and went home in the same taxi. When I said goodbye to the driver, he commented, "The old lady summed it up just right. Honestly, how we Russians kick each other in the teeth!" The next day I told her this and she was pleased, but remarked, " 'Bivouacker' was better. She really was a bivouacker."

In her lifetime she had accumulated a number of versatile expressions which she used to label vast areas of human experience and indeed the human condition itself; there was a regular demand for one from Vyazemsky or possibly Gorbunov: "and it's good for the bown brear". This was one of the few which she liked to accompany with the story from which it came. "One winter a peasant gallops up to the Shere-metevs' town mansion to tell the ladies and gentlemen that they have tracked down a brown bear and the whole village has it cornered. The ladies and gentlemen begin getting their things together quickly and send the messenger off to the kitchen to have a glass of vodka. There all the servants crowd round him, asking questions and mulling things over. 'It's a good thing for you—the ladies and gentlemen have noticed you.' 'Yes, it's a good thing for me,' he concedes languidly, flattered by all the attention. 'And it's a good thing for the ladies and gentlemen, they'll enjoy themselves.' 'Yes, it's a good thing for the ladies and gentlemen.' 'And for the peasants—no doubt they'll get a silver rouble each.' 'Yes, it's a good thing for the peasants.' 'And it's a good thing for the womenfolk—they'll feed everyone and get a present or two.' The servants gradually tire. 'Yes, it's a good thing for the womenfolk,' agrees the hero. 'And it's a good thing for the bown brear!' 'Yes, of course it's a good thing for the bown brear!' he confirms authoritatively."

She was sometimes capricious, despotic, and unjust to people, she behaved selfishly at times, and she collected, as if for show, her readers' latest raptures, the shyness and trepidation of her admirers, and admiration itself as the definitive attitude to her, adding them to the phenomenon and concept of "Anna Akhmatova". Consciously or unconsciously she encouraged people in their desire to see in her an exceptional figure of greater stature than themselves, someone unique, important to them as a living example of the superiority and stature which human beings can attain. And the fact that she really was a figure of this kind was apparently the motivation for her behaviour, her behaviour seemed to be the most important thing, important in itself.

As the years went by, her essence and her behaviour, put themselves into proportion. Attracting admiration and repeated compliments now seemed not a manifestation of or tribute to egoism, but rather the contrary—a constantly troubling reminder of the necessity of giving "one's life for one's friends". She did not exclude herself from the axiom that the disciple is not greater than the teacher. She knew that she was inferior to Vyacheslav Ivanov in erudition, to Nedobrovo in subtlety, to Gumilyov in confidence—the names and qualities are here taken almost at random—but she surpassed them in talent, and Time had put the demand for talent above all else. Different periods value different things, and now the need was not for prodigious knowledge, philosophical systems, religious or moral teachings, etc., but, primarily, for talent, for talent and an audacious manifestation of it; Akhmatova possessed both the talent and the necessary boldness. It thus fell to her to speak for all to hear on behalf of those from whom she had learnt things, and who, for one reason or another, had not spoken themselves, those on whose drafts she wrote, as she says in *Poem without a Hero*. And she succeeded in so doing. It was for them, all those on the oddly assorted list, from her mother and father, Olga Glebova-Sudeykina, and Lozinsky to Dante and Homer—via herself—that she collected glory.

However, the knowledge, principles, and criteria which she had assimilated from and through living teachers (combined with her powerful and flexible intelligence) and, most important, her common sense, which matched her talent in its extent and comprehensiveness, set boundaries to the freedom and unpredictability of her writing, and thus to her genius. "An everlasting childhood is his prize," she wrote of this aspect of Pasternak's gifts, with admiration but also condescension, and not without a hint of sarcasm, as if to say, "How long can one be like this for?" His poems bubbled over the edge of an Acmeistically structured universe; he declared provocatively that Goncharova, who did not understand her husband, was a better wife for Pushkin than Shchegolev and recent Pushkin scholars, and that Shakespeare was a long time in finding the right word and therefore dragged his scenes out; his lapses of taste, such as 'Oh, those love bites around women's necks' or 'Hops', which she did not forgive him for, were just as striking as his undoubted successes. In short, he "put himself above art", as Chukovskaya records her saying. She said that Mandelstam's "stale staircases" ("on stale staircases, on city squares . . . Alighieri sang the rounds of Florence . . . ") were legitimate, justified by Dante's "strangers' bread", but "bareheaded grass" was a taboo device.

When a book of translations of Rilke came out, undertaken by a person she knew well and respected, she said sadly that everything was as it should be, but he had not caught the greatness of the poetry. We talked about 'Requiem für eine Freundin', which was not in the book. I said this was a poem of sheer genius: she dies, but she remains part of life, she is resurrected, and the poet begs her not to come to him . . . "That is terrible," Akhmatova responded directly. "And it is the *sine qua non* of genius. She comes to him after she has died and he says, 'No, I'm sorry, please don't'. Or there's Tolstoy who fails to notice *what* he makes the woman in *Father Sergius* do. And then Sergius cuts off his finger, or doesn't—as if I need that after what has happened already.

But Tolstoy is only interested in what happens at a distance, out there ... Dostoevsky, though! Mitya Karamazov is a real murderer: he hits Grigory so hard that he falls to the ground with his skull split open. But geniuses—because they are geniuses—do this in such a way that no one notices ..." I said that, dispensing with flattery, Akhmatova was not a genius but some kind of *anti-genius* ... She listened to this with displeasure and growled, "I don't know, I don't know." I explained that I had used this term in a positive sense, using the analogy of the antiproton, for example: "It doesn't imply anything offensive, still less anything bad ..." She ended humorously, making peace: "I'm almost sure that it can imply, but there's no one to ask."

Need one say that these boundaries did not in the least constitute an obstacle to art? They lay within it, and marked internal limits, but did not fence it in. She said that, strictly speaking, Dostoevsky did not write a single novel apart from *Crime and Punishment*: in the others "the main events take place before the beginning, somewhere in Switzerland; but in that book everything is topsy-turvy, the reader gasps for breath, everything is dreadful ..." And she immediately added: "But generally speaking real prose-writers have the devil's own kitchen. In the course of their lives they write five times more than eventually gets into their complete collected works. That is why I don't believe one writes a major novel and nothing else after it, like Sholokhov." (This observation may have been inspired by Kafka's *Diaries* which she was reading in a French translation at the time. The entry for 17 December 1910 reads: "I am also greatly hindered in writing by the fact that I have thrown so much out and crossed so much out—and this I have done with practically everything I have written this year. There is a whole mountain of it, five times bigger than the writing I have ever finished, and by virtue of its very mass it runs away with everything I write, straight from beneath the pen.")

She explained that Pushkin studies were unlikely to have any very significant results in the near future because Pushkin scholars needed not only the flair, talent, diligence and other qualities which all scholars must have, but also a good knowledge of French, English and the history of the period, and this combination was now so rare. She insisted that a writer should have the erudition of a Thomas Mann and she quoted his *Der Zauberberg* as an example, with the reservation, to be sure, that the disquisitions on time were not on the same level as the rest of the book, for which she seemed to have a specifically personal affection, perhaps on account of the descriptions of life in a sanatorium for tuberculosis sufferers. I read it when I was in hospital, and she said, "It's just the thing to read in hospital."

But even so she singled out Kharms as a prose-writer: "He had great talent. He succeeded in writing what hardly anyone else could: so-called 'twentieth-century prose': when they describe, let's say, the hero going out of the house and suddenly flying through the air. No one else has him fly, but Kharms does." She said, "Freud is art's enemy number one. The light in art saves people from the darkness within. But Freudian theory seeks an explanation for all that is gross and foul on the level of the gross and foul—and that is why it is so beloved by the man in the street. Art wants to cure people, but Freudian theory leaves them with their illnesses, having driven them down more deeply inside. In Freud's view there are no purgative sufferings, no journeys from darkness into light as in *Brothers Karamazov*, but only a few rather disgusting reasons why, given certain relations between father and mother and particular childhood experiences, nothing could have happened except what did happen. And what use is that?" She told me about a letter one of her female friends had written to another, Nadezhda Yakovlevna Mandelstam, on the subject of a book written by Khazin, N.Ya.'s brother. "He had written a novel—about 1812, I think: what do people write about to save themselves from dying of starvation? And she said amongst other things, in praise of the author, that he knew how to prattle, and that this was indispensable to a real writer. And then she said—I read it with my own eyes, because Nadya wanted to set me against her and showed me the letter: 'Everyone knows that, even Anna Andreevna.' I must admit that she was the one who set me against Nadya." She chuckled, but the fact that prose needs to prattle, that it requires superfluity, "gratuitous detail", was for her an absolutely elementary fact about art. It was, perhaps, because "everybody knows this" now that she considered the prose written in the middle of the century superior to that written in her youth, which produced such shining pearls as "The steppe was tactfully silent", some author's gem subsequently taken up by Mandelstam. She liked Aksyonov's story 'Victory' and Rid Grachev's 'Suspicion' a few years earlier. But "superior" and "inferior" referred to the overall standard of prose writing at those times—in 1910 Lev Tolstoy was still writing: "all ze same", as she joked.

She put most store not by freedom, which is not bound by rules, nor by the unpredictability of genius, but by mystery. "There is mystery in this poem," was her first *real* plaudit. Another, "There is song in this poem," was spoken exceptionally rarely and I heard it only twice, in connection with Blok and Brodsky, apropos of the latter's 'Christmas Romance' and his poetry in general. Brodsky once began arguing heatedly that some of Blok's books of poems were entirely unsatisfactory. "That is not true," Akhmatova objected calmly. "Like every poet Blok has unsatisfactory, middling and good poems." But after he had gone, she said, "There is song in his poems too"—she had said the same of Blok previously—"perhaps that is why he attacks him like that."

As Louis Armstrong remarked, "At first I thought people needed a song, but I soon realised they needed a show." As far as mystery is concerned, in Akhmatova's lifetime it began to give way to hinting, and after her death the poetry of hints became generally accepted and recognised. In the 1970s such poets had a large devoted audience, educated by themselves, which understood perfectly what political event or personality was intended in a poem about angling: the "tiddlers" meant the young people and the "nets" the censor. This was Symbolism in reverse, the poetry of the second half of the twentieth century.

❖　　　❖　　　❖

It is true that she endowed the trifles which entered her sphere of attention with a grandiosity which seemed excessive to those around her. This was the result of the scale of her personality, the effect of opening the dividers too wide: we imagine that one thousand millimetres is much less than one-thousandth of a kilometre. When she needed confirmation of some fact in the history of the 1910s, she telephoned Olga Nikolaevna Vysotskaya, formerly an actress, whose son by Gumilyov was a little younger than her own son Lev Nikolaevich, and she asked her to come to see her. Boris Ardov and I brought her from Polyanka Street to Ordynka Street by taxi. Akhmatova sat in majesty, with her hair carefully combed, wearing an attractive dress and lipstick, surrounded by respect and consideration, but her erstwhile rival was feeble, old, broken by fate, as it were. She confirmed one of the facts of the kind which is described in Akhmatova's poem 'Can you really leave gaping lacunae in the glorious tale of your life?', in my view a fact of secondary importance, and Akhmatova arranged for her to be

215

taken home; she had confirmed the fact—and confirmed Akhmatova's victory. This sector of the front was also of secondary importance and did not require such high-calibre artillery, but she had no other.

This goes a long way towards explaining her so-called exaggerations and her conclusions which "did not follow from anything". In 1940 Chukovskaya recorded some words spoken by V. G. Garshin, who was intimate with Akhmatova at that time: "Have you noticed that she always takes some highly dubious fact as her foundation, and constructs arguments upon it with cast-iron consistency and incontrovertible logic?" And Isaiah Berlin recalls the same thing:

Her accounts of the personalities and acts of others were compounded of sharp insight into the moral centre of characters and situations [...] together with a dogmatic obstinacy in attributing motives and intentions [...] which even to me—who often did not know the facts—seemed implausible, and indeed, at times, fanciful [...] It seemed to me that upon dogmatically held premises Akhmatova constructed theories and hypotheses which she developed with extraordinary coherence and lucidity. Her unwavering conviction that our meeting had had serious historical consequences was an example of such *idées fixes*; she also believed that Stalin had given orders that she should be slowly poisoned, then countermanded them; that Mandel'shtam's belief, shortly before his end, that the food he was given in the labour camp was poisoned was well founded; that the poet Georgy Ivanov (whom she accused of having written lying memoirs after he emigrated) had at one time been a police spy in the pay of the tsarist government; that the poet Nekrasov in the nineteenth century must also have been a government agent; that Innokenty Annensky had been hounded to death by his enemies. These beliefs had no apparent foundation in fact—they were intuitive, but they were not senseless, not sheer fantasies; they were elements in a coherent conception of her own and her nation's life and fate, of the central issues which Pasternak had wanted to discuss with Stalin, the vision which sustained and shaped her imagination and her art. She was not a visionary, she had, for the most part, a strong sense of reality.

Nedobrovo, writing about a different matter, but describing the same characteristic, says of the young Akhmatova, who was then just beginning her career: "Unhappy love, which has pierced the innermost core of her personality, and which at the same time by virtue of its strangeness and propensity to disappear without warning *inspires the suspicion that it is fantasised*, so that it seems a *self-made* spectre, torments her soul even to bodily pain—this love calls much into question for the person who must undergo it . . . " [italics mine.]

The words of Garshin and Berlin would also serve to explain much of what happened in Akhmatova's later years, as well as unexpected twists in situations and conversations, and several letters. The words and phrases which I have emphasised in Nedobrovo's article describe one aspect of the reality behind *Prologue*, 'Midnight Verses' and other poems relating to that cycle. One might be inclined to say that her behaviour was *inadequate*, did not the *general direction* of her behaviour consist, on closer scrutiny, of a multitude of responses to what was happening, all of them absolutely adequate to the specific event. Everything she did was spot on and had the exactness of medicine or of the police. A few tiny brown specks on the eyeball, linked into a circle by the finest of veins, formed "that wreath all rusty and barbed"; and indeed a chiromancer could read "those same miracles upon her palm".

She observed these and other less distinct details of reality all the more acutely because her whole life was lived, from her earliest youth, under the sign *memento mori*. Perhaps the fabric of her later poetry is so fine because death had taken on irreversible and indisputable features—those of old age and illness.

I received two letters from her while she was in the Botkin Hospital, where she was taken in November 1965 when she had a heart attack. There were several patients in the ward, and because she was hard of hearing one had to speak loudly to her; we therefore wrote each other notes on scraps of paper when necessary, but these two were sent by post when I had left for Leningrad.

2 January 1966

Dear Tolya,

I am writing to you because you wanted me to, and Marusya makes me, but I do not feel ready to write letters yet.

You know all about me, and Joseph saw that I could walk, read a little, did not sleep all the time, and had started to eat.

217

Thank you for the letters and telegrams, the last telegram even brought me some happiness.

Moscow has been a good mother to me, everyone here is kind.

I am expecting the lyrics of Egypt.

Regards to all.

Akhmatova

31 Jan 1966

Dear Tolya,

Have forgotten your address and am therefore intending to trouble Asya Davydovna.

Thank you for your fairly intelligible telegram.

Yesterday Misha Meylakh and Arseny were here, but I was hardly functioning. This was because of the medicine, wh. has been stopped today. No news, of course, apart from one thing, of a surprising kind. Don't be inquisitive.

Am writing my recollections of Lozinsky, but they are coming out flabby and just a little tearful.

For my part I send greetings to my dear fellow-citizens.

Give my respects to your parents [...] Please ring Nina.

A.

[On the reverse is my mother's address and the return address:]
From Akhmatova A.A., Block 6,
Botkin Hospital, Moscow

Arseny is Arseny Aleksandrovich Tarkovsky, a poet who first won recognition in the 1960s, when he was already over fifty, had come through a war which maimed him, and had been writing poetry for more than a quarter of a century. By this time he had known Akhmatova for several years. He read her poems written at various times, and she once said affectionately, "With these very hands I dragged Arseny from the pyre of Mandelstam"—that is, she had helped him to free himself from Mandelstam's influence.

When she was a little better and was about to be discharged, I went to the hospital several times, dropping in at the racecourse nearby on my way. One day when it was frosty and cold I went in and, thinking that she might smell the brandy which I had just downed in the snack bar to get warm, I decided to avoid an explanation with the not very inventive, "You'll never guess where I've just been." Her expression showed that this was of no interest. I said, "At the racecourse!" She replied indifferently, "That's all I ever hear about you". And with a hardly noticeable wave of the hand she gave me to understand that both the explanation and its clumsiness were over and done with, and she began talking about something more important. Betting on the horses was a game, perhaps a failing, but not a vice, and in any event nothing to do with ideas. When she read the line "We shall fight a war at cards" in a love poem of Brodsky's, she frowned and voiced her disapproval.

The Flight of Time had only just come out and she was inscribing several copies a day. A fair number of poems of central importance had not been included in it, and she still nourished the hope of printing many of those which had been removed; a note of bitterness could clearly be heard in the words of gratitude with which she responded to compliments. She was confident that they would be published sooner or later and she wanted this to be done now, in her lifetime, while the poems were still alive and fierce, "with horns, hooves and a tail" and not reduced to sacred (least of all, edible) cows, modelled out of the sausage-meat which the publisher would churn out of the mincer of his own times.

The nurses, cleaners, and her fellow patients from the ward who had been, or were being, deserted by their husbands and lovers came to talk to her as "an authority on women's experience of love" and, to quote *Requiem*, they spoke the "poor words" which she had "overheard from them" and in part taught them. Each said the same as the next, and the same as Akhmatova, only less clearly and rigorously. She was "an authority on love" because love was her poetry: "one less hope, one more song", as she wrote in one poem. Love as experienced by women was not a special kind of love distinctive to the female, but a more deeply felt, profound and complete love, a better love, as Tiresias attested long ago. "It's a scientific fact that men are an inferior race," she declared. Or: "If one thinks about it, ewes are also to be pitied: they only have one husband between them, and he's a ram." She took pity on all those who came to her bedside, and "rendered them first aid"—and laughed a little both at them and at herself, quoting a phrase which I had heard and which she had immediately "taken into her arsenal": "I'm not jealous, I'm just disgusted." She took pity on women in general and comforted them all. Her own early poem 'I do not ask you for your love' irritated her:

> These little fools have greater need
> Of knowing that the triumph's theirs
> Than sharing friendship's joyous talk
> Or treasuring those first sweet days.

"Why 'these little fools'?" she asked with exasperation. "If he's transferred his feelings to another woman, must she then automatically be a fool?" That is why she disliked Tsvetaeva's poem 'An Attempt at Jealousy' ("How are you doing with that trash?", "How are you doing with that mass-production female?")—"the tone women market-traders use".

In mid-February, on the 19th I think, she was discharged, and places had been obtained for her and Olshevskaya at a sanatorium for the beginning of March. During those ten to twelve days at Ordynka Street she sometimes got better and sometimes worse: they had to call the emergency medical team, she would be given injections, they would hurry for the oxygen supplies.

On 5 March I set off for Domodedovo with a bouquet of narcissi. When I was saying goodbye to her on the 3rd we had arranged that I would come and make a fair copy of her memoirs of Lozinsky before they were sent in to the journal. They were ready in draft and required only finishing touches and collation. Midday was sunny and carried the promise of spring, then a grey shroud began to spread across the sky—I later observed that this often happens on this day in March and just before and after. A woman in a white coat met me in the vestibule and walked down the corridor with me, saying something anxious, the sense of which I did not understand. When we went into the ward, Nina Antonovna was lying in bed and breathing with difficulty—she had been given a sedative, I discovered. By her side stood a tear-stained Anya Kaminskaya who had just arrived. The woman in the white coat closed the door behind me and said that Akhmatova had died two hours before. She was lying in the next ward, her face covered by a sheet. When I kissed her forehead it was already quite cold.

The celebration of International Women's Day on 8 March put the funeral back by several days. The fact that she had died on the anniversary of Stalin's death was recalled only later. On 9 March there was a civil funeral in the morgue of the Sklifosovsky Institute, then the coffin was sealed and flown to Leningrad. There was a burial service on 10 March in the Naval Cathedral of St Nicholas and for many hours people came to pay their last respects, then in the second part of the day she was buried in the cemetery at Komarovo.

Two of the books which she gave me are linked by her inscriptions. On *Anno Domini MCMXXI*: "To Anatoly Nayman as he sets out on his path. Anna Akhmatova, 23 April 1963, Leningrad". And exactly two years later on an offprint from *Apollo* of her poem 'At the Edge of the Sea': "To Anatoly Nayman—and now my path begins at Crystal Bay. A. 23 April 1965, Leningrad". She had brought her time with her and had taken it away: if she were alive today, there would be no place for her—"we would not even recognise" her if she returned, as she wrote in her elegy. In her last inscription the letter "a", written as a small letter the same size as a capital, is lightly crossed through with a horizontal stroke.

1986–1987

Notes

1. The ghosts of 1913, which Akhmatova evokes in *Poem without a Hero*, are the shades of the people she knew in Petersburg before the revolution.
2. The theme of the double pervades Akhmatova's poetry.
3. Nikolay (Kolya) Stepanovich Gumilyov (1886–1921), poet, member of the Poets' Guild and writer of a manifesto for the Acmeist school. Akhmatova's first husband (married 1910, divorced 1918). Fought in the White Army, arrested and executed by the Bolsheviks on false charges.
4. Akhmatova and Modigliani ("Modi") met in Paris in 1912, before either was well known. Modigliani did a series of drawings of her, of which only one survived.
5. Joseph Brodsky (b. 1940), poet, in his youth Akhmatova's protégé and friend. Tried and sentenced for parasitism in 1964, emigrated to the United States in 1972. Awarded the Nobel Prize for Literature in 1987.
6. Osip Emilevich Mandelstam (1891–1938), poet, essayist, and friend of Akhmatova. A member of the Poets' Guild, the nucleus of the Acmeist movement in poetry. Sentenced to internal exile, arrested, and died in a labour camp.
7. After the death of Stalin the truth about his gross abuse of power, hitherto spoken of only by a few and in private, began to be spread. Khrushchev made his secret speech to the Twentieth Party Congress in 1956. Millions returned from labour camps and exile and the extent of collaboration with or opposition to the Stalin regime became clear.
8. Boris Leonidovich Pasternak (1890–1960), poet and prose-writer. Akhmatova and Pasternak were not close friends, but met and corresponded periodically. In spite of her criticisms of Pasternak, Akhmatova held him in high regard and viewed him as one of "us four" poets, along with Mandelstam and Tsvetaeva.
9. Marina Ivanovna Tsvetaeva (1892–1941), poet. Until latterly in official disfavour for her politics and her emigration from the Soviet Union. Wrote poems to Akhmatova before the revolution. Met Akhmatova after she returned to the USSR in 1939, when Akhmatova celebrated their spiritual closeness in a poem. Committed suicide.
10. Maxim Gorky (1868–1936), writer of autobiography, novels, plays, and short stories, was held up from the 1930s onwards as a model for Soviet writers, largely on account of his explicit commitment to the Party. The political enthusiasm of his novel *Mother* (1906) was considered all-important. Its literary quality is poor.
11. Akhmatova consistently quashed stories about her supposed affair with the most famous poet of the time, Aleksandr Aleksandrovich Blok (1880–1921), inspired by the

223

(few) poems they addressed to each other. Blok was one of the younger generation of Symbolist poets, whose later poems record the moral and spiritual decline of Imperial Russia.

12.   Akhmatova's connections with Tsarskoe Selo, the little town in which the summer residence stood, subsequently provided her critics with ammunition for their denunciation.

13.   Grand Princess Anna of Kashin (d. 1368) became a nun and was canonised. Her life had something in common with her namesake's, whose husband was put to death on false evidence, and whose veneration was partially banned for a long time. Princess Anna, the wife of Yaroslav the Wise, was also a Russian saint (d. 1051). Anna the prophetess, referred to in the New Testament (Luke chapter 2, verses 36–38), lived her life entirely in the temple.

14.   Vladimir Vladimirovich Mayakovsky (1893–1930) was a member of the Cubo-Futurist group which called for the abandonment of the traditions of Russian literature; after 1917 he harnessed his poetry to the cause of the revolution, though besides propagandist verse he also wrote some fine love poetry, which escapes political didacticism. He lived for some years in a *ménage à trois* with Osip and Lili Brik. Finally, unhappy in love, disillusioned with the Soviet literary establishment, and despairing at the slow progress of the revolutionary transformation of society he committed suicide. He was hailed by Stalin as "the best and the most talented poet of the Soviet epoch".

15.   Nikolay Mikhaylovich Karamzin (1766–1826), poet, writer of Sentimentalist prose, and historian of the Russian Empire. Karamzin's family were thought to have been Pushkin's friends, especially when the latter was under pressure in circumstances which led to his death in a duel. Akhmatova's research on Pushkin's death showed, however, that his trust in them had been sadly misplaced.

16.   A line from Pushkin's poem 'The Prophet' (1826), describing the vocation of the poet as a divine calling.

17.   Author of epic poems depicting the achievements of the Young Communist League in building socialism. His reputation has not stood the test of time.

18.   Pushkin (1799–1837) was descended from a Negro whom Peter the Great brought to the Russian court during his reign.

19.   Gumilyov had had an affair with E. I. Dmitrieva for which the poet Voloshin took him to task, and as a result the two fought a duel.

20.   In Blok's poem *The Twelve* (January 1918) the marauding and murdering band of Red Guards is led through snowstorms by a hidden figure who turns out to be Jesus Christ. Blok was himself surprised by the appearance of Christ in the text.

21.   In Lermontov's poem 'The Demon' (1829–41) the Demon, cast out from heaven, seduces the beautiful Tamara and kills her with his passionate embrace. Akhmatova's lines quoted here allude to a speech by the Demon in the same poem.

22.   Chekhonte was a pseudonym used by Chekhov when he first began to write. *The Bear* is a vaudeville. 'Disarray' is likewise an early cycle, and Akhmatova is a pseudonym.

23.   In Russian Brodsky advocates the "Astroumie" article; his coined word consists of *astro-* "stars" and *-um-* "knowledge" and is phonetically identical to the word *ostroumie*, meaning "wit". Translation cannot do justice to the neatness of the pun.

24.   Meshchaninov was also an academician though more distinguished and respected.

25. The trial of the writers Sinyavsky and Daniel which took place in the mid-1960s signalled an unexpected return to the rigours of Stalinism during a time of political change.

26. Some of the Futurists attempted to create, and write in, a new language whose words they coined, sometimes by combining Russian prefixes, roots and suffixes into novel conglomerations. The aim was to liberate words from meaning and cultivate their aural and visual characteristics.

27. Mayakovsky, Akhmatova suggests, very soon recognised that the policy of the state was to harness literature to the cart of politics. Thus he produced the kind of poems required for propaganda purposes, deliberately closing his eyes to actual conditions. However, the dichotomy between the assertions of his conformist writing and his own insights into the nature of Soviet society in the 1920s eventually led him to commit suicide.

28. *The Tales of the Late Ivan Petrovich Belkin* are a set of short stories by Pushkin in which the authorship of the tales is obscured by the claim that Pushkin heard them from Belkin, who himself heard them narrated by various other people. Akhmatova refers to the multiple veils thrown over the person of the author in her poem.

29. Sofya Vasilevna Kovalevskaya (1850–1891) was an eminent mathematician who, in spite of being unable to obtain a higher education on account of her sex, became Professor of Mathematics at the University of Stockholm.

30. Genrikh Grigorevich Yagoda (1891–1938) was Chief of Security Police in the Soviet Union. He organised the first of the show trials and was later himself purged, tried and executed.

Biographical Guide

Akhmatova, Anna Andreevna (Anya, A.A., Akuma; pseudonym of Anna Gorenko) (1889–1966) Poet, founding member of the Acmeist school.

Annensky, Innokenty Fyodorovich (1856–1909) Poet, predecessor of the Acmeist school.

Anrep, Boris Vasilevich (1883–1969) Poet and mosaicist; had an affair with Akhmatova.

Ardov, Boris (Borya) Viktorovich (1940–) Actor, son of N. A. Olshevskaya.

Ardov, Mikhail (Misha) Viktorovich (1937–) Son of N. A. Olshevskaya.

Ardov, Viktor Efimovich (1900–76) Writer, humorist, husband of N. A. Olshevskaya.

Arens, Lev (Lyova) Evgenevich (c. 1895–c. 1970) Brother of Punin's first wife; helped to look after Akhmatova at Komarovo.

Arens, Sarra Yosifovna (c. 1900–c. 1970) Wife of L. E. Arens, Akhmatova's housekeeper at Komarovo.

Basmanova, Marina (1939–) Artist, former partner of Joseph Brodsky.

Batalov, Aleksey Nikolaevich (1928–) Film actor, son of N. A. Olshevskaya.

Blok, Aleksandr Aleksandrovich (1880–1921) Poet, initially a Symbolist.

Bobyshev, Dmitry Vasilievich (1936–) Poet.

Bolshintsova-Stenich, Lyubov (Lyubochka) Davydovna (1908–1983) Gave Akhmatova hospitality in Moscow.

Brodsky, Joseph Aleksandrovich (1940–) Poet.

Chukovskaya, Lydia Korneevna (1907–) Writer and diarist.

Glen, Nika Nikolaevna (N.N.) (1928–) Editor at State Literary Publishing House; gave Akhmatova hospitality in Moscow.

Gorenko, Viktor Andreevich (1896–1976) Akhmatova's brother.

Gumilyov, Lev (Lyova) Nikolaevich (1912–   ) Akhmatova's son.

Gumilyov, Nikolay (Kolya) Stepanovich (1886–1921) Poet, founding member of the Acmeist school and Akhmatova's first husband.

Ivanov, Vyacheslav Ivanovich (1866–1949) Symbolist poet.

Kaminskaya, Anna (Anya) Genrikhovna (1940–   ) Daughter of Irina Punina; lived in the same flat as Akhmatova.

Khardzhiev, Nikolay Ivanovich (1903–   ) Art historian and literary scholar.

Lourié, Arthur Sergeevich (1892–1966) Composer; lived with Akhmatova for a time.

Lozinsky, Mikhail Leonidovich (1886–1955) Poet, translator, member of the Poets' Guild.

Mandelstam, Nadezhda Yakovlevna (Nadya, N.Ya.) (1899–1980) Memoirist, wife of O. E. Mandelstam.

Mandelstam, Osip (Oska) Emilevich (1891–1938) Poet, founding member of the Acmeist school.

Mayakovsky, Vladimir Vladimirovich (1893–1930) Futurist poet.

Nayman, Anatoly Genrikhovich (Tolya, A.G.) (1936–   ) Poet and Akhmatova's literary secretary.

Nedobrovo, Nikolay Vladimirovich (1882–1919) Critic and poet.

Olshevskaya, Nina Antonovna (Ninochka, N.A.) (1908–   ) Actress; gave Akhmatova hospitality in Moscow.

Pasternak, Boris Leonidovich (1890–1960) Poet, novelist and translator.

Petrovykh, Mariya Sergeevna (1908–1979) Poet and translator who gave Akhmatova hospitality in Moscow.

Punin, Nikolay Nikolaevich (1888–1953) Art critic and historian, Akhmatova's third husband.

Punina, Irina (Ira) Nikolaevna (1923–   ) Daughter of N. N. Punin; shared her Leningrad flat with Akhmatova.

Ranevskaya, Faina Grigorievna (1896–1984) Actress.

Shileyko, Vladimir Kazimirovich (1891–1930) Assyriologist and Akhmatova's second husband.

Sreznevskaya, Valeriya Sergeevna, née Tyulpanova (c. 1887–1964) Life-long friend of Akhmatova.

Zhirmunsky, Viktor Maksimovich (1891–1971) Literary critic and historian.

Chronology

11 June 1889	Anna Gorenko born near Odessa.
1890s–1910s	Silver Age of Russian literature.
1893–1905	Gorenko family live at Tsarskoe Selo, near St Petersburg. Holidays on Black Sea coast.
1905	Parents separate. Mother and children move south to Eupatoria. Anna subsequently at school in Kiev.
Autumn 1907	Takes law course in Kiev.
25 April 1910	Marriage to N. S. Gumilyov. Conflicts soon follow.
1910, 1911, 1912	Visits to Paris, Italy, Switzerland. Gumilyov also travelling in Africa for long periods. A.A.'s friendship with Modigliani.
Autumn 1911	Foundation of the Poets' Guild. Akhmatova acts as secretary. From this group emerges the Acmeist school, also known as Adamism (members: Gumilyov, Mandelstam, Akhmatova, Gorodetsky, Narbut, Zenkevich). Manifestos published belatedly in 1913.
Spring 1912	Publication of first book of poems, *Evening*, under pseudonym Anna Akhmatova.
1 October 1912	Birth of son, Lev. Lev soon put into care of Gumilyov's family, who bring him up.
1913	Events referred to enigmatically in *Poem without a Hero*, involving the suicide of a young officer on discovering the infidelity of Akhmatova's friend Olga Glebova-Sudeykina. A.A. frequents the Stray Dog cabaret.

March 1914	Publication of second book, *Rosary*.
July 1914	World War I. Beginning of "The Real Twentieth Century" in A.A.'s view. N. S. Gumilyov volunteers and goes to the front.
1914–16	A.A. close to the poet and critic Nedobrovo. His article on her poetry published 1915.
February 1916–17	A.A. intimate with Boris Anrep.
1917	Final break with Gumilyov. Publication of third book, *White Flock*. Revolution, followed by civil war. A.A. refuses to join those emigrating.
1918	Divorce from Gumilyov and marriage to Shileyko. Widespread cold, hunger and deprivation, plus personal unhappiness.
1921	A.A. leaves Shileyko and lives with Lourié and Glebova-Sudeykina. Stays behind when they emigrate. Publication of fourth book, *Plantain*. N. S. Gumilyov executed for alleged anti-Bolshevik plot. New Economic Policy (NEP) begins.
1922	Publication of fifth book, *Anno Domini MCMXXI*.
1925	After politically motivated criticism of her poetry A.A. banned from publishing.
1926	Goes to live with N. N. Punin at the House on the Fontanka. Writes very little while living with him. Begins her research on Pushkin's poetry.
1928	Son, Lev, comes to live with her.
1935–1941	Stalin's terror increasing its grip on Soviet life.
1935	Arrest of Lev Gumilyov and Punin. A.A. writes to Stalin and they are released. A.A. begins *Requiem*.
1938–39	Lev Gumilyov re-arrested and imprisoned in Leningrad; deported from Leningrad August 1939 after his death sentence commuted; first in a camp, then in exile.
1938	Beginning of A.A.'s friendship with Lydia Chukovskaya. A.A. leaves Punin but housing shortage obliges

229

her to continue living in same flat. Later agrees to marry V. G. Garshin but plans disrupted by the war.

Death of Mandelstam in prison camp.

1940	Ban on publishing lifted. *From Six Books* appears but is soon withdrawn.

"Reaps a great harvest" of poetry. Begins *Poem without a Hero*.

Winter war with Finland.

1941	Soviet Union goes to war with Germany. Leningrad under siege; A.A. invited to make radio broadcasts. Leningrad Party officials arrange for A.A. to be evacuated.

A.A. living in Tashkent, along with Ranevskaya, Chukovskaya, N. Ya. Mandelstam. A.A. often ill.

1944	A.A. returns to Leningrad and the House on the Fontanka.
1945	Lev Gumilyov returns home.

A.A. prepares major collection of poems for publication.

Visits from Isaiah Berlin.

14 August 1946	Central Committee Resolution describing A.A.'s poetry as ideologically harmful. Ban on publication. Expelled from Soviet Writers' Union. Print run of collection of poems destroyed. This signals return to strict control of the arts after the more liberal war years.
1949	A.A. becomes part-time professional translator.

Arrest of Lev Gumilyov and Punin.

1950	A.A. unwillingly writes cycle of poems in praise of Stalin in an attempt to save her son's life.
1952	Leaves the House on the Fontanka and moves with the Punins to Red Cavalry Street (also in Leningrad).
1953	Death of Punin in prison camp.

Death of Stalin.

1956	Khrushchev's secret speech to the Twentieth Party Congress beginning de-Stalinisation.

Release of Lev Gumilyov. Quarrels follow and the two cease to meet. A.A. has a heart attack.

A.A. refuses to see Isaiah Berlin for fear of the consequences.

Some poems published.

1959	Nayman meets Akhmatova.
1961	A.A. moves with Punins to Lenin Street (Leningrad).
1962	*Poem without a Hero* completed.
	Visit from Robert Frost.
	Nayman becomes A.A.'s literary secretary.
1963	Publication of *Requiem* in Munich without A.A.'s consent.
1964	Fall of Khrushchev.
	Joseph Brodsky tried for parasitism and exiled.
	A. A. goes to Italy to receive Etna-Taormina prize.
1965	Travels to England to receive honorary degree at Oxford. Returns via Paris. Meets Anrep, Isaiah Berlin and other old friends.
	Publication of *The Flight of Time*.
	Another heart attack.
	Brodsky released.
5 March 1966	Dies in sanatorium at Domodedovo near Moscow. Civil and church funeral services. Buried at Komarovo.

Appendix

Excerpts from Zhdanov's speech to the Central Committee,
14 August 1946

I will now take up the question of the "creative" writing of Anna
Akhmatova. Lately, her work has been reprinted in Leningrad
journals in "mass produced editions." This is as astonishing and
unnatural as the republication of the work of Merezhkovsky,
Vyacheslav Ivanov, Mikhail Kuzmin, Andrei Bely, Zinaida
Gippius, Fyodor Sologub, Zinovieva-Annibal and so on, would be,
in other words of all those who were always considered by our
progressive society and literature as representatives of reactionary
obscurantism and a negative attitude to politics and literature.

Gorky, in his time, used to say that the decade between 1907–17
deserved to be called the most untalented and despicable decade in
the history of the Russian intelligentsia, when after the revolution
of 1905, a large part of the intelligentsia turned away from the
revolution and plunged into the bog of reactionary mysticism and
pornography, made a banner out of its lack of ideas, concealing its
negative attitude with a "beautiful" phrase: "I have burned everything that I revered, and made a farewell bow to everything I was
burning." Just at this time there appeared such renegade work as
"The Pale Steed" of Ropshin, the work of Vinnichenko and other
deserters from the revolutionary camp into the reactionary one,
who were hastily trying to bring down the high ideals for which the
best, the most progressive part of Russian society was fighting.
Symbolists, imaginists, decadents of all shades and colours rose to
the surface, disavowing the people, acclaiming the slogan of "art
for art's sake," actually preaching a lack of ideas in literature,

hiding their ideological and moral rottenness by seeking a beautiful form without any content. They were all united by their animal fear of the coming proletarian revolution. May I remind you that one of the outstanding "ideologists" of these reactionary literary trends was Merezhkovsky, who called the coming proletarian revolution "The Coming Hamite", and who greeted the October Revolution with savage hatred.

Anna Akhmatova is one of the representatives of this empty reactionary literary bog. She belongs to the so-called literary group of Acmeists, who emerged from the ranks of the Symbolists, and is one of the standard-bearers of empty, aristocratic, drawing-room poetry, lacking in ideas, and totally alien to Soviet literature. The Acmeists represented an exclusively individualistic trend in art. They preached the theory of "art for art's sake", "beauty for beauty's sake", they did not want to know anything about the people, their needs or interests, nor anything about social conditions.

In its social origin this was a literary trend of the bourgeois-nobility, at a period when the power of the bourgeoisie and the aristocracy was ebbing, when the poets and ideologists of the governing classes were trying to escape from the unpleasantness of reality into the cloudy heights and fogs of religious mysticism, into the narrowness of their private emotions, by delving into their petty little souls. The Acmeists as well as the Symbolists, the decadents and other representatives of the ideology of the bourgeois nobility, preached pessimism and faith only in the other world.

The contents of Akhmatova's poetry are personal through and through. The scope of her poetry is wretchedly limited, it is the poetry of a lady foaming at the mouth, and constantly dashing from drawing-room to chapel. Her basic theme is erotic love, interwoven with motifs of sadness, sorrow, death, mysticism and doom. The feeling of apprehension permeating the social consciousness of this dying group, the gloomy tones of death-bed despair, mystical emotions mixed with eroticism—this is the spiritual world of Akhmatova, one of the fragments of the old culture of the nobility lost forever, "of good old Catherine's time". She is neither a nun nor a fornicator, but really both of them, mixing fornication and prayer.

Anatoly Nayman

I swear to you by the angels' garden
I swear to you by the miraculous ikon,
Any by our burning passionate nights ...
(Akhmatova, *Anno Domini*)

This is Akhmatova with her insignificant narrow personal life, insignificant emotions and religious eroticism.

Akhmatova's poetry is remote from the people. It is the poetry of the ten thousand members of the upper class, the condemned ones who had nothing else left but to sigh, remembering "the good old times". The estates of Catherine the Great's time, with their avenues of old lime trees, fountains, statues and stone arches, orangeries, love bowers, and obsolete coats of arms on the gates. The St Petersburg of the nobility. Tsarskoe Selo, the station at Pavlovsk and all the other leftovers of the culture of the nobility. All this has disappeared forever! Leftovers from this far-off culture, alien to our people, who by some miracle have suvived to our days, have nothing else to do but retreat into their own narrow world and live in dreams. "Everything is stolen, betrayed and sold," writes Akhmatova.

What is the reason for the sudden popularization of the poetry of Akhmatova? What has she in common with us, Soviet people? What is the reason for offering a literary tribune to all those decadent and deeply alien currents in literature?

From the history of Russian literature we know that on many occasions reactionary literary movements such as the ones to which the Symbolists and the Acmeists belonged have tried to start campaigns against the great Russian revolutionary democratic traditions of Russian literature and its progressive representatives; they tried to deprive literature of its high ideological and social meaning, and to plunge it into the bog of ideological emptiness and common-place triviality. All these "fashionable" trends have been flung into oblivion together with the classes whose ideology they reflected. All these Symbolists, Acmeists, "yellowjackets", "Jacks of Diamonds", "Nothingists"—what is left of them in our native Russian Soviet literature? Absolutely nothing, although their campaign against the great representatives of the Russian revolutionary democratic literature of Belinsky, Dobrolyubov, Chernyshevsky, Herzen and Saltykov-Shchedrin—were planned with great noise and pretension, and foundered just as noisily.

The Acmeists proclaimed: "No corrections should be made to life, and the latter must not be criticised." Why were they against introducing any corrections into life? Because this old life of the nobility suited them, and the revolutionaries were on the point of disturbing it. In October 1917 the governing classes, as well as their ideologists and those who sang their praises, were thrown into the garbage heap of history.

And then, suddenly, in the twenty-ninth year of the Socialist Revolution, some museum rarities from the world of shadows appeared on the scene and started to teach our youth how they should live. A Leningrad journal opens its doors wide to Akhmatova, and she is left free to poison the minds of our youth by the corrupting spirit of her poetry.

In one of the numbers of the journal *Leningrad* there appears something like a summary of all Akhmatova's work written between 1909–1944. Amongst other rubbish, there is one poem written during the Great Patriotic War [World War II], when she was evacuated from Leningrad. In this poem she describes her loneliness, which she is forced to share with a black cat. The black cat looks at her with the gaze of centuries. This is not a new theme. Akhmatova already wrote about a black cat in 1909. The atmosphere of loneliness and despair, so alien to Soviet literature, permeates the whole of Akhmatova's "creative work".

What can there be in common between such poetry and the interests of our people and our state? Nothing at all. The work of Akhmatova belongs to the long forgotten past; it is totally alien to the contemporary life of the Soviet people and cannot be tolerated in the pages of our journals. Our literature is not a private enterprise aimed at catering to the various tastes of the literary market. We are not in any way forced to find a place in our literature for tastes and customs that have nothing in common with the morals and qualities of the Soviet people. What can the work of Akhmatova give our youth? Nothing but harm. This work can only bring depression, low spirits, pessimism, a wish to get away from all problems of social life and activity into the narrow little world of personal emotions. How can one entrust her with the education of our youth? Meanwhile the work of Akhmatova was being published with eagerness now in *Zvezda*, now in *Leningrad*, sometimes even in anthologies. This was a grave political mistake.

Index